"The greatest opportunity for us in this digital age is the technology that is now available to us, yet this creates the biggest divide in business. I am often asked, what's the ROI of social media and digital? After searching for a great quote I came across this quote, "the ROI for utilising the digital and social media tools is that your business will still be here in 5 years". To ignore the importance of digital assets in your business is acutely naive and something that any investor, supplier or client should be wary of. Cheryl has immense experience as a researcher, writer and as a practitioner and her words will inspire and guide the beginner and the experienced business person."
Penny Power, Founder and CEO of Ecademy and Digital Youth Academy

"If you read just one book on digital business, make it this one. This must-read workbook is brilliantly practical and, vitally, very readable. It is inspirational, informative and interactive in equal measure. Highly recommended!"
Rowan Gormley, Founder and CEO of NakedWines.com

"Cheryl Rickman knows her stuff. What makes this book stand out is that it takes you on a real journey of digital business start-up and beyond, that any digital entrepreneur will relate to; from having an idea and building your business and website, to running and selling it. The case studies are engaging and thought-provoking, the exercises are action-oriented and engaging. The result is an inspirational, practical and excellent book. I've always loved Cheryl's writing, and this book confirms why."
Thomas Power, Chairman of Ecademy

"Digital success is all about the customer – you need to excel in web experience / delivery / returns / customer service, but it's vital to remember it's about the customer. This book excels in providing practical guidance on how to create a successful digital business which exceeds customer expectations and keeps customers happy each step of the way. Tips, case studies and exercises within the book show you how to turn your customers into raving fans who spread the word – making this a must-read book for budding web entrepreneurs."
Scott Weavers-Wright, CEO of Kiddicare.com, and MD of Morrison.com (non-food)

"It's a golden moment for start-up entrepreneurs in the WIRED world – and Cheryl Rickman provides many of the tools and inspiring stories that could help launch the next digital success stories."
David Rowan, Editor of Wired UK

THE

DIGITAL

BUSINESS

START-UP

WORKBOOK

The Ultimate Step-by-Step Guide to Succeeding Online from Start-up to Exit

CHERYL RICKMAN

CAPSTONE

This edition first published 2012

© 2012 Cheryl Rickman

Registered office

Capstone Publishing Ltd. (A Wiley Company), John Wiley and Sons Ltd, The Atrium, Southern Gate, Chichester, West Sussex, PO19 8SQ, United Kingdom

For details of our global editorial offices, for customer services and for information about how to apply for permission to reuse the copyright material in this book please see our website at www.wiley.com.

The right of the author to be identified as the author of this work has been asserted in accordance with the Copyright, Designs and Patents Act 1988.

Wiley publishes in a variety of print and electronic formats and by print-on-demand. Some material included with standard print versions of this book may not be included in e-books or in print-on-demand. If this book refers to media such as a CD or DVD that is not included in the version you purchased, you may download this material at http://booksupport.wiley.com. For more information about Wiley products, visit www.wiley.com.

Designations used by companies to distinguish their products are often claimed as trademarks. All brand names and product names used in this book are trade names, service marks, trademarks or registered trademarks of their respective owners. The publisher is not associated with any product or vendor mentioned in this book. This publication is designed to provide accurate and authoritative information in regard to the subject matter covered. It is sold on the understanding that the publisher is not engaged in rendering professional services. If professional advice or other expert assistance is required, the services of a competent professional should be sought.

Library of Congress Cataloging-in-Publication Data
Library of Congress Cataloging-in-Publication Data is available

A catalogue record for this book is available from the British Library.

ISBN 978-0-857-08285-5 (paperback) ISBN 978-0-857-08304-3 (ebk)

ISBN 978-0-857-08305-0 (ebk) ISBN 978-0-857-08306-7 (ebk)

Set in 10.5 on 13 pt Adobe Caslon pro-Regular by Toppan Best-set Premedia Limited

Printed by TJ International Ltd, Padstow, Cornwall, UK

Contents

Dedication and Acknowledgements

I dedicate this book to the memory of my warm, inspirational and courageous mother, Denise Rickman, née O'Farrell. Thank you for smiling, believing, encouraging and loving.

I'd like to thank the two most important people in my life for bearing with me while I wrote this book – my wonderful daughter, Brooke Denise and my brilliant 'mister', James Suddaby. Thank you both for being there, being you and being awesome. Thanks also to my additional support network of friends and family.

Many thanks to all of the inspirational and successful digital entrepreneurs who have given their time to be interviewed for this book, and to Holly and Jenny at Wiley/Capstone for believing in me, guiding me and publishing the book. Thank you all.

Foreword

I am lucky enough to hold the slightly grandiose title of 'UK Government's Digital Champion' and as such I often meet people who are not online or who have recently started using a computer for the first time. Here in the UK, 8.4 million adults are yet to experience the wonders of the web. In stark contrast, the UK is top of its league for e-commerce with online retail now accounting for 17% of total retail sales – higher than any other country in the world – and with the rise of mobile commerce and the huge numbers of tablet devices sold last year, these figures can only keep increasing.

This epitomizes the dichotomy that existed when Brent and I co-founded lastminute.com in 1998 – for a long time, it was tech evangelists vs. technophobes. We spent countless hours trying to convince investors, theatres, hotels and airlines that the internet wasn't going to blow up – and now I am having the same conversation with offliners across the UK – but in the world of business, my, how things have changed! Last year more than one billion parcels were shipped from online purchases in the UK. That's hyper growth.

We have a great opportunity to build on the success of existing digital sector successes. I believe that by embedding digital thinking in more of business, more of government and more of the charitable sector, we can create a truly remarkable digital UK. Starting a digital business, even if it fails, is a great grounding for a career. Don't go into a bank, don't go into accountancy, go into a start-up. You will learn a bucket load more and you will gain solid experience. We don't encourage enough in people to take the risk and go it alone. Whether you are in education, in work or unemployed there may well be an idea burning in you or there may be someone that needs your help. Now, more than ever let's encourage digital start-ups.

The UK has created so many world class tech businesses – from moshi monsters to autonomy to tweetdeck, but there are certainly many more that we should all take every opportunity to encourage. The current economy creates the necessity for much more entrepreneurial and digital thinking from everyone. Whether you are looking for work, struggling to cut your cost base or launching a new product, creativity, boldness and the ability to deliver astonishing things on shoestring budgets are all more important than ever.

I am often asked what we can do to encourage the next wave of digital entrepreneurs, particularly women, of whom there are still far too few in the technology sector. My advice is 'be bold'. This is a rallying cry for you to make that first scary step; I won't pretend it's easy so anything that can make it less scary is worth trying. You will need to be agile and hard working and you will never stop learning. Cheryl's workbook will help you on your first steps towards the roller-coaster start-up journey that is both exhilarating and terrifying in equal measures. I highly recommend it.

Martha Lane Fox
UK Digital Champion and Co-founder of Lastminute.com

Introduction

Generation Entrepreneur: Open For Business

This global village of ours is now virtual, digital and mobile. The omnipresent World Wide Web has enabled anyone to access revenue-generating audiences from anywhere with an Internet connection at anytime, 24–7. Ultimately, where there's an Internet connection, there's a potential enterprise and, where there's scale, there's colossal opportunity.

With more people starting their own businesses to regain control of their lives rather than work for someone else to make a living, this new vast and permanently wired world is exciting for entrepreneurs. As someone who is reading this book, you probably don't need persuading about the benefits of the digital revolution. You already know that wider access, opportunity and connection are the vital fruits of its existence; that despite not existing 20 years ago, the World Wide Web presents an unmatched opportunity for entrepreneurs to sell their products, services and expertise to a larger yet more targeted market than ever before.

Thanks to technology and the digital revolution, global web operations can be orchestrated from any location. (Amazon and Google started life in their founders' garages, eBay was established in a spare bedroom).

Today, when start-ups open their doors for business, they can do so to the world. Indeed, living in a global village means that, as well as seizing the chance to sell, entrepreneurs can also tap into a global talent pool and source low-cost supplies from far-flung corners of the planet. The world is quite literally an entrepreneur's oyster.

Distributed teams, suppliers, partners and customers can be effectively managed and coordinated from a single location. Workforce productivity can be boosted as enhanced mobility makes us more able. We can perform tasks from anywhere – on the move, from home, on a train or plane . . . And, by using advanced technology, we can perform those tasks better and faster than in previous decades.

Consequently, entrepreneurship has been enabled. We can better connect, engage, interact and collaborate with target consumers and business partners on both a local and global scale. We can involve consumers in the decision, selection and marketing process. We can analyze and fine tune our marketing messages to better inform, educate and sell to others.

Generation E (Generation Entrepreneur and Generation Web) is an 'open' generation. For, not only are we as human beings more open and receptive to new ideas than we have ever been, today the world's information, products, people and opportunities are openly accessible to all.

The open participatory platform of the Internet has opened the doors to opportunity, something that entrepreneurs embrace, while the market for online trade is continuously growing. Indeed, as the physical world metaphorically shrinks and gets smaller, the world of opportunity grows in size.

Greater Opportunity = Greater Competition

However, while opportunities and the ability to leverage them have increased, so has the threat of global competition. As such, opportunity in the digital world is mutual. So, while technology provides us with the opportunity to compete on a level playing field with companies of all sizes across the globe, it enables our competitors to do the same. We share that opportunity.

Ease of access has therefore created hyper-competition, particularly in the digital space. It has created an abundance of content producers and online enterprises as everyone strives to take advantage of the digital revolution and seize their slice of the digital pie. As such, in an increasingly competitive world, where local competition has become global, digital businesses face significant challenges as they strive to survive.

And therein lies a core reason for writing this workbook: to provide a truly comprehensive guide on how to start, build and sustain a successful Internet enterprise that will stand the test of time and stay ahead of the competition; to equip entrepreneurs with a blueprint and toolkit to start up, survive and succeed in the ever-changing super-competitive realm of digital enterprise.

That said, while competition and opportunity have increased in parallel, the fast-changing nature of the digital realm has created an ideal time for enterprise to thrive.

The Perfect Storm for Digital Enterprise

Over the past decade conditions have changed. These changing conditions have created the perfect storm – a time when a culmination of events creates a unique situation. According to Skype founder, Niklas Zennstrom, 'now is the healthiest [the European start-up market] has ever been.'[1]

Costs of communication, production, distribution and marketing have all been dramatically slashed, while consumers and companies alike can save time and money by comparing prices and doing things faster. Technology has evolved and become lighter and more accessible; open source software, VoIP, video conferencing and cloud computing, have all come of age. Globalization has made the worldwide talent pool, supplies and services readily available to anyone. Furthermore, the way we access the web has changed. Today you can access the Internet via a number of devices, not just via a web browser and a dial-up connection. In the early days we had to go to the Internet. Today, the Internet comes to us, wherever we are. Ultimately then, the Internet and digital realm has facilitated entrepreneurship for all.

What's more, while the growth of digital and access to technological tools enables a faster speed to market whereby entrepreneurs can experimentally dip their toe in the water for minimal cost, entrepreneurs can also apply digital DNA to each strand of their business, not just their sales channel. Digital can filter through to each business function from data storage and telecoms to fulfillment and recruitment, making each area more efficient, productive, secure and scalable.

In order to take advantage of the technological tools at your disposal it's vital to learn all you can about each area of digital enterprise to thoroughly enhance your chance of prosperity. This road-map to digital success will therefore equip you with the knowledge and focus you need to achieve your goals.

What You'll Learn

180,000 people per minute search Google and visit a website following their search. This book aims to help you ensure that as many of those people as possible find *your* website and buy from *you* rather than from your competitors. It includes everything you need to know about search engine optimization (SEO) and marketing (SEM) plus easy-to-implement strategies to drive high quality traffic to your site along with tips on converting those visitors into paying customers.

From having the right idea and hiring the right people at the right time; to rolling out the right business model to the right niche audience to create rapid growth; there are many variables that can impact the level of success or failure that an entrepreneur achieves.

In this book you'll learn the do's and don'ts of raising capital to finance an Internet venture, discover how to manage relationships with a growing team and investors alike, plus learn how to implement sustainable online revenue streams to generate the best return on investment for both you and your financiers.

You already know how fast the digital world is moving and how quickly things change. We've frequently had to realign our goals and adapt with speed to market challenges and changes. As such this book recognizes the importance of being nimble and will explain how plans of action are as important as business plans to digital entrepreneurs.

We'll also review traditional and emergent disruptive business models. Where entrepreneurs feel that consumers are getting a raw deal at the hands of big brands and the high street, new business models are emerging. We'll examine these methods of enabling consumers and enterprise alike, from Freemium and Revenue Share models to Me-tail, E-tail and Apps.

Furthermore, you'll notice that I've chosen the word 'digital' over 'Internet' for the title of this book. That's simply because we no longer merely access the web through a browser. We can now connect to the Internet and interact with other forms of digital media in a number of different ways and through a number of different devices. There are now more mobile phone users in the world than Internet users (up from 12.4 million – 0.25% of world population in 1990 – to 4 billion – 67% of the world population). Subsequently, the Internet has become the 'Splinternet' – a term which describes the splintering of Internet technology and a move away from standardization. This means a well-rounded approach is needed to cover all aspects and device standards within the digital realm, from m-commerce to mobile apps; from interactive TV and radio to GPS and beyond. Forward-thinking is prerequisite to seizing digital opportunities.

So this book will guide you through the entrepreneurial journey: from concept and validation to commercialization and exit via 12 key steps. Because, while starting-up your own business can seem a daunting process, the biggest dreams are achievable if they are approached one step at a time.

This workbook will give you a master class in digital enterprise enabling you to take advantage of the digital opportunity, avoid costly marketing mistakes and, ultimately, gain and sustain that all-important competitive advantage. You'll effectively learn how to put a great idea to work on the web. Each stage: from planning and assessing your idea through to building your website, your team and your brand, and then making plans to sell your business will be covered.

- In **Step 1** you'll examine your big idea, what makes an idea a good one, and how to evolve your idea from 'light bulb moment' and 'process of elimination' to 'vision' and beyond.
- **Step 2** will encourage you to think about your idea commercially, as different digital business models will be examined in detail and you'll figure out how your big idea will make money.
- In **Step 3** you'll discover how to validate your opportunity, plot a clear path, research your customers and competition and ultimately decide whether your idea is likely to work or not.
- In **Step 4** you'll learn how to fund your venture, assess sources of available finance and understand how best to prepare and pitch for that finance.
- **Step 5** will guide you through the process of building your website, outlining the key variables to get right from engaging content and intuitive navigation to persuasive web copy and clean design.
- **Step 6** will talk you through how to build your mobile site and/or mobile application.
- From product to people, **Step 7** will show you how to build your team and fill the gaps by sourcing, recruiting and retaining the best talent you can find to help you create a successful digital enterprise.
- **Step 8** will take you through the ins-and-outs of building an engaging purposeful brand that people will relate to, believe in and, crucially, trust.
- In **Step 9** we'll examine how to drive traffic to the website you've built through effective traditional online marketing, from affiliate and e-mail marketing to online advertising and search engine optimization.
- **Step 10** reveals how to harness response-boosting web analytics and testing methodologies to increase conversion click-through rates and generate the best return on investment (ROI).

- **Step 11** explains how to create a buzz using people power. From social networking and building hives of influencers to reputation management and buzz monitoring. The importance of collaborative partnerships is also explored, including how to make them work for both/all parties.
- Having validated and implemented your ideas, built and promoted your business, the final part of your journey is **Step 12**, which explores the final destination: selling or passing your business on. It examines the best time to sell, how to prepare for a successful exit and how to reduce owner dependency.

In 1999, after writing a couple of booklets on the subject of Internet business and online marketing, I founded my own digital business as a sole trader: Web-Critique – a business which reviewed other people's websites and provided appraisals on what people were doing right and wrong. I sold the business in 2005 to concentrate on my writing. In 2000 I co-founded online music magazine, I Like Music (ilikemusic.com) with my partner, James. Eight years of organic growth later, the company merged with a music service provider and moved operations to London. James continues to run the company alongside his CEO. This all puts me in the fortunate position of being able to share my experiences, insights and lessons learned with those embarking on their entrepreneurial journeys.

However, I have also interviewed a number of digital enterprise leaders, successful entrepreneurs who share their insight; from the founders of Moonpig.com, and Kiddicare.com to the founders of iwantoneofthose.com and NakedWines.com. From Martha Lane Fox and Brent Hoberman to Sarah Beeny and Saul Klein. Everyone contributing to this book has succeeded in digital business. So, here's your opportunity to gain insider insight and learn from them all – both from what they've done right and, crucially, what they've done wrong.

'Never believe anyone who says they've not made mistakes', says Martha Lane Fox. 'We made mistakes all the time. We hired the wrong people at the wrong moment, we put technology live too early before we'd tested it; we bought companies that weren't very easy to integrate; we spent too much money on bits of technology . . . you should be very suspicious if you're not making a mistake at least every month and learning from it.'

Ultimately this book condenses a wealth of entrepreneurial expertise and real-life experience (warts and all) into an easy-to-digest guide to help you to pursue your dreams of succeeding in digital business and learn from the mistakes and achievements of those who have gone before you.

In a culture of enterprise and media with such a plethora of participants, this book will help you to stand out from the crowd. Some might choose to lament such a culture that enables everyone to be expressive and entrepreneurial but that world exists, whether we like it or not. So it's time for you to optimize that opportunity, use the tools at your disposal properly, and win!

Part 1

Starting Up

Your Own

Digital

Business

Step One

The Big Idea – Create and Evolve Your Concept

'Just as our eyes need light in order to see, our minds need ideas in order to conceive.'
Napoleon Hill

We all have ideas, some of them brilliant. However, an idea is merely an idea and nothing more until it is acted upon. Ultimately, the difference between those who build their own businesses and go on to sell them and those who don't is very simple . . . the former do it. They act on their ideas; they just get on and make it happen. Simply put, there are two types of people in the world: those who make stuff happen and those who don't. If you've had an idea and bought this book, you're on your way to being part of the former group.

Certainly, as soon as you had an idea and decided to act on it, you've taken the first step on the journey of The Big Idea from imagination to reality, from thought to action, from idea to business. What matters now is how you deal with your idea; how you fertilize the seed that your mind has sown; how you convert your idea into being.

By the end of this chapter, you should understand:

☐ **The journey you will need to take your idea on, from light-bulb moment to vision.**

☐ **How to fertilize the seedling of your idea and enable it to grow and flourish.**

☐ **Why it's OK to change your mind, evolve an idea and 'pivot' accordingly.**

☐ **What criteria to follow to create an idea that is commercially viable in the digital realm.**

☐ **The type of ideas that tend to work well on the web.**

Sowing the Seeds of Success

Ideas drive innovation. They stimulate creativity. They furnish enterprise. Ideas are essentially the seeds of success that, when nurtured, turn into seedlings, grow and thrive. According to research by Dr Fred Luskin of Stanford University, the average human has as many as 60,000 thoughts per day. Many of them are fleeting. Within those thoughts, new ideas spring into our heads in the shower or whilst driving; some (frustratingly) arrive just as we're drifting off to sleep.

Wherever we are when we have ideas, our day-to-day experiences, both positive and negative, our reactions to problems and thoughts about how we might solve them, our drive and ambition to fund the life we wish to live, all of these things fuel great business ideas.

Entrepreneurs, of course, have ideas aplenty. The crucial element is weeding out the poor ideas from the brilliant ones without dismissing early variations of concepts which may lead to something great. In general, the good ideas stick in our minds and we respond by devoting more attention to them.

For example, when it comes to an idea for a digital business, you might have been inspired by your own experiences browsing the web. Perhaps your positive experience at a particular website has encouraged you to create something similar. Or, conversely, the negative experiences you've had online may have spurred you on to create something better. You might wish to turn your hobby into a business; perhaps you have a new invention or service that would solve a common problem; or have a wealth of expertise on a specific topic that you are keen to exploit. Maybe you have lamented the absence of a product in the market that you feel would fill a gap.

Whatever has inspired you to have an idea in the first place must mean something to you, otherwise you'd have shunned the idea and it would have simply wended its way to the back of your mind, along with countless other concepts that enter our imagination in any given day.

If you're reading this book, you should already have at least the basis of an idea, no matter how sketchy that is. So, you've envisaged the fledgling beginnings of an enterprise that could give you the freedom to achieve your lifelong dreams. Now it's time to embark on a journey of idea evolution: from light-bulb moment to formulating a valid vision which you can implement and commercialize.

Stepping Stones: The Journey of an Idea

Just as there is an entrepreneurial journey, as noted in the Introduction, I believe that ideas go on a journey and evolve through four main stages:

1. **The Light-Bulb Moment.** The moment that you first spot an opportunity and envisage a solution is often your light-bulb moment. You may experience additional 'light-bulb' or 'eureka' moments as your idea evolves. Your concept may be very sketchy with the 'light-bulb' moment not happening until later down the line, once you've had a chance to gather feedback, flesh the idea out, give it definition and build momentum. At this first stage of idea evolution, your idea will be relatively unpolished.
2. **Process of Elimination.** This step involves committing to your idea and taking action by exploring it. You then build upon your idea by seeking out what is and isn't possible, what is needed and what isn't. Rather than over-analyze at this point, you simply gather data to support your idea, to justify briefly why it should work.
3. **Vision.** As you polish your idea and crystallize it, your long-term vision will develop from that initial spark of the light-bulb flickering on inside your mind.
4. **Validation.** This involves discovering whether there is a real need for your product or service and whether you're solving a real problem. Fortunately, in the digital world, you can figure viability out very cheaply and get the

bare bones of your digital business idea up and running for little or no cost. The biggest cost of proving whether there is a genuine opportunity to be had will be your time.

In this chapter in particular we'll focus on the first three stages of concept evolution: Light-bulb Moment, Process of Elimination and Vision. We shall cover the final step of idea evolution, Validation, in Step Three.

So let's examine the first three stages of idea evolution in more detail: from initial spark to fully defined, long-term vision.

The word 'evolution' is vital here because the only constant, the only certainty in business, is change. Sure, that may be a cliché, but only because it's true. As an entrepreneur, you must be able to adapt to change. So, while your idea may be a sufficiently stonking one, it needs to be pursued by someone who can execute and deliver upon it and, crucially, by someone who is not averse to change. Why? Because business ideas, like the markets in which they operate, change; they evolve and morph into strategically improved versions. They shift direction or are fine-tuned to suit the changing needs of all stakeholders in the business.

That's certainly what happened with Moo.com.

Moo-ving On: An Evolutionary Idea

Founder of Moo.com, Richard Moross, took his idea on a journey before hitting the jackpot. Today the company makes well-designed business cards to order and grows at 100% each year. Its primary customer base is small businesses. However, it wasn't always that way.

The first version of Moo.com was targeted at consumers. Furthermore, the business started life in 2004 as a social networking site which enabled users to send their details to each other using real physical cards, like business cards but 'social cards'. Richard initially named the 'Facebook with cards', business 'Pleasure Cards'.

In 2003 Richard had his light-bulb moment while working for design company, Imagination. Part of his job remit was to spot upcoming trends in social networking and the Internet.

'I remember being unable to sleep and, rather than counting sheep, I starting thinking about product development, in particular Coca Cola's vision for the world which is 'everyone within an arm's reach of a Coke'. This slightly scary concept of conceiving and making a product that everyone would want to have around them interested me. So I thought about objects that people already have around them, in their pockets and wallets: keys, wallet, money, key chain, bus pass, credit cards and business cards. These seemed quite strange pieces of analogue technology that most people have.

'The business card is a professional tool that's been around for 300 years, it's still around in the digital age for good reason.' But Richard wondered, 'Why don't consumers have access to this?'

Richard's 'light-bulb moment' took shape as he noted the opportunity created by the fledgling 'online identity' social phenomenon, to create a personal version of the business card. 'Something which said 'here is my blog, email address, mobile, website and social network URL. And that was how the idea was born.'

Subsequently with his core vision of 'great design for everyone' (his Coca-Cola motto paraphrase), Richard launched forth with his social network and trendy-looking MiniCards – a third of the size of a traditional business card. However his idea stalled. He needed to take drastic action. 'The life of the business was dependent [on changing direction] as we'd all but run out of money,' says Richard. 'People loved the little cards, but they didn't want to join another social network. That's why it didn't work. They had their own social networks already. What they wanted was the physical product, but a better version.'

'Failure is simply the opportunity to begin again, this time more intelligently.'
Henry Ford

The Pivotal Moment

With inconsistent demand, Richard realized, in order to create a sustainable digital enterprise he'd need to generate repeat custom so, having gained attention with a unique product, (the high-quality MiniCards) Richard shifted focus to a core niche to fill the recurrent need of business people who had grown tired of traditional business card print quality.

Rather than give up, Richard tweaked his original idea by 'pivoting', a term that comes from the way that basketball players quickly shift direction on court.

He dropped the social network element and the name and relaunched in September 2006 as Moo.com, working with established social networks, such as photo website, Flickr, enabling users to upload images onto their business cards. 'That really catapulted us into the limelight to their customers and then on to many others', explains Richard. That year the company raised £2.75 m from Atlas Venture and Index Ventures. Later, Richard extended Moo's range of cards from MiniCards to a variety of sizes and types, all made to order, with a variety of USPs (unique selling points) including high quality paper selection; the chance for customers to order each card in a pack to be different; plus pre-designed templates and self-uploaded image options.

However, what Richard learned through that evolution of his idea from light-bulb moment through a process of elimination (which he had done live on the web) was this:

'It was a survival situation and, thanks to the good and prudent advice of the people around me, we started to look for where people already were, made the customer the centre of gravity and brought the product to them. That

(Continued)

realignment of the business plan was the catalyst for the fundraising and the vehicle from which we've driven the business ever since.'

Evolving his initial idea has certainly paid off. Moo.com has been profitable since 2009. The company has printed and delivered over 10 million MiniCards to date to over 100,000 customers, disrupting the traditional business card printing industry by creating something better. Growth is so significant, with revenues doubling every year since it relaunched, that Moo.com opened a production office in Rhode Island, USA to reduce costs and delivery times to US customers who now make up nearly half of all sales.

Yet, despite his idea evolution, Richard's core vision remained unaltered and resolute. 'Great design for everyone' the motto that stemmed from his original sleepless night analysis of Coca-Cola's motto has always applied. In fact, subsequently, in January 2012, Moo.com joined forces with Faceboook to launch Facebook cards as a way to "take your Facebook Timeline offline". Evidently, Richard's initial 'Facebook with cards' idea has seen the light, albeit in a differenet manifestation.

Great sustainable business ideas need not be entirely revolutionary and pioneering; the lesson here is that you need not be first, but you absolutely must be better!

Exercise

In order to succeed and sustain success, your product or service must be better than the rest. We shall examine this point in more detail in the following few chapters, however, at this initial idea stage consider:

1. What can you do via your online business that traditional businesses cannot? For example can you:
   - Offer a wider range of products or services than a physical shop could stock? (e.g. Borders bookstore with its 100,000 book titles could never hope to compete with Amazon.com's 3.7 million books).
   - Provide a personalization service or personalized experience which traditional outlets are unable to provide?
2. How can you evolve your idea to create something that is ultimately better than everything else out there?
   - List ways that you might make your product/service: look or feel better, be of better quality, make the customer experience easier, more enjoyable, quicker, safer?
   - Outline what will make your product or service truly remarkable.

Moonpig: Laughing All The Way To The Piggy Bank By Creating Something Better

Founder of Moonpig.com, Nick Jenkins, realized early on that, in order to create a successful digital enterprise, he'd have to create something that was differentiated and fundamentally better than what was available on the high street.

After leaving Glencore where he'd worked as a commodity trader, Nick did an MBA and applied logic to selecting his business idea. 'It was a lot more of a logical process than thinking "ooh Eureka, here's a good business idea",' Nick told me. After coming up with five ideas initially (from teaching English to Japanese businessmen online to growing exotic mushrooms) and brainstorming those, he examined Internet business models and went through a process of elimination.

Nick didn't want to rely on the advertising model because 'I realised I would spend more money attracting people to my website than I was going to make from the advertising'. Nick also avoided selling digital products such as images, news subscriptions or music as 'everyone was giving stuff away so it was very difficult to charge for anything.'

Furthermore, he didn't merely want to sell something that could be bought from a traditional shop. 'Then there's a price comparison issue where people would only buy online if it was cheaper and would compare prices to find the cheapest place to buy. In that case your margins get squeezed, so that wasn't terribly attractive either.'

'I thought about doing something physical which I could change and adapt using the Internet, to make it into a better product than the high street. The idea of a personalized greeting card – a Moonpig card – is much better than a card you'll get on the high street where it is unavailable. So you can charge more for it, break away from the price comparison issue and give people a reason to go online to buy a product. What's more, the economics of producing a single, personalized card simply do not work outside of the Internet.'

From the outset, the long-term vision was clear: 'I wanted to create a household brand that people would go to for the best greeting cards,' says Nick. And so he did.

Nick steadily grew Moonpig.com into a household name and grabbed 90% share of the British online card market sending around six million cards out each year (a big leap from the 40,000 sent out in its first year). The company, 12 years after launch, is turning over £32m and making £11m profit. Nick sold the business in summer 2011 for £120m to Photobox.com.

The Long-Term Vision

Once you have dreamed your dream, discussed, tweaked, defined and refined your idea, you need to create a long-term vision that encapsulates your ultimate end-goal and feeds your strategy, your business plan, and your mission; your very purpose for being in existence.

All successful entrepreneurs have a strong vision, bar none. Richard Moross wanted to create 'great design for everyone'. Nick Jenkins wanted to create 'a household brand for the best greeting cards'. The long-term vision for Bill Gates was famously to put 'a computer on every desk'. The woman who runs the flower shop down my road wants to 'brighten up people's lives'.

Exercise

What's your vision? Encapsulate your vision in one or two sentences here:

I want to create: _____

Where do you hope the business will be in three years time (e.g. leading the market? Sold to the market leader? Entering new markets?)

_____

The point is: good entrepreneurs start with the end in mind. All good entrepreneurs have a purposeful, well-defined, long-term vision. They start with a light-bulb moment which, following further thought and discussion, evolves into a powerful long-term vision.

Take Amazon founder, Jeff Bezos. His light-bulb moment came when, back in 1994, he noticed how fast web usage was growing (2300% annually) and decided to sell something over the Internet. That 'something' evolved into a vision: to sell books direct to consumers online which grew into a wider long-term vision: 'to be earth's most customer-centric company; to build a place where people can come to find and discover anything they might want to buy online.' The site he subsequently created became the definitive point of reference for online retailers across all sectors. And today, almost two decades after launch Bezos says he knows that, in a decade's time, his customers are still going to want low prices, fast delivery and vast selection. No matter what direction he takes his business and no matter how diversified his product strategy becomes, that vision remains strong and stable.

'I find that most of the initiatives we undertake may take five to seven years before they pay any dividends for the company,' he says. 'They may start paying dividends for customers right away.'[2]

When you start up your own business you need to think big – not only in terms of your ambition, but also in terms of seeing the bigger picture and wider vision which informs your strategy and your decision-making process.

Exercise

Create a vision board:

Write your business vision in the centre and get creative. Cut out and stick brands, colours, photos, messages, adverts, words, images that relate to that vision. From people who epitomize your target audience to images of a tropical beach to inspire where you'll be when you sell your business.

Next, stick a piece of paper onto the bottom of the vision board and jot down your notes so far about why you believe in your idea, why it is different and better, who your customers are likely to be and who you know who might help you achieve your vision. Empty your brain of all the bits and pieces flooding your mind relating to your idea, including the 'what if?' scenarios, doubts and unique selling points. Get it all down. Use both the pictorial and textual representations of your vision when you come to flesh out your idea, assess its viability and write your business plan.

! Top Tips for Taking your Idea on the Right Evolutionary Journey

1. **Pay attention to ideas that you instinctively give more mind-time to.** Your instinct is telling you that these ideas are worth evaluating further.
2. **Nurture your ideas and be prepared to adapt.** Allow your ideas to evolve from inception and sketchy outline through a process of questioning and elimination to a crystallized vision that you should be passionate about. Remember, people buy from/supply/invest in people who are passionate about what they are offering.
3. **Get digging.** Sketch ideas, ask questions: pitch to friends, family and potential customers; get feedback – learn.
4. **Seek out windows of opportunity that you have the competencies to take advantage of.** Consider how you can create a better, unique, differentiated, useful product or service with a fantastic value proposition. Seek out problems that you might be able to solve. Consider how you might make a group of people's lives/tasks easier. What can you offer that traditional businesses cannot? Personalization? More product choice via a wider range? Faster turnaround? Easier purchasing? A brand new solution?
5. **Think big, start small (and grow fast).** Visualize your long-term goals to create a focused vision.

(Continued)

6. **Let your vision guide your strategic decisions.** Your long-term vision should inform your choices as you move onwards and upwards, relating to growth, international expansion, product sets, value proposition, strategy, financing, purchasing choices, and so on.

7. **Uncover problems and discuss how you might solve them.** Don't be too stubborn or precious when it comes to your ideas. Think practically. How do people respond to your idea? Do they like it? Is it commercially viable i.e. will it make money? Is it sustainable? Can your idea generate repeat custom by fulfilling an existing need/unmet demand? If not, you may need to uncover what's missing or what needs changing.

8. **Listen to people's reactions when you explain your idea.** 'My worst decision was being too stubborn in the early days and not listening to people', admits Moo.com founder, Richard Moross.

9. **Do not fear failure or mistakes.** Failure provides valuable feedback. As such, mistakes are fantastic learning tools for entrepreneurs. They provide insight and help you make better informed choices as you progress.

10. **Go round brick walls.** If you come up against an obstacle, take the necessary action to shift direction and pivot on your original idea if necessary.

If you follow these tips you are more likely to find a great idea that works. You can also check that your idea fulfils certain criteria and has the following indicators of success.

Good Idea Checklist

Sir Richard Branson has incorporated five key criteria into each business and joint venture that he has started. Virgin-associated products/services must:

- be high quality
- be innovative
- be good value for money
- challenge existing alternatives
- have a sense of fun.

These are certainly worthwhile criteria to follow. However, in order to survive in a highly-competitive, fast-changing, digital climate, as well as being commercially viable by operating within a growing market with demonstrable demand, the best digital business ideas are:

1. clear and simple
2. useful, innovative and differentiated
3. disruptive.

So let's examine what this means to you and your idea . . .

1. Clear and simple

Once polished, your idea should be simple to explain and easy to summarize in one sentence. It must be understandable at a very basic level so you can explain your idea in no more than 60 seconds. If you can't do that, you'll find it difficult to pursue. A common way to explain this notion is through what's known in the business world as the 'elevator pitch'. It essentially means that you should be able to pitch your idea to a potential investor or partner in a lift or 'elevator' before they reach their floor and leave you and your opportunity behind.

In order to achieve this simplicity, your idea must have a clearly defined value proposition, i.e. a summary that explains what it is that you do and why customers choose you rather than your competitors. For example, in very simple terms both Tesco and easyJet's value proposition is 'low prices', while BMW and Bang & Olufsen's is 'quality'.

Many entrepreneurs try to develop all of their ideas or multiple products from day one and choose to do everything at once. This is a mistake. Not only does it take far more effort and dilute the potential success of the business by spreading efforts and resources more thinly, it also clouds the clarity of the value proposition. It therefore makes far more sense to start with a single product, focus on the detail, do it well and then expand from that product base over time.

The best ideas are simple and easy to explain.

Fundamentally, if you can deliver a simple idea with a clear value proposition providing something better than your competitors, you are onto a winner. In order to do this your idea must stand out from the rest.

> *'The key thing we have done and the reason we have been successful is we've focused entirely on creating a value proposition for the customer,'*
> **Jeff Bezos, Founder of Amazon**

Exercise

Define your value proposition here

_____

_____

_____

_____

2. Useful, innovative and differentiated

While the birth of the web opened up the world's information to all, it presented problems, the key issue being that the information was disorganized. Larry Page and Sergey Brin realized this and pursued their idea to create a solution to this problem and organize the world's information – the resulting enterprise is the world's largest search engine, Google (originally called BackRub!). Its mission/ vision: to organize the world's information and make it universally accessible and useful. 'The perfect search engine', says co-founder Larry Page on Google's 'Our Philosophy' web page, 'would understand exactly what you mean and give back exactly what you want. When Google began, you would have been pleasantly surprised to enter a search query and immediately find the right answer. Google became successful precisely because we were better and faster at finding the right answer than other search engines at the time.'[3] Ultimately Google provided something incredibly useful and differentiated itself by being better than anything else out there.

And therein lies the key: great ideas are *useful* and *better*. They provide a solution to a common problem. The best ideas do so in a way that has not been done before or certainly not in the way that you intend to do it. As such they meet a previously unmet demand and fill a gap by doing something better, quicker, cheaper than existing providers, by providing an attractive alternative solution. Great ideas effectively serve a previously underserved market and/or a gap in the market: a sure-fire way to reap rewards in business.

- Anything Left-Handed was the first specialist left-handed business in the world. AnythingLeftHanded.co.uk provides a single location for the global niche market of left-handed people (15% of the world's population) to buy items especially designed for them: from scissors and tin openers to golf clubs and mugs. It provides products and information to make life easier for left-handers around the world, solving problems encountered by left-handed people in a predominantly right-handed world. This had never been done before.
- MySingleFriend.com is a digital enterprise idea which was borne from founder Sarah Beeny's irritation with the options for online dating. She spotted a gap in the market and built a site around her ideas. According to the site, Sarah is notorious for setting her friends up with each other (with mixed consequences) so it occurred to her that, if she could create an online resource where she and her friends could describe their fabulous single friends, they could all 'check each other out'. So, Sarah and her school friend, Amanda Christie, created the antidote to the solitary 'online dating' experience, as friends join the site together.
- TheGadgetShop.com founder came up with his business idea after leaving his Christmas shopping to the very last minute and being

unable to find what he wanted. He provided a solution to a problem he encountered.

- When Hugh Chappell launched TrustedReviews.com with the Editor-In-Chief of *Personal Computer World* Magazine, he made sure his online publication was better than the rest. Unlike traditional computer magazines, TrustedReviews was free to consumers, there were no space limitations so reviews would be as long as they needed to be. Furthermore, new products were reviewed and published immediately compared to traditional magazine content which was often out of date by the time it hit the shelves. TrustedReviews published several reviews per day, seven days per week, which magazines simply couldn't compete with. Consequently, by the time Hugh sold the business to TimeWarner/IPC Media in October 2007, the site was attracting two million unique visitors per month, more than the circulation of all the computer magazines put together.

- Vision Express founder, Dean Butler, took advantage of a gap in existing offerings by establishing an opticians that solved a common problem. His wife, like many other spectacle wearers, was upset when her optician informed her she'd have to wait seven days for new glasses. Dean created a business from a missed opportunity to ensure that his wife never had to face that problem again.

- James Murray-Wells spent the last £1000 of his student loan setting up GlassesDirect.co.uk – solving the common problem of overpriced spectacles. When he needed a new pair of reading glasses he was staggered by the £150 price tag for what was essentially a piece of wire and two pieces of glass. He was studying for his finals and thought there must be a way of making glasses less expensive. He discovered that the glasses market hadn't changed in 50 years. Despite huge opposition from the high street he found a way to provide consumers (who were used to spending £150+ on a pair of spectacles) with an affordable alternative. His range starts from £15 with lenses. Three years after launch he had sold 150,000 pairs of glasses and has since secured two rounds of funding totalling £12.9 m. By uncovering a gap in the market he broke the mould of the traditional optician and turned a mature and established industry on its head.

Each of these people spotted and/or developed a solution to a problem experienced by many people.

Ultimately business is about providing a better choice and providing better solutions, often where there was previously limited choice (such as the market for spectacles). By addressing the needs of spectacle wearers, noticing where customer frustrations lay, and recognizing what was missing in the marketplace, such as cheaper and faster-made glasses, both Dean and James were able to reap significant rewards.

Differentiation and innovation are critical in business, particularly in the fiercely competitive digital marketplace. Digital businesses must stand out from the crowd by providing one or more Unique Selling Points (USPs). With the competition literally only a click away, you must have a differentiator that makes you stand out in some way; there must be a reason for your customers to choose you over anyone else.

Evidently, ideas need not be entirely unique or ground-breaking; they just need to be better than those ideas which have gone before them. Being first to market can be problematic as someone with bigger budgets and braver backers may follow, copy and win the race.

Fortunately, you don't need to be pioneering to succeed in business. Modification of existing successful ideas is generally the norm in the world of enterprise. If a market is large enough, there's enough room for everyone.

'We're not going to be the first to this party, but we're going to be the best.'
Steve Jobs

Google was not the first ever search engine and, as such, did not invent search engines or the pay-per-click model. Excite, Yahoo, AltaVista, and Infoseek, among others, were up and running before Google launched in 1998. However, Google's founders created a search product that outshone the others. It presented a better offering by using its link rating and relevance system, PageRank and developed a superior AdWords product from the existing pay-per-click concept, pioneered in the US by GoTo and in Europe by eSpotting. This strategy of differentiation and creating a better and more intuitive product has turned Google into the biggest media company in the world, with a value of $170bn, almost six times that of Rupert Murdoch's News Corp!

It's also worth looking laterally to find good ideas that exist in other parts of the world but have not yet entered your own country's consciousness. If you can capitalize on an opportunity ahead of the crowd, you need not have invented a brand new product or service to reap rewards. For example, importing something not yet seen over here can be a great way to offer a differentiated product without reinventing the wheel. As an observant 13-year-old, Dominic McVey spotted a trend for collapsible scooters in America. He ordered one over the Internet, sold it and bought two more. The trend translated well to UK shores and, after selling the new type of scooters over the Internet to a public that was hungry for a new gadget, Dominic became a teenage millionaire. This was an innovative and shrewd move, which bypassed the high risk and cost of launching a brand new product or service.

Ultimately, ideas are about finding the link in the chain, uncovering what's missing in existing 'solutions' or coming up with a different or new way of doing something. Being an entrepreneur is about creating your own thumb print and going in the opposite direction (or at least in a slightly different direction) to the majority to persuade customers to choose you over the competition.

Your USP might be that you can provide things faster, at a lower cost, or provide better premium quality, customer service, or after-care. You might be able to provide a larger or more focused range of products or might be able to source your products from a more ethical supply chain. Whatever you do, if your business idea is uniquely differentiated in some way – and protected too – you'll have immediate competitive advantage.

Exercise

Define your key competitor's value proposition here

How do you intend to differentiate yourself from their value proposition? What steps will you have to take?

- Think about how you can provide something better, faster, cheaper, safer than the rest?
- List existing areas of frustration for consumers or businesses within the marketplace you intend to target. Can you spot any windows of opportunity?
- Think laterally. Can you import something and refine it to suit the UK market? What's hot in the world today? What's going to be hot tomorrow?

---

3. Disruptive

Of course there are some entrepreneurs who are born to be pioneering. For them it helps if they are daring too. For instance, some businesses take the notion of differentiation to the next level and challenge existing alternatives in a way that drastically improves and shakes up entire industries and traditional business models. Such companies are called 'disruptive' and these ideas are not just good, but truly great!

Disruptive ideas tend to occur within markets where there are many unsatisfied customers. Take game changers such as Skype, which entirely disrupted the telecommunications industry and became the world's largest telecoms business, with over half a billion users, or eBay's redefinition of the second-hand goods industry. It can pay dividends to be a game changer. These types of business seek out traditional set-in-their-ways sectors that are failing to satisfy their disgruntled customers and come up with a worthwhile alternative. If your business idea is disruptive, all the better.

The likes of Google completely disrupted the *Yellow Pages* and traditional advertising industry. Amazon disrupted the retail status quo in terms of the way consumers buy products. Virgin Airlines and easyJet disrupted the air travel industry, so much so that existing players in the market had to drastically change the way they did business in order to compete.

NakedWines.com founder Rowan Gormley disrupted the wine industry by selling 'better wines at lower prices.' He did this by removing the middleman from the equation, and enabling the wine consumer to connect directly with the wine maker and pre-order their wines in advance of the wine-maker making it. This gives the wine maker back the time they'd have spent marketing/selling to focus on making delicious wine/improving their products. Consequently, the customer gets a better tasting wine for a lower price, exclusively.

Can you think of ways to turn an established industry on its head?

Whatever idea you have, if it ticks these indicators of success and has evolved well, it's likely to succeed, as long as it adheres to a proven model. So, having explored the evolution of ideas and what makes a business idea a good one, it's time to focus on the commercial side of things. Now you can answer the question: what's the big idea? It's also time to answer the next burning query: how will it make money? So, let's explore the different types of digital business model available to you.

Step Two

Choose Your Business Model

'Business models doing well today are those which have exclusive products or exclusive pricing; the flash sales models or sites like Made.com.'
Brent Hoberman

Old economy or new economy, digital or otherwise, there are a number of ingredients which are vital determinants of success. From impressive products and services which delight customers, to sustaining a competitive edge and having a top-notch team; from having financial discipline of the bottom line (i.e. generating more money than you spend) to having strong foundations and processes – each one is mandatory.

There's little point having an impressive workforce if you don't have an equally impressive product to sell. Just as there is little value in having an outstanding product if you have no financial discipline. Of course there are some exceptions to the rule of starting out with no business model. Twitter, for example, which was five years old in 2011, attracts 200 million users and sits on a goldmine of personal information, only announced its business model – advertising via Promoted Tweets and B2B subscription via charging for commercial accounts – in 2010. However long you take to instate your model, it is critical to choose it wisely, for it is this – your business model – which will determine how profitable your business is likely to be.

This chapter will:

- **Walk you through the variety of business models that currently exist within the digital space.**
- **Help you to select the most robust revenue streams to suit your idea which best adheres to the needs of your customers.**
- **Understand the pros and cons of each model, and how to implement them successfully.**

All Change: The New Digital Currency

Books written more than five years ago on the topic of online business state that there are only three main models for online business, namely: e-commerce, subscription and advertising. That's because, a decade ago, Internet businesses used to sell stuff or banner ads. That was it. Today though, in an era of the cloud and the crowd, digital enterprises can sell data and downloads; apps and content, leads and licenses. They can attract users with freemium offerings before selling them premium versions, or involve users in choosing what they actually sell. They can sell through a computer or mobile device.

Not only *what* is sold and *how* it is sold has changed, but the way in which digital businesses build their very foundations has also altered. In recent years, attention and reputation have prevailed as new forms of digital currency (see the following table).

Whether you focus on attention or revenue (or both) as currency, the key point here is that, in order to take this trajectory of wowing consumers before

	WEB 1.0	**WEB 2.0**	**WEB 3.0**
Type	Semantic Internet (interaction between machines)	Social Internet (interaction between people)	Semantic + Social Internet (rise of machine-to-machine applications and social networking)
Elements	Directories	Tagging	Geo-social tools
	Content stickiness	Content syndication	User generated content
			Augmented reality
	Publishing	Participation	Personalization
	Content management	Wikis	Community
Typical business models	Create monetization opportunity first	Attract traffic (attention/reputation) first, then monetize	
	E-tail	Me-tail, flash sales and daily deals	
	Sell traditional goods	Sell traditional goods plus data, downloads, apps, content, leads, licenses, APIs, services, platforms, virtual goods	
	Advertising (page views)	Advertising (CPC)	
	Affiliate	Freemium and revenue share	

profiting from them, you must come up with something that is compelling enough to gain traction.

Monetization methods

Digital companies have monetized their large user communities in various ways, using different models, from e-tail and revenue share to freemium and advertising. Some have sold services to them directly, such as Salesforce.com which sells services to enterprises. Some have generated revenue by taking a share of each transaction that occurs on the platform that they have provided, such as eBay. Others, from Google and Skype, MySQL to Last.fm and, more recently, to Doodle.com and GroupSpaces, have provided products or services entirely free of charge to individual consumers, in order to build huge audiences. They have then generated revenue by selling premium versions of their offerings to a sizeable fraction of their customer base, sometimes to consumers, other times by selling 'enterprise versions' or B2B (Business to Business) products to companies.

Others building equally huge networks of users, have monetized their traffic by selling behaviourally targeted ads and sponsorship such as Facebook and Myspace. In fact, as Facebook surpassed 800 million global users in 2011, it secured its place in history as a digital phenomenon. Half of Britain uses the site. Indeed, cliché though it is, if Facebook was a country it would be the third largest in the world, larger than the USA! And it is able to sell incredibly well-targeted advertisements due to the sheer volume of personal data (from likes and pastimes to status updates and musical preferences) that it has collected from its loyal, open, participatory and active user-base. It generated $3 billion ad revenue in 2011 by getting the right content to the right people, providing a blend of non-social ads and social ads, (the latter tell you which brands your friends like) and ultimately creating an eco-system and social platform which enables word of mouth at scale.

People powered models

Indeed, the digital space has become far more participatory and open. Users/consumers have their own identities and are in control. People are connecting, reconnecting and interacting. Companies are having richer conversations with those whom they target their wares at. Command and control has effectively become collaboration and communication.

Digital entrepreneurs can use this openness and rise of people power to their advantage. How? By enabling users to become evangelists for their offerings, by creating things of brilliance, putting them in front of a large community of users and interacting with those users to improve those offerings further.

The core requirement – to differentiate from the rest – has encouraged entrepreneurs to think outside the box and give existing business models a new twist. Many of these tweaked business models have emerged as a direct response to the increasingly open, user-led Internet experience. Consequently, the digital universe has enabled entrepreneurs to create business models which cut out the middleman to save their customers' money.

For example, me-tailers Made.com have halved the price of contemporary furniture by stripping the wholesaler and retailer from the equation, empowering consumers to get involved in the process of selection by connecting consumers directly with the furniture makers, many of whom make furniture for designer brands.

The founders of Made.com use their website cleverly as a platform to showcase furniture designs and then encourage consumers to vote on their favourites. The pieces voted as most popular go into production as a manufacturer makes the exact number of items ordered. Using 'crowd-sourcing' to choose its range results in no waste or unsold stock, while voters are rewarded for their participation with a discount. The company's ambition is 'to bring original design to the masses by revolutionizing the furniture retail market.' By tapping into the opportunity of linking the consumer to the manufacturer, Made.com has revolutionized the way people buy furniture by offering high quality at a more affordable price, while maintaining design integrity. Customers pay upfront and the exact number of pieces are ordered and sent direct to the customers' homes, so there is no inventory and no need for a warehouse to store anything. A win–win operation.

Another online retailer – Naked Wines – takes a similar approach, creating a virtuous cycle where independent winemakers pitch directly to NakedWines.com customers (known as 'angels') who select their favourites. The customers sponsor the winemakers who make the wine for Naked Wines exclusively.

'It is a completely new way of buying wine, where everyone wins', says founder Rowan Gormley. 'It's not just a case of a traditional wine merchant advertising wine and telling people to drink it, we're saying to customers "it's your money, you decide where we are going to invest it,"' he adds. In harnessing that people power, Rowan and his team have grown the company to £20 m turnover in just three years.

Linking the consumer to the manufacturer/producer directly, by providing a link in the chain, is a huge business opportunity; but the NakedWines.com business model goes beyond introducing them directly.

'Our customers actually invest in our winemakers and fund them, which is why we call them angels and, by doing that, they transform the winemaker's business. In exchange for changing their lives, the winemaker gives them their wines exclusively and at a preferential price. So it's not just a marketplace, it couldn't exist without the customers' support. So it's much more of a virtuous circle.'

'The Internet has opened up possibility for small companies to beat the giants at their own game', says Rowan. 'It's opened up a whole new way of doing business.'

'Historically supermarkets used their size as their biggest asset, because buying power means low prices and high sales volume, which means more buying power. The Internet has tilted the see-saw back again so that, for the first time in hundreds of years, little companies have got as much of a shot, if not more, than the big companies.

'The fundamental principles of this new way of doing business are:

1. You give your power to the customers (i.e. the right to decide what you're selling, how you sell it, what goes in to the site, how it's priced and everything else).
2. In exchange they give you their support, which could be financial, as in our case.
3. You take that support and transform the suppliers business by passing it on to them, and you create a virtuous circle where everyone's a winner.'

Evidently, the masses matter more than ever before. They have a voice. And savvy digital entrepreneurs are now harnessing the power of those voices to directly impact what they stock, sell and do over the Internet.

Consumers are holding the cards in the digital universe. Me-tail crowd-sourcing models, flash sales models and group discount models, all new twists on existing 'e-tail', enable consumers to get what they want for lower prices. Customers are driving stock choices and discount levels.

These modern models work because today's digital world is primarily about connection. For LinkedIn.com that's about connecting business contacts. For eBay.com that means connecting sellers with buyers. For Made.com and Naked-Wines.com that involves connecting consumers directly with the furniture makers/wine producers.

Connecting people essentially enables people to do something they couldn't do previously. These models of connection cannot be easily replicated in the bricks and mortar world. It's not merely taking a traditional offline business and sticking it up online, it's about becoming an enabling conduit to create win–win business models where consumers and suppliers benefit, thus creating a sustainable competitive advantage.

Exercise

Connect

Consider the connections that you might use to optimize, enhance or modify your chosen business model.

List target audiences, suppliers, customers, partners, acquaintances, contacts, friends... can you provide a link in the chain? Can you make life easier for anyone by connecting them with someone else? Can you introduce or get introduced to someone for mutual gain?

Digital Business Models Explained

There are a variety of business models available to entrepreneurs starting up a digital business. So let's examine these in detail:

1. The Freemium Model
2. The E-commerce Model
3. The Advertising Model
4. The Affiliate Model
5. The Revenue Share Model
6. The Subscription Model
7. The App Store Model

Clearly there are a variety of business models available to entrepreneurs start-ing up a digital business. So let's examine these.

1. The freemium model

This means providing a free version and selling a premium version. Doodle.com, Skype, MYSQL and GroupSpaces all provide products or services entirely free of charge to individual consumers in order to build huge audiences.

Many savvy digital enterprises have harnessed the power of free to their advantage. By focusing on large reach and consumer uptake above all else, some of the world's most successful pioneering companies have achieved prosperity by giving stuff with inherent value away for free.

The freemium model is where a paid-for premium version supports a free version of a product or service. This is nothing new. Gillette gave away free razors and sold all-important (and expensive) razor blades at a premium as early as the 1920s. By putting your product or service in the hands of the maximum number of people (i.e. by giving it away) you can convert a percentage of those people into paying customers.

> 'For the Google Generation, the Internet is the land of the free.'
> **Chris Anderson, editor-in-chief of *Wired* magazine,**
> **and author of *The Long Tail* and *Free***

Google provided the world with a free search engine, offered e-mail (or G-mail) free of charge along with a multitude of other valuable and popular services, from Google Maps to Google Docs; from Google Chrome (the fastest growing web browser) to its Android OS (half a million Android devices are activated each day). All of their consumer-facing offerings are entirely free of charge. They charge businesses instead: a strategy that has undeniably paid off.

As a direct result of their generosity they have shrewdly accrued an outra-geously large user base. This has made their paid-for B2B offerings such as Google Adwords extremely attractive to companies wanting to advertise on the world's most popular search engine. So attractive that Google today generates billions in net profit ($6.5 billion net profit in 2009) and revenue (setting a revenue record at $9.03 billion for the quarter ended June 30, 2011) with 98% of its revenues coming from advertising.

'Our emerging high usage products can generate huge new businesses for Google in the long run, just like search,' says Google co-founder, Larry Page. 'And we have tons of experience monetizing successful products over time. Well run technology businesses with tremendous consumer usage make a lot of money over the long term.'[4]

Google's business model is to create amazing products for free which drive rapid and vast global adoption over the long-term, *before* monetizing. In order for this strategy to work, however, it's vital to be providing something truly amazing.

Skype, too, opted to offer their services for free, charging only for their premium version. They were only able to do this because their service didn't cost much to provide. Customers downloading their free software (to make free calls via their computers) use their own bandwidth and peer-to-peer software. It therefore doesn't cost Skype anything to serve users, making their customer acquisition and distribution costs minimal.

Crucially, because they had created an innovative and disruptive service that provided users with a very attractive free alternative to the traditional telecoms model, Skype created a product that had huge viral potential and spread via word of mouth across the globe. This kept their marketing costs to a minimum, as is the case with virally endorsed products. Consequently, hundreds of millions of people downloaded the free version of the software, while 12% of those paid for premium mobile and landline calls. In essence the minority of paying customers partially subsidized the non-paying ones. Perhaps even more importantly, with such a huge database of users they became an attractive acquisition target. eBay bought Skype in 2005 for $2.6 billion!

Similarly MySQL, the open source software business, gave its software away for free and charged businesses for maintenance and support. MySQL was acquired by Sun Microsystems in 2008 for $800 million.

If you give consumers something fantastic for free, you not only lower the barriers of adoption and encourage rapid uptake, those consumers will often show their gratitude by spreading the word, becoming evangelical about your proposition and providing you with much-needed feedback to help you tweak and improve your offerings.

Exercise

Freemium implementation

Consider how you might implement the Freemium model, e.g. by offering:

1. A free version of a product and a better/upgraded version of the product at a premium, as with Skype. A free version to one type of customer (individual consumers or early stage companies) and a paid-for version to another type (businesses of a certain size/revenue base) as with MySQL, Twitter or Google.
2. One licence for free and subsequent licenses for a fee.
3. A free time-limited trial (so customers can sample your wares, enabling them to discover that they simply must have it and, when the trial period runs out, happily pay up).
4. A free feature-limited subscription (so customers can get basic features for free but must pay to use the more attractive, useful, added-value features).

As illustrated by point 4 above, Freemium also works with the subscription model. For example, MySingleFriend.com works on this basis. The site uses a subscription model as its revenue stream; however it attracts users by offering a 'free profile'. As such, it is free to join and users can gain certain limited benefits from their free membership, such as searching, inviting friends to make recommendations to them, receiving messages and seeing who they are from. However, with a free profile you cannot send, read or reply to messages unless you upgrade to become a paying member, subscribing for anything from one month to six months at a time.

While the freemium business model is a viable one, particularly to those with deep-pocketed financial backers who can fund any early losses, it is worth using a revenue-generating model alongside freemium in order to keep innovating products and building a strong team.

Ultimately today, in the land of the free, as Chris Anderson says, 'Web entrepreneurs have to not just invent products that people love, but also those that they will pay for. Free may be the best price, but it can't be the only one.'[5]

That's why sites such as FourSquare and Spotify use a blend of advertising *and* freemium models. Foursquare charges local businesses to use its dashboard service while Spotify uses a 'buy now' feature so users can download tracks using a micro-payment model, along with an ad-funded model to complement its freemium model, so users of their free version must be prepared to hear an ad between tracks.

Whatever your premium product is, it must compel people who have the free version to pay.

2. The e-commerce model (E-Tail)

This means selling stuff or services as a merchant or broker including variations such as me-tailing (crowd-sourcing), flash sales, and digital media downloads (micropayments). Moonpig, Naked Wines, iTunes and Gilt Groupe all sell directly to end users.

Straightforward products

Products that sell well online via web browsers (e-commerce) and via mobile phones (m-commerce) include items that have historically sold well via mail-order; from cards, books and clothes to gifts, gadgets, games, software and hobbyist products.

By targeting a large yet focused niche audience you will have a good scope to earn repeat custom and maximize revenue by up-selling to customers. For example, if you choose to set up a business selling electric guitars over the web, you might also sell guitar lessons to those customers or partner with an instrument insurance provider in a revenue-share deal.

Ultimately, if you can

* source or create something at a lower price than the price you then sell it for;
* justify there is enough demand from a growing/niche market; and
* package and distribute your products easily . . .

. . . you can sell pretty much anything over the Internet.

Virtual goods and digital downloads

In fact, you can even sell virtual goods. Zynga, the company behind social farm game, Farmville, for instance, sells virtual crops. The company has made tens of millions by selling digital goods such as corn and sweet potato seeds to users of its free social game. Indeed, social gaming such as Farmville has become successful as a business model because it enables a wider market (non-gamers) to get involved in gaming in little windows of time they might have. And it's certainly grabbing significant market share. Of Facebook's 500m monthly users, around 250m play social games. That's a huge market to sell virtual goods to, even if you offer the game itself for free download via the freemium model and pay sites like Facebook a 30% commission.

iTunes brought micropayments for digital products to the mainstream by selling singles for 99c. However, it is important to note that, in the case of music, license fees that the record labels charge iTunes are astronomical. So much so that, despite selling 2.4 billion tracks in 2008, iTunes, whilst profitable, is primarily about pushing adoption of the real revenue driver of Apple, namely its hardware: iPods and iPads. Digital downloads are a viable business model, but only if you can get enough scale.

Customer-led: me-tail and flash sales

Sites like the aforementioned Made.com and NakedWines.com have developed a twist on the traditional e-tail model via me-tail. As a me-tailer you are not only listening to your customers, you are putting crucial decisions (about what stock you sell) into their hands.

Another retail twist has come in the shape of the flash sales model which is gaining in popularity with discount-hungry consumers keen to snag a bargain online. The flash sales e-commerce model sells products directly to consumers on behalf of a brand or brands by providing invitation-only access to top brands, from fashion to furniture, at highly discounted prices. After notifying members of upcoming sales via e-mail and SMS, their high-speed 'flash' sales, which last just a few days, provide aggressive discounts to members who are quick to snap up the limited quantities on offer.

Flash sales drive down prices by helping brands to offload excess, unsold or introductory inventory to an exclusive and discerning audience, harnessing the power of urgency and scarcity.

The flash sales model requires a method of generating large databases of users in order to persuade brands to participate and tends to work best within markets such as retail and electronics where new season lines, versions and models make existing stock obsolete.

The potential pay-off can be attractive as investors are certainly taking note. Founded in 2007, flash sales site Ideeli has so far raised $70 million funding. It currently provides its four million members with 50–70 percent discounts on clothing and accessories during its private member-only flash sales.

Profitable flash sales site Gilt Groupe has so far raised $100 million in investment and has been valued at $400 million, while HauteLook was recently acquired by Nordstrom for $270 million. However the flash sales model is not a new phenomenon. It was pioneered by sites such as vente-privee.com which was founded in France in 2001 and recently teamed up with American Express to launch the site in the USA.

We'll cover how to build a great website in Step Five. However, you may decide not to have your own domain/website, instead opting to use existing tried-and-tested platforms from which to sell your wares, such as eBay, Amazon Marketplace or art and crafts sites, Etsy.com or Folksy.com. Not only does this enable you to start selling online almost immediately, you can test what sells the best, and won't need to fork out for website design, development, hosting, security, payment gateways and so on. You can also deal with as high quantities as are demanded.

According to eBay there were 127 eBay enterprises turning over at least £1 m in 2010, double the number of eBay millionaires from the previous year. Similarly, F-Commerce (Facebook Commerce) shouldn't be ignored either. While there is not yet the ability to sell direct from Facebook, you can set up a free storefront on your Facebook page to showcase your goods via iFrames (in the central Facebook page column) or via Facebook apps. Some brands enable their users to select products and view delivery dates and do as much as is possible on Facebook before taking them off to their own secure shopping sites.

Of course, you need not sell actual *stuff* to make money online.

Selling expertise

You could monetize your expertise by creating information products and content based on your specialist area. Take Paulette Ensign of Tips Products International (TipsBooklets.com), who I met back in 1999. She has sold well over a million copies of her booklet *110 Ideas for Organizing Your Business Life* in various languages and formats, and made a good living by recycling the same 3500 words since 1991, without spending a penny on advertising.

She did this initially by sending copies to magazines and inviting them to excerpt from her booklet in articles with an invitation for readers to send $5 plus an SAE to her. She then licensed the booklet to companies that wished to customize it with their own logos. Once she had achieved success in this way she then had a new specialist area to monetize – how to make money from 'tips products'. Subsequently Paulette went on to sell audio and video workshops teaching others how to profit from publishing their own booklets and then paid commission to others selling her booklets, adopting the affiliate model by going where the traffic was. Paulette created a mini empire from one 16-page booklet.

Selling services

You may have skills and expertise that you can sell as a service. From management consultancy and accounting to web design or copywriting.

If this is the case, your website and mobile site will act either as a compelling brochure persuading visitors why they should use your services over your competitors, or will enable people to order your services directly. If the latter is the case, you will need e-commerce functionality in order to take payment for your services. If the former is true, you won't need such functionality as customers will pay you via traditional means, via cheque or bank transfer.

Regardless of how you are paid, your service should harness the demands of a growing market. For example, you might set up your own business producing apps for mobile phones, developing websites and/or m-commerce sites. For every website that goes up, there's someone who's got to design and build it, provide the content for it, represent the advertising for it, create mobile versions of it, and so on. Indeed, for those with the right skills and areas of expertise, the opportunity to service the digital space in itself is huge.

Back in 1999 I used my own expertise, having written a number of booklets on the topic of Internet business as an employee, to start my first digital enterprise, WebCritique. I critiqued websites for a living by providing Website Appraisal Reports for people wishing to improve their websites. I sold the business in 2005 to focus on my writing, but it was a worthwhile growth market to enter into, and still is.

Selling data

You might gather competitive intelligence data by analyzing your own users' data or data that you pay others to monitor, whether that is Internet usage data (as Hitwise have done) or market research data (as collected and supplied by companies such as Mintel). Property website Zoopla also charges for the data it captures via its website, using an infomediary model, among others.

Selling data, whether it is about usage, behaviour or geo-specific, works best if you have enough traffic, just like the advertising model. If you can collect and analyze data in a structured and segmented way, and produce reports that clients within your industry will be interested in buying, the infomediary model may be worth exploring.

The benefit of selling information or services is that you need not stock any inventory, may not have to take payment online and won't need to fund fulfilment. The same is true of selling leads which comes under the bracket of the affiliate model, explained below.

Selling licensing

Just as Paulette Ensign licensed her tips booklet to others, and MyDeco.com licenses its 3D technology, if you can provide a white label solution whereby you license your product, software or service to another company, this can be particularly profit-worthy. That's what pay-per-click pioneer, eSpotting did. They licensed their technology and their results to Yahoo, Google, AltaVista and Ask, so their results appeared within those companies search results, giving them an additional revenue stream. They also licensed the whole back-end of the eSpotting platform to a company in Sweden enabling that company to have their own pay-per-click engine.

Exercise

E-Tail implementation

Consider which way you might implement the e-tail model, e.g. by offering:

1. Straightforward products for sale via e-commerce and m-commerce (on your own site or via a partner's marketplace, such as eBay, Amazon or Etsy.com) which can be packaged and distributed easily and target a niche audience.
2. Low cost virtual goods and digital downloads such as 'ingredients' or 'tools' for digital social games, social games themselves, 'gifts' and e-greetings or digital products such as e-books, white papers, podcasts, videos and music.
3. Products via the customer-led me-tail or flash sales models whereby customers either vote on what you sell or flock to buy heavily-discounted, limited-number, quality goods via invitation-based online sales.
4. Expertise via selling physical or downloadable information products, training courses or software as a way to earn additional revenue (on top of money earned from speaking engagements, face-to-face training and so on). You might even license your products to someone else or sell in bulk to a like-minded company.
5. Services that help others to fill the gaps in their own skillsets either for a flat fee, hourly/day rate, per word rate, payable in instalments as the service is provided or instantly on ordering or completion.
6. Informative data that you have legally collected, analyzed and segmented which other companies can use to their advantage, be it statistical, about industry trends, preferences or usage.
7. Licensing your technology, product, software or service directly by providing a white-label solution to another company so that your product/service appears with their branding rather than your own.

3. The advertising model

This means selling advertising space. Google and TrustedReviews.com are examples of sites which provide advertisers with a targeted platform on which to advertise.

Many digital businesses use the advertising model as a secondary revenue stream rather than the primary one; however many commentators deem it

---

Securing Your First Advertisers

Hugh Chappell's TrustedReviews.com website, for example, is highly targeted within a specific niche and generated significant user numbers which exceeded the circulation of the computer magazines combined. Gaining traction to create a market leader gives advertisers scale.

After examining types of ads and ways of selling that traditional publications and online magazines were doing, Hugh Chappell went against the grain to get initial advertisers on board.

'I introduced forms of advertising that others were not doing', explains Hugh. 'The typical way of selling advertising online is CPM (cost per thousand impressions). In 2003 that was primarily how people did it. But I had the conundrum that, on day one, my traffic was zero. So one example was how do I get advertising customers from day one when I've got no traffic?'

Hugh's solution harked back to a time when, aged 21, he signed up as a member of a new club in town. The club offered a 'founder rate' to its original members. 'I joined and, many years later, they kept that founder rate the same, even though the cost of joining became several times higher.'

'So I offered a founder rate to a limited number of advertisers, those who came on board first.' Years later, when Hugh sold the business most of the founder members remained. 'I never forgot the fact that they supported me at that very early stage and in return, they continued to pay that founder rate.'

With TrustedReviews.com, Hugh chose the advertising model as the key revenue driver because he knew that, in order to gain market share from the traditional publishers who had controlled the print market, he would have to make his product free to consumers. 'We made a decision very quickly that we couldn't charge people to read it', says Hugh. 'For the print magazines that option wasn't possible.' Their circulation had been falling since 1999, thanks, in part, to the rise in computer literacy, but also due to Internet uptake. By providing a better product (better quality reviews which were longer, more detailed, and available to read instantly), TrustedReviews.com gained traction. Ultimately, by providing something better, his site attracted a substantial readership. And by growing a large and targeted readership, they naturally attracted advertisers.

unwise to sell advertising space if you are selling a product, as well-designed compelling adverts will take visitors away from your site. Conversely, some sites such as online magazines, subscription sites or social networks with large user numbers find the advertising model to be the best way to monetize their well-targeted web traffic, particularly if they have a compelling user base within a niche market. Certainly, the advertising model works best with highly specialized, high-volume traffic.

If offering a free service to users, unless you intend to offer a premium version, the advertising and affiliate models will probably be your main revenue generation methods.

Advertising formats

The regular advertising model uses the CPM (cost per thousand impressions) method of charging advertising clients, so the advertiser receives an invoice based on the number of times their ad has been displayed. If your CPM rate is £1 per thousand page impressions and your home page generates 150,000 page impressions per month, the advertiser would be charged £150.

Whether you choose an advertising model as your primary or secondary revenue stream, be creative in integrating advertising into your website. Many people simply stick a banner advert at the top of their site and leave it at that. Yet there are many alternatives to standard formats of display advertising.

For instance, you can create different sponsorship levels and customized channels or pages, or you might include paid links and buttons, text ads, or advertising integrated within rich media, such as pre-roll and post-roll video opportunities and branded players where ads or sponsor messages appear before or after useful video content or are embedded into the design of a video player.

You can also earn revenue from placing Google ads on your site, via their Adsense programme: enabling Google to populate certain areas of your site with relevant text ads.

The expenditure on online advertising has now overtaken that of television advertising for the first time. According to the UK's Internet Advertising Bureau (IAB), Internet advertising has the highest market share of any other country (23.5%). While these statistics sound encouraging for those seeking to earn revenues from digital advertising, it's important to note that:

a) online display advertising (banners, MPUs and leaderboards, etc) decreased by 5.2%;

b) Google takes the lion's share of all advertising revenue (62.6%); and

c) generating a large, scalable and highly targeted audience to appeal to advertisers takes a lot of resource, both in terms of time and money, although if you have something uniquely differentiated that appeals to users, you could gain traction reasonably quickly. It took Hugh Chappell just four years to grow his readership from zero to two million unique visitors per month.

If you do sell advertising space on your website, as well as needing decent traffic numbers, there are some important rules to remember:

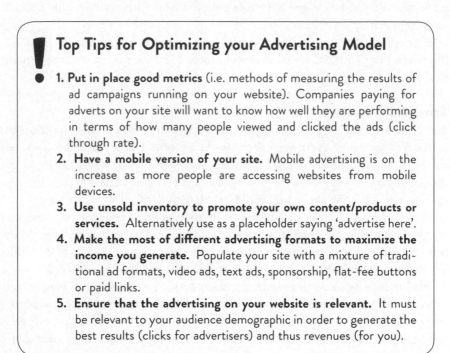

! Top Tips for Optimizing your Advertising Model

- 1. **Put in place good metrics** (i.e. methods of measuring the results of ad campaigns running on your website). Companies paying for adverts on your site will want to know how well they are performing in terms of how many people viewed and clicked the ads (click through rate).
- 2. **Have a mobile version of your site.** Mobile advertising is on the increase as more people are accessing websites from mobile devices.
- 3. **Use unsold inventory to promote your own content/products or services.** Alternatively use as a placeholder saying 'advertise here'.
- 4. **Make the most of different advertising formats to maximize the income you generate.** Populate your site with a mixture of traditional ad formats, video ads, text ads, sponsorship, flat-fee buttons or paid links.
- 5. **Ensure that the advertising on your website is relevant.** It must be relevant to your audience demographic in order to generate the best results (clicks for advertisers) and thus revenues (for you).

4. The affiliate model

This means selling leads, products or services for which you earn a commission, or providing a commission to other parties. Sites such as Cheapflights, Parkatmyhouse and MyDeco follow this model.

This model is inherently well-suited to the Internet because of the web's ability to match intending buyers and sellers. There are a number of variations of this model.

You might, for instance, generate revenue by matching buyers in a particular sector with sellers; charging companies for providing them with valuable leads (intending purchases). You can charge a commission of a sale (cost-per-acquisition), as a broker (as eBay and Parkatmyhouse.com do), or charge per-click (as Cheapflights.co.uk and MyDeco.com do). With the pay-per-click option, a company charges its advertisers each time an 'intending purchaser lead' clicks through to the advertisers website or calls its call centre. With cost-per-acquisition, the customer is charged each time a user actually buys from the site, rather than merely clicks through to it.

The brokerage affiliate model sees buyers and sellers brought together through a website which facilitates transactions, whether that is via a fee or a commission, through a marketplace, auction or other method.

Take Cheapflights.co.uk which pioneered online flight and travel price search and comparison back in 1996. Four years later it was the first UK dotcom to introduce pay-per-click as its advertising affiliate business model. As it explains on the Cheapflights.co.uk website: 'The model enables advertisers to publish their offers on Cheapflights sites for free, and to pay only for those highly qualified leads that click through to their own sites or telephone their call centres.'

UK property websites often use this model too. For example, RightMove charges advertisers a subscription fee. While Zoopla provides free information to the consumer and then monetizes its traffic using various business models: the affiliate model (by selling leads to estate agents, charging £1 for every possible buyer and £5 for a potential vendor, along with charging for listings and advertising) and data sales (selling market information from its extensive data gathering platform).

Many people use the affiliate model (cost-per-click or cost-per-acquisition) as a method of implementing a secondary revenue stream to earn extra money by linking to other people's sites. In simple terms, you earn commission should anyone click or click and buy from that trackable link on your site. This certainly worked as a secondary income stream for Hugh Chappell of TrustedReviews.com.

TrustedReviews reviewed technology products which generally fall in price rapidly, particularly as new models are frequently released. Hugh's reviews listed the price on the date the product was reviewed so he decided to offer a price comparison engine which featured live feeds from a specialist in the sector, Price Grabber.com. 'Every review would have "price as of date of review" and then "price now,"' explains Hugh. 'To the reader it was a TrustedReview price comparison engine, but if someone clicked to look at all the prices and then clicked through to a store, there was affiliate revenue for us. The revenue from price comparison was significant.'

Additionally, the affiliate model works the other way round. So, if you sell your own products or services you can join an affiliate network as a *merchant* rather than as an *affiliate* to boost your own product sales and enable other people to earn commission by linking to *your* site with a trackable link. So you pay others for generating sales or leads for you. When customers buy something via that link, they earn a cut of that sale – a sale you may never had received had it not been for your affiliate's link to your site.

Unfortunately, the straightforward traditional affiliate model of placing affiliate links to other websites and earning commission from orders placed via those links (and vice versa), is currently in jeopardy for both merchants and affiliates alike. This is due to something called the Google Panda project – a Google algorithm aimed at improving the relevance of its search results (great for Google users) by tidying up and removing from their search results 'low quality' links to websites which are deemed by them as not relevant or as duplicate content (not so great for some webmasters). In the process thousands of affiliate links have vanished from Google's search result pages.

As Brent Hoberman commented, 'I think the affiliate model is getting more and disseminated by Google. So what we've seen with Shopping.com and others is that they have lost a tremendous amount of traffic recently since Google's latest updates.'

The biggest hit sites/models have been content farms such as ehow.com; price comparison sites such as Ciao; voucher code and affiliate sites such as myvouchercodes.co.uk, and even review sites.

One of the criteria which now holds more importance than ever in terms of Google assessing which links and sites are high/low quality is the time spent by users on a particular site. So the length of time that a user interacts with content proves to Google that users value that content.

How much users value content is thus the biggest driver for Google when deeming how relevant pages are. Content rich sites such as econsultancy.com, mashable.com and metro.co.uk have therefore fared well since the Panda updates.

We shall examine the value of content in more detail in Step Five. However, while focusing on business models, it is important to understand how these changes may affect those pursuing an affiliate model.

❗ Top Tips for Making your Affiliate Model Work

● **1. Operate a broker or 'per-click' affiliate model (matching buyers with sellers as with** Cheapflights.com, MyDeco.com **or** Parkatmyhouse. com**).** This is preferable to a straightforward traditional affiliate model 'per-acquisition' as the latter method means you are dependent on the conversion rates achieved by your retail partners. That's why MyDeco.com has recently moved away from CPA to CPC.

2. Consider alternative models. To avoid being penalized for 'duplicate links' consider other ways to drive up sales than being an affiliate merchant and supplying others with links to your content.

3. Choose other business models as primary revenue drivers where possible. Unless you are certain that your affiliate model will not be affected by Google updates due to your high quality content.

4. Keep an eye on changes that Google makes. Read Google's 'webmaster guidelines' regarding content quality. Ultimately, if you deliver content that serves your customers' needs and develop a content strategy based on insights you gain from engaging with your customers, while simultaneously ensuring that your content is sharable, you should be able to stay in Google's good books, whichever model you choose.

One such company is Parkatmyhouse.com, founded in 2006 by Anthony Eskinazi. The site uses the broker affiliate model by matching buyers and sellers of car parking spaces.

Listing a parking space is free, but owners pay a fee to the site – which manages the booking and payment process – when their parking space is successfully rented out. The company has 125,000 drivers registered with its service. Additionally the site takes a commission on every parking space booking and is due to add advertising to the site as an additional revenue stream.

'We allow space owners to upgrade their listing so, if you've got a free listing, it'll appear in our search results, but if you want to make it stand out by making it bold, highlight or enhance it, you can pay a monthly fee which varies between £2 and £15', Anthony explains.

As such, the site uses a combination of brokerage affiliate and subscription models.

While those revenue models are his main focus, Anthony says that he also intends to talk with department of transport and local councils to offer a revenue share model to help them help their residents to make money, 'rather than the general council reputation of taking money out of home owners' pockets, this could be a way of putting it back in.'

Revenue share models are generally seen as a variation of the affiliate model.

Exercise

Assess merchants to pursue and affiliate schemes to join

- Consider which intending buyers you might match with which sellers. List the companies you might approach who may wish to sell goods or services to your captive audience. Are they likely to provide you a commission on leads you can generate for them?
- Consider whether brands you provide leads for would be most likely to pay a commission for each sale made (cost-per-acquisition) or for each time the link to their site is clicked (cost-per-click).
- List products or services which complement your own. Visit affiliate marketplaces such as AffiliateWindow.co.uk and TradeDoubler.com to see if you can sign up to affiliate programmes to earn extra revenue via lead generation.
- Evaluate revenue generated from bespoke lead generation partnerships and automated affiliate programmes to maintain the right balance between driving traffic away from your own site to the merchants site. Make sure it's worth it.

5. The revenue share model

This means providing a share of revenue from products/services that you sell, in exchange for something of benefit, such as exposure to a large targeted audience; or earning a share of revenue by providing exposure to a large reach as in the case of Daily Deals sites such as Groupon.

The mutual back-scratching model can be particularly useful for small start-up businesses with great ideas. It enables you to share risk, pool resources and spread costs with other enterprises. It also affords you with the chance to gain instant access to a large target audience and reap mutual rewards. All small enterprises need to do in order to enjoy these benefits is to share, collaborate and cooperate with a larger business which has considerable resources and reach.

Certainly, in today's economy, value is created through collaborative networks that open up a wider pool of talent, resources, ideas and knowledge. Julie Meyer, founder of FirstTuesday.com and investment firm, Ariadne Capital, calls this 'network orientation'. It's where small innovative companies, often start-ups operating in high growth sectors, partner with larger corporations to leverage the reach and resources of the big business for mutual gain. The small business brings to the table the opportunity (the innovative product/service) along with creativity, flexibility and talent; while the larger business provides access to their existing audience, distribution and corporate infrastructure.

By aligning themselves towards a shared purpose the big company can increase their margins, fill gaps in their portfolio or enter new growth markets, while the smaller company gets the opportunity to gain credibility within a sector and sell to a large existing customer base. Both parties share revenue created by their collaboration.

Julie Meyer suggests some ground rules to maximize success within the revenue sharing model. She warns small businesses against charging upfront fees 'for use of their clever monetization opportunity' and warns big businesses against 'imposing their business model on the start-up'.

Collaborative revenue-share partnerships are primarily about sharing the upside for mutual benefit and being clear about expectations and roles from the outset, i.e. who does what and why so. The win–win must work for everyone involved.

Since merging with and becoming a music service provider, I Like Music operates a partnership approach by building revenue-generating strategic alliances with large brands that have an audience to add value to their existing products and/or engagement plans through music.

For small digital businesses with unique or interesting added-value products, the revenue share model can be an attractive method of selling to a large audience that it would not have ordinarily had access to without the help of the company they are sharing revenue with. They then share revenue with that company as a way of thanking them for the exposure to a large reach of targeted people. While the large company benefits from content or products it would not have ordinarily had access to, or cannot recreate itself.

Sites such as Groupon use the revenue share model from the perspective of the large company providing the large reach. Groupon makes 50% of what each customer pays for a deal. By connecting merchants to customers via collective buying, daily deal sites like Groupon (just like retail flash sales sites) drive down prices by harnessing the 'value of volume' to encourage brands to provide large discounts to their large user bases. Like the flash sales model, discounted deals are time-limited and need a large database of users in order to persuade brands to participate and share such a hefty slice of the revenue (generally 50%).

6. The subscription model

This means selling subscriptions to content, such as news, or services, such as dating. The FT.com, Mysinglefriend.com and Lovestruck.comall sell subscriptions, payable annually or monthly.

Many sites combine subscription and advertising models. The monetization of content by charging users a periodic fee (daily, monthly or annually) to subscribe works well digitally because of the low-margin cost of information. The *Financial Times* and *New York Times* are good examples of the subscription model at work with hundreds of thousands of subscribers between them. Some sites opt for data over revenue by offering a free subscription to services, products or content in exchange for personal data. Such data can be valuable when it comes to selling targeted ads and products/services at the most likely customer sets and adding value to your site as an asset with a large user database that a potential acquiring company might be interested in.

Other sites bundle services and information together and charge for this premium content. The *New York Times*, for instance, offers free content on the day that news items are added to its site but, should you wish to access back articles, you must pay for them and are provided with access for 90 days. They also provide a personalized e-mail topic alert service to keep you posted when content of specific interest to you has been posted to the site. The *Wall Street Journal* and *Financial Times* have a subscription service where users pay to subscribe to premium information and services. The downside is that premium/paid-for articles don't appear on search engines. Another method is to charge per-article rather than a fixed rate, which is easier to implement by using micropayment options.

Many commentators have suggested that web users won't pay for information when so much is available for free, but the aforementioned popular publications have validated the subscription model of charging for access by offering unique bundles of information and interactive services such as e-mail notifications. However, they initially created value in the marketplace by offering a free time-limited trial to their subscription service.

In order to charge for content, the information and tools that the consumer is paying for must be of premium quality and, in some cases, might be customized or tailored to suit each specific customer.

In general, though, the revenue generated from subscriptions alone is not enough to sustain success. Hence the reason that subscription sites tend to boost their subscription revenues with classified, behavioural and display advertising, just as traditional print publications do.

Mysinglefriend.com operates a subscription model, engaging potential subscribers with a free profile but encouraging them to upgrade and pay to subscribe in order to gain access to the full site features (and ultimately be able to communicate with admirers who have sent messages or indicated interest, and so on).

'A huge proportion of our approved members go on to become regular paying users, a testament to what they get out of the website', says Sarah Beeny. 'It's important to make life easy, and ensure your product or service does what people need it to. On Mysinglefriend every profile is checked manually, and we take people off the site if they haven't logged in for a few months', adds Sarah. 'This means the quality of the profiles and response rates are significantly higher than on other sites.'

Lovestruck.com is another dating site, this time aimed specifically at busy single city professionals, which follows the subscription model. The site matches time-strapped city singles to others who work close by for quick coffee, lunch or after-work dates. Like MySingleFriend.com, Lovestruck.com attracts users by offering a free-to-browse version which can be upgraded at any time to take full advantage of the service.

As a Free Member of Lovestruck.com you can add your profile and up to four photos, browse the entire 'little black book' member base and wink at members that you fancy. However, the site offers Connect or Elite Membership which enable paid-subscribers to send unlimited messages, add more photos, view members' photo albums, see who's listed them as a favourite, receive email alerts about new matches and get instant alerts when someone is 'Free For Lunch' or 'Free Tonight'.

Aside from subscription and events revenue streams, Lovestruck.com also earns additional revenue from its advertising model. The site's busiest territories are London, Hong Kong and Singapore, and has over half a million visits a month generating 12 million page impressions. As such it enables advertisers to put their brand in front of locally-targeted or national audiences that can also be split by gender and age. This means that advertisers can achieve an optimum ROI by targeting the exact audience.

Lovestruck.com is now turning over £150k a month in subscriptions and is profitable following investment from various business angels, including Hugh

Chappell, wishing to take advantage of the online dating sector which, according to Mintel, is set to be worth £150 m by 2014.

Co-founder of the site, Brett Harding has the following tips on making the subscription model work:

1. 'Reduce payment friction by removing as many unnecessary fields as possible – if you're not posting it to their house, no need for an address.
2. 'Start with the most expensive package at the top, as consumers will "adjust" to your prices quicker as they scan downwards.
3. 'Keep prices to £xx instead of £xx.xx – it's psychologically smaller', advises Brett.

While Sarah Beeny of MySingleFriend.com provides the following Do's and Don'ts:

Do

✓ 'Set everything out clearly: length of subscription, cancellation, terms', says Sarah. 'Tell a user what payment you're taking and when and how to cancel. Hiding this away or making it difficult to get out of can cause problems. Be transparent and fair.'
✓ 'Thorough research into pricing and how price sensitive your users are.'
✓ 'Make sure subscription levels attract the right quality of listing or profile.'

Don't

✗ 'Hide anything from your users or, worse still, trick them into anything.'
✗ 'Continually change prices, or give too many offers, devaluing the offering.'
✗ 'Assume it's all about numbers. Quality not quantity comes out on top.'

7. The app store application model

This means selling applications via smart phones and tablet computers. Rovio and Tapulous are well known successful app creators.

The media has enthusiastically reported on people who've made a fortune from their iPhone apps. From lone programmer Ethan Nicholas's artillery combat game, iShoot, which made $600,000 in one month by securing #1 ranking in the App Store, to Fieldrunners which has been downloaded over 1.6 million times. Stories of striking it rich within the apps model are fuelling a second digital boom.

The best-selling apps have, according to Comscore, been downloaded by 30% of iPhone users. From such a large user base, it's little wonder that top titles such as Tap Tap Revenge, in which players tap on-screen balls in sync to the beats of a song, have been downloaded over 20 million times with over four million active users per month.

However, while the 'hits' have been duly given prime coverage, what has been less prevalent in the press is the 'misses'.

Indeed, while over three billion apps have been downloaded to the iPhone in just over 18 months (200 apps per second), the majority of the 100,000+ apps in Apple's pioneering app store make minimal money.

According to a blog post at iReaderReview.com, 'The very good businesses (top 1%) in any niche find a ton of success. The next 4–9% do OK, and everyone else does terribly. The press fixate on the 1% and make it seem as if your 14-year-old brother could make a million a month – all he has to do is write an app.'

Certainly, there are apps performing almost every imaginable function. There's even a Mosquito Buster app which emits a high-frequency sound to keep mosquitoes away (created by Japanese software maker, Sea's Garden).

Yet, while iShoot netted its developer a tidy sum ($900,000 in eight months), the level of success slowed from $600,000 in the first month to an additional $300,000 in the seven months that followed. This demonstrates that there is a shelf-life for apps. For some apps this is less than 30 days with only a small percentage of users returning to use applications after that period is over. Indeed, the top app creators have proven that success is only sustainable by regularly updating applications to keep sales coming and customers satisfied.

It's an app eat app world

Before bounding headfirst into developing an app strategy, it's important to recognize that, once developed, app store competition is significantly brutal. To have any kind of chance of making it big, an app needs to make it in to the charts, and not only that, it must secure a high ranking. According to a study by mobile advertising platform AdMob, only the top five per cent of apps have over 100,000 monthly users, the next 14 per cent have between 10,000 and 100,000 active users with the middle 27% securing between 1,000 and 10,000 monthly active users. The remaining 54% have less than 1,000 monthly users. As such only the top 20 paid apps are making thousands of pounds per day.

As LA developer, Rick Strom, told the *Guardian* in March 2009, while his applications often chart in their categories, they only generate a relatively passive income for him. For example, one in particular (Zen Jar) charts at number 30, yet it is generally downloaded around 35 times per day, netting him just over one dollar per hour.

For that reason, apps must achieve success in order to drive and sustain that success. As such, apps need to gain significant exposure, not only by being ranked in the top 25 of their category and gaining 'What's Hot' listings, but also by gaining positive reviews on websites such as TouchArcade.com. Additionally, successful apps must adapt to the changing needs of their users in order to maintain success.

The most successful apps (think Rovio's Angry Birds game app which is downloaded over one million times per day) are frequently updated and free of charge, to maintain loyalty and satisfy users.

Furthermore, it's worth noting that the majority of million-dollar apps have been developed by proven and experienced programmers, with most (almost half of the top 100) created by the big publishers, such as Electronic Arts or at least having some business heavyweights involved. For instance, the co-founder of Tapulous, the company behind Tap Tap Revenge was part of the launch team for Firefox. Another co-founder came from McKinsey & Co. While makers of top selling Engimo game, Pangea (which in late 2009 had achieved sales of over $2.5 million) have been developing for Mac for over a decade.

However, this reality check doesn't mean that the applications model opportunity should be ignored. If you see through the hype and know the rules, you can generate an income from developing apps. Just don't expect to become a millionaire by doing so.

We shall examine the kinds of content, tools and ideas which make sustainable apps, the secrets of app building success and how to build a great app in Step Six: Build Your Mobile App and Mobile-Friendly Site. For now though, it is worth reviewing what exists in the market and where there might be a gap for your app.

Exercise

Go online. Look at your favourite websites. What model are they operating? What makes their value proposition stand out?

Check out the best apps in your market on your smart phone. What makes them easy to use and compelling?

Exercise

Choose your business model and define it here. Outline each potential revenue stream for your product/service in detail.

_____

_____

As well as potential revenue streams, consider other sources of value/non-financial benefits that strategic partners may gain by partnering with you and that you may gain by partnering with others (e.g. reach to a specific target market, data, promotion, credibility, and so on).

Go Forth and Multiply

The digital marketplace is attractive for consumers and entrepreneurs alike. And it enables entrepreneurs to generate multiple revenue streams and adopt multiple business models.

A site selling content or membership subscriptions may also generate revenue from selling advertising space and by earning affiliate income.

Take MyDeco.com for example, Brent Hoberman's latest venture. While it is not yet profitable, it is growing at a rapid rate and does have multiple revenue streams in place. It is the largest aggregator of furniture in one place in the UK so, as Brent explains: 'there is the affiliate stream which is cost per click or cost per sale, there is ad revenue and there is the sale of 3D models. There is also the licensing of the 3D technology and we also have our own MyDeco boutique where we source products directly.'

The web gives you the opportunity to put in place multiple revenue streams stemming from a singular idea. Yet only a few act upon those ideas to turn them into reality. Yes, action is a vital tool in any entrepreneur's armoury and a key stage in formulating and taking forward a business idea. But, before you can implement your idea, you need to make sure it is commercially viable. It's time to do your homework.

Step Three

Assess Viability and Create A Customer-Centric Business Plan

'Before everything else, getting ready is the secret to success.'
Henry Ford

Having created, evaluated and evolved your idea and chosen your business model, you need to start assessing viability and planning your routemap toward success. In doing so you must ensure that your customers are at the heart of everything you do to create and maintain a healthy buzz and reputation from the moment you launch onwards. As such, you should create a customer-centric business plan. We shall focus in more depth on delighting and taking good care of your customers in Step Eleven. Right now though, Step Three will help you to:

- **Assess the viability of your idea by gathering market data, competitor analysis, facts and figures to back up your assumptions and justify why your idea will work.**
- **Understand who your customers are and what makes them tick.**
- **Uncover demand and untapped customer needs.**
- **Uncover gaps in the market and growth sectors.**
- **Test, justify, validate and substantiate your business opportunity.**
- **Create a clear and simple customer-centric business plan.**
- **Create an action plan to help you bring your vision to fruition.**
- **Decide on your brand name, register it and protect your intellectual property.**

Diligence: The Importance of Planning

In business, growth can kill; over-trading or under-trading can cause havoc. As the cliché goes, 'fail to plan, plan to fail'. And that's why a business plan is an essential piece of kit in an entrepreneur's armoury. It enables anticipation. It provides foresight rather than hindsight (or oversight). It enables you to see and evaluate what is going on around you. As a result, relevant opportunities can be more readily noticed and seized, threats tackled and financial frenzy avoided.

An effective business plan enables you to anticipate potential growth and avoid over-trading to ensure that you're properly capitalized to cope with the growth.

Plans essentially provide early-warning systems; they act as integral communications tools and can be the difference between securing an injection of much-needed capital or being under-capitalized and subsequently doomed. In performing such fundamental functions, business plans not only help to guide businesses towards reaching their objectives, they also enable you to pursue valuable opportunities, rather than mediocre ones.

'You need capital ovation to be able to take a certain view on opportunities and, if you're not properly capitalized, you may have to grab revenue short term,' says founder of FirstTuesday.com and Ariadne Capital, Julie Meyer. 'The more you don't have a plan, the more you're going to be swayed by opportunities and the more you can't assess how far an opportunity will take you off-piste.'

'Ultimately', says Julie, 'the better the plan, the surer your success is.'

Fortunately, a robust road-map can prevent these issues of over-optimism and under-education by providing a reality check and by equipping entrepreneurs with knowledge. Ultimately then, whilst you can never totally be rid of risk, planning de-risks. By increasing awareness effective planning also helps entrepreneurs to set, achieve (and sometimes supersede) goals, define priorities and gain focus.

In business, as many entrepreneurs will tell you, everything always takes longer and costs more than you think it will. So planning prepares you and prevents the fire-fighting that comes from lack of planning. In this way, planning informs and enables.

It's quite surprising, then, that research carried out by business insurance comparator, SimplyBusiness.co.uk showed that 54 per cent of the 400 surveyed companies had no written business plan.

Jason Stockwood, CEO of SimplyBusiness.co.uk, says: 'Limited time and resources are characteristic of growing businesses, and the recession will have stretched UK entrepreneurs further than ever before. Understandably, many have become so focussed on working in their business that their time working on their business may have suffered as a result.'

However, once you have a business up-and-running, time resources are pushed to the limit. Start-ups should therefore make the most of the time they have BEFORE they launch – to create a roadmap which addresses *what* you intend to do and *how* you'll do it. As well as informing you and de-risking the business, planning reinforces your passion. 'It's far easier to be passionate about the future if you can see where you're going and how you're going to get there', says Keith Milson, CEO of AnythingLeftHanded.co.uk. 'A clear business plan tells you how you're going to get from where you are to where you want to be.'

Destination and Direction: Plotting a Clear Path

Fundamentally, if you take a wrong turn, face an uphill struggle or get caught up in a race with a competitor, you'll be glad you've got a map to help you make informed decisions along the way, and to take a different route if necessary. Furthermore, in establishing credibility and defining opportunities, a business plan helps to reinforce your belief as an entrepreneur and that of other stakeholders that you are, in fact, making the right moves toward success. In the fast-paced environment of digital enterprise a business plan helps you to:

- Set key targets and assess how to achieve them – and by when – so you can allocate the right resources to required tasks at the right time.
- Benchmark performance by providing a snapshot of your current position.
- Improve that performance plus operational efficiency, productivity, your value proposition and product/service itself. Planning does this by encouraging you to assess resources, processes, strategies, operations and competencies in order to gain clarity, prioritize tasks and tactics and optimize time and margins, while also evaluating what's out there in the market; what the market has, wants and needs.
- Persuade investors to provide the capital and added value resources (contacts and knowledge) that you need to reach your destination, and enable you to figure out how much money/time you'll need to achieve your goals and how best to allocate the funds you raise.
- Outline the potential risks and rewards that your venture presents along with the market scope and threats, so that you are in the best possible position to enhance your strengths and maximize opportunities.

Creating a Customer-Centric Plan

If, as outlined in Step Two, you are thinking of adopting an approach where you attract a vast following of adopters *prior* to putting in place revenue streams, you absolutely must ensure that you develop innovative products to enrapture your customers by exceeding their expectations, causing them to return frequently and bring their friends. Equally, if you are intending to put revenue streams in place from the outset (which is what the majority of entrepreneurs would advise) you need to create amazing customer-focused products and services in order to gain and sustain the competitive edge.

Attracting customers by creating an expectation-exceeding proposition is known as the mousetrap approach. With it you can blow your competition out of the water and generate that all-important customer loyalty (possibly the most valuable element in any digital entrepreneur's armoury) to grow your user base rapidly and thus create a sustainable business.

Exercise

Define your mousetrap

1. Describe clearly exactly what it is that your customers want/need.

    _____

    _____

    _____

2. List every compelling benefit that your product has which meets those needs.
    - What exactly is it about your value proposition that makes it remarkable? What will compel your customers to shout from the rooftops and enthuse about how wonderful your product/service is?
    - What's in it for your customers? What benefits will they gain from their purchase? Being able to send email while on the train home might appeal to me more than the easy-to-use trackpad features of a Blackberry, for example.
    - What solutions do you provide to problems?
    - What advantages will customers gain from buying what you offer, instead of buying from your competitors? – Why are you better? What gives you that advantage? (Skills, service, product, operations, location)?

    _____

    _____

    _____

    _____

    _____

    _____

    _____

    _____

3. Explore what you hope customers will say about you and why?
    - List adjectives that describe your product/service that make it better and more compelling than existing alternatives. (e.g. enabling, convenient, cost-effective . . .)

    _____

    _____

    _____

4. Outline specific actions you will need to take in order to make this differentiation happen.

    _____

    _____

    _____

Exercise

Hit the streets (physically or virtually)

Get out there and ask potential customers what they like best about your products and why?

Identify which product features/benefits are the most remarkable and will enable your products to promote and sell themselves.

_____

_____

Are your customers likely to recommend your product/service to their friends?

YES	NO
What tools will you supply them with to make remarking upon your remarkable products/services easier? Note them down here.	If not, what changes can you make to turn this answer into a 'yes'? Write down these changes and actions here.

_____ _____
_____ _____
_____ _____
_____ _____
_____ _____

How will you connect customers with people they know who are most likely to buy?

_____

_____

Ask people to list their top ten sites and blogs that they subscribe to, at least five of which should be relevant to your own product/service. You'll refer back to this information in the marketing chapter, Step Nine.

Remember, crucially, as founder and CEO of Made.com, Ning Li, says, 'What we think is good for the consumer doesn't matter – it's what the consumer thinks is good that matters.'

So, you need to verify what your customers actually think and examine their core needs to really understand their mindset regarding what you intend to offer them.

No matter which business model(s) you choose for your business there is one rule that every single business must follow in order to grow – the customer retention rule. Retaining your customers is a vital determinant of success if you want to maintain and grow a business, no matter what you are selling or doing, no matter which industry you enter into and no matter which business model you select.

Particularly on the Internet, it is imperative to earn your customers' trust. If you don't, you won't have a digital business for long. However, in order to retain customers you first need to attract them. Fortunately, you can both attract *and* retain customers if you do one simple thing: make what you sell them utterly brilliant in terms of perfectly fulfilling their needs.

Ultimately in order to be rewarded for your efforts, your goal in business is three-fold:

1. Attract customers.
2. Retain customers (gain loyal evangelists of your product/service).
3. Ensure those customers return frequently and recommend you to their friends.

This is particularly important in the digital sphere because of the hurtling rate of change. Customers can click away and move on to the next big thing very quickly. Industries advance and evolve. Technology emerges and converges. As such, in business, a stationary non-agile business is a dead one. You have to move with the times and make sure that you continue to attract, retain and gain referrals from customers in order to sustain competitive advantage amongst the metamorphosis of the market place.

One method of quantifying growth and measuring customer loyalty is discovering your 'net promoter score' and doing everything you can to maintain and increase it. Your net promoter score is the number of promoters minus the number of detractors of your product. Many businesses use this only once their business is established. However, this exercise is worth using at planning and development stage to gauge interest and ensure that you focus on the right areas of your product and service going forward.

> ## ❗ Top Tips for Establishing, Maintaining and Improving your Net Promoter Score
>
> 1. **Create an exceptional and memorable product.** 'The most important element of our growth has been the product', says Moonpig. com founder, Nick Jenkins. 'That's been 75% of it because people like it and they want to spread the word.' Benchmark your success based on how exceptional, exciting, remarkable and memorable your products and company are.
>
> *(Continued)*

2. **Be transparent and open with customers.** Start a conversation and maintain an open dialogue with them.
3. **Understand people.** Understand what makes them tick and why. In doing so you will be far better placed to deliver and exceed their expectations.
4. **Put the customer at the heart of what you do.** Provide unrivalled customer service that goes the extra mile to please your customers and turn detractors into promoters.
5. **Collect data from your customers about how they perceive your products, services and brand and also how they perceive your competition.** Do this from the outset, before you even launch. Once you have launched, invite your customers to regularly rate your products, customer service, website, delivery and so on. Focus on weak areas and poor ratings to discover how to improve and turn weaknesses into strengths.
6. **Be innovative.** 'Innovate around things your customers care about', says Amazon founder, Jeff Bezos. Then keep on innovating. 'Business is incredibly complex at the moment and it's difficult to be aware of all the new trends, so a new company must concentrate on creating a niche and get very good at what it's doing, then just try to stay ahead of the competition and keep innovating', advises leading business thinker, Judy Piatkus who sold her publishing company, Piatkus Books, ahead of the digital boom.

Everything you do should stem from your customers' needs. So listen to your customers to gain a deep understanding of those needs to identify the opportunities to pursue. So many entrepreneurs focus on raising capital before they have perfected the product. Yet, if the product is phenomenal, the funds will follow. Great ideas and great execution of those ideas are the first part of the entrepreneurial pie to get right (which is why I'm devoting so much page space to these topics). And the only way to get it right is to *listen to your customers*!

If you do this well, you will generate a virality because people will like your product so much they will simply *have* to tell other people about it. This in itself will make your business far more resilient and, by being close to the consumer, far more agile if and when their needs change.

Knowledge Is Power: Gathering Evidence and Understanding

In order to establish what your customers need, why they need it and how you might fulfil those needs, you first need to establish who your customers are, where they go, what they do and why they buy. You need knowledge, first and foremost.

With limited resources, it is often wise for start-ups to focus first on a single customer segment and being the absolute best you can be at doing what you do specifically for them. In business, if you target everybody, you are likely to attract nobody. If you segment your customers based on age group or other criteria, you can then figure out how best to attract and serve that specific audience group.

Research your customers: Uncovering demand, uniqueness and untapped needs

The first course of action to is create a customer profile based on who they are and their buying habits.

Exercise

Get to know your customers so you can define a profile of your best customer

Try to uncover:

Who Are They?

* Who are your customers? Are they commuters? Students? Tourists? Office workers? Supermarket buyers? Publishing companies? Newly-weds? Retired couples? Mums? Seek out niches and common characteristics within your target audience segments, but ensure those niche markets are accessible and large enough to generate ample revenues.

_____

* Where do your customers live and work? Where are the most responsive geographical regions?

_____

* What do your customers do for a living? What is their level of income and education?

_____

* What are their values? What kind of lifestyle do they lead? What makes them tick? What do they enjoy doing? What are their hobbies and habits? What do they spend their hard-earned cash on?

_____

* How do they see themselves? How do they hope to be seen?

_____

(Continued)

* How old are they?

* What gender/race/nationality are they?

* What is their family status and size?

* What magazines and media do they read/listen to/watch? What websites do they visit?

Buying habits

* Where do your customers go to source and purchase products/services like yours and how often do they buy? How might you be able to reach them?

* Why do they buy existing alternatives currently in the market and what do they think about those in comparison to what you are offering? (For example, as Hugh Chappell of TrustedReviews.com discovered from his research: 'People reading reviews do it for two reasons, they are either thinking about buying something or they like to be up to speed on everything and hence recommend to their family, friends and colleagues.' Knowing why people used services such as his helped Hugh to build up a strong profile of customers for advertising clients.)

* What is their opinion about your product and service? What would encourage them to switch? Is this something you can provide?

* What are their key expectations around price, quality and service? What holds most importance to them: saving money, status or long-lasting quality?

Once you have developed a strong profile of your best customer types it's important to uncover their needs, problems and aspirations to make sure what you offer them fits with those requirements.

Exercise

In a nutshell, in order to create a successful digital business you must match what you offer with your customers' needs that are currently not being satisfied. So:

Discover what people need and help them to get it

- Post messages on relevant online discussion groups and forums and listen to responses.
- Commission students or the NOP to carry out surveys.
- Establish focus-groups.
- Set up in-depth interviews.
- Start conversations with suppliers and stockists as well as consumers. Ask them what their best-sellers are and what they can tell you about the market in terms of demand and customer needs. Cover every angle.

Your objectives should be

1. Define what makes your core customer segment tick? What are their aspirations? What pain do they feel that you might resolve? What do they want and need? Sniff out dissatisfaction.

   _____

   _____

2. Sketch out your customer vision. What will your product/service enable your customers to do? For example, Martha Lane Fox's customer vision was 'spontaneous, romantic adventurous behaviour'. Everything else focused around that. 'We had to make sure we had a really tight plan that fitted with the idea around getting our customers to live their dreams', says Martha. 'That customer vision was always absolutely core'.

   _____

Testing Times: Get Your Product Out There

'Don't debate. Prototype', says NakedWines.com founder, Rowan Gormley. 'There's a saying, "Launch early, launch often." Companies waste so much time and energy debating. They lose their best ideas because they go into a committee and go around and around, and the essence of the idea gets lost. What the Internet enables you to do, is to prototype. If you've got an idea which you feel has any kind of legs at all, you build something that, to the outside world, looks like a proper business and you stick it out there and see what happens. And if people like it then you know it's worth going through an industrial phase to handle the volume, if people don't, give them a freebie and say sorry for the distraction.'

Rowan points to his own site's Marketplace as a case in point. 'It's a place for winemakers we don't normally do business with to pitch their wines at our customers', explains Rowan. 'It's taken us four attempts and three and a half years to get it right. But we did it by prototyping, by getting it live, trying it, seeing what worked, taking it down, putting up something slightly different. Yet we would have never got to the answer had we sat round and talked about it or even researched our customers.'

Henry Ford once pointed out that if he had asked his customers what they wanted, they would have said 'a faster horse'. While you should put your customers' needs at the forefront of everything and listen to their feedback, you should also get on with what it is you believe is a remarkable offering for them. *Then* see what they say about it and tweak accordingly.

Essentially, if you are in tune with the needs of your market place, you can figure out what customers want before they know themselves. For it is not only understanding customers' *existing* unmet needs that fuels growth, it is understanding their *future* needs that creates competitive advantage. That's what true innovation is all about. No consumer group articulated the need for tablet or mobile based technology. It was a combination of internal and external insight and empathy that created the foresight that led to the creation of the iPad, iPod and iPhone. And it was Apple's depth of understanding of the user experience and how they could improve on it that enabled such innovation. As Steve Jobs famously said, 'Our job is to figure out what they're going to want before they do. People don't know what they want until you show it to them. Our task is to read things that are not yet on the page.'

'It's only by building something, showing it to customers and seeing what they actually do or don't buy that gives you the answer', says Rowan. 'That's very Internet specific. If a traditional retailer wants to try out a new store front they can't build something that looks like the shop; they have to physically build the shop.'

'My advice would be get out there and have a go on the web at low cost to test and validate your ideas', suggests Martha Lane Fox. 'Talk to people in your networks and encourage them to help you think through', she adds. 'Our first customers were mostly family and friends. Talking to friends about whether it was a good idea certainly helped us to refine it.'

Hugh Chappell agrees: 'We're fortunate today, particularly in the start-up world, there are lots of mentors and organisations where you can stress test your business before you take the final plunge.'

'It's always worth researching your market, but there's no better way than to actually get out there and ask people if they agree with your concept', adds Sarah Beeny. 'Both mysinglefriend and Tepilo were really created to solve a personal need, and we then took this further and opened them up to others.'

Exercise

Test the market and validate your business opportunity

1. Get in front of potential customers, to find out how they react and assess their level of interest.
   Ask them questions about:

   - How they'd use your product/service.
   - What key features/benefits they'd most like to see and why.
   - How much they'd consider paying for it.

   As well as helping to justify your belief in your product or service, this exercise will help you to determine the key functions/features/benefits that you should focus on straight away and whether other areas can wait until you gain more traction.
   Also speak to potential suppliers and assess how you will reach your target audience.
   Your goals from this exercise will be to discover:

   - Who will buy what you are selling and why?
   - How much they will be willing to pay?
   - What will it cost you to provide your product/service and acquire that customer?

2. Trial your products/services live online. The beauty of the web is that you can test your ideas without incurring too much cost. You can set up a blog and use free open source software to build a site; you can join forums and networks, access information and take payment using Paypal.

The Right Market

When developing a better product within a specific market, you essentially need to find out:

1. The size of the market in terms of monetary value. (For example, the greetings card market is valued at £1.7 bn while the spectacles market is valued at £4 bn).
2. How the market is segmented. (For example, the spectacles market can be broken down into fashion and functional segments, high price and low price segments, and segments for different types of vision problems.)
3. Whether the market is growing, declining or static.

Exercise

Assess the market overall

- Visit competing websites as well as traditional stores where your products/services might be sold. Examine what is currently being offered within the same market and jot down the brand names of suppliers/manufacturers where possible.
- Visit supplier websites and refer to corporate information. Check whether they share details about their market share percentage or estimations of the size of the market within their corporate pages, press sections or in downloadable annual reports within the CEO's statement. Seek out their revenue figures, either within this data, or by downloading information from Companies House. If you can access their sales turnover figures and their market share percentage, you can work out the approximate size of the market overall.
- Dig deep for market information from Mintel report headlines, via exhibitor information from places such as the NEC; via Google NewsAlerts for your chosen market, (using search terms such as 'greetings card market' or 'greetings card industry').
- Figure out the entire market size, the share of the market you aim to seize and what direction the market is headed in.
  - Is the level of demand and market size large enough to support your objectives?
  - Are customer trends and tastes working in your favour?
  - In which direction is the market going in terms of growth: up, down or stationary? Seek out market opportunities and threats.
- Determine how much of your product/service you need to sell in order to achieve the market share you are hoping for. Use this to figure out your sales targets.

If you are operating in a niche market, it can be relatively easy to establish the size of the market. For example, when Keith Milsom of AnythingLeftHanded. co.uk researched his market, while he couldn't find a definitive survey about how many left-handers there are in the world, he could find anecdotal evidence, including a few population surveys.

Says Keith, 'It's generally accepted that between 10–15% of the population are left-handed and that's worldwide across all cultures and countries, with some exceptions, where left-handedness is suppressed.'

Based on this, Keith created a business plan board which displayed the size of the market for his business. 'It shows the number of people with web connections in developed countries who've got credit cards and can buy stuff, and how many of those are left-handed, plus how much the net connection rate is growing', explains Keith. 'So we've got a fairly easy total target of 46 million left-handers who are already online with web connections in developed countries.'

Based on that market size, Keith created an initial target of 50 orders per day. 'That's 0.4% of our immediate target market, four people in 10,000, so we haven't even scratched the surface.'

Research Competition: Uncovering Gaps in the Market and Growth Sectors

In order to match your proposition with your customers' unmet needs, researching your customers is only one part of the market research pie. To source windows of opportunity and gaps in the market you also need to evaluate in detail what your competitors are doing.

Exercise

Analyse the competition so you can differentiate accordingly

Try to uncover:

- Where is the pulse of the industry?

- Who are the most successful competitors within your market and why are they successful?

- What exactly does the competition offer? And, vitally, what *don't* they offer? Look for gaps in the market where customers' needs are not being met. Can you find competitors who are over-charging or under-serving? Their weaknesses can become your strengths – can you uncover any untapped niche markets? Are they providing something that you don't or vice versa?

- How do your competitors market themselves? Examine their collateral and press pages.

(Continued)

- How well do they perform? Order products from them directly to assess their sales cycle and customer service.

  _____

- How do they price their products?

  _____

- Who are your competitors' largest customers and partners?

  _____

- Who supplies your competitors and who distributes their products?

  _____

- How does their offering compare to yours?

  _____

- What can you do that is superior to their offering? How can you gain and maintain competitive advantage?

  _____

'A company needs to figure out what its unfair advantage is', explains Julie Meyer. 'You need to play to your strengths. You need to find out what your strength is as a business; what is it that you do extremely well? I find frequently that [companies are] trying to do too many things and not really having an effect in any one quadrant. One of my top tips would be to find out what your unfair advantage is and to really deepen that advantage.'

That's what Jamie Murray-Wells did with Glasses-Direct.co.uk. Yet he could only achieve that competitive advantage by being thorough with his research, by digging deep and being relentless in his questioning of the market's existing offerings so he could make a real difference by satisfying consumers unmet needs.

Looking Through a Lens to Uncover a Competitive Advantage: Glasses Direct

Convinced there must be a way of making glasses cheaper, Jamie Murray-Wells contacted glazing laboratories to find out the price of manufacturing. To his frustration, he was met with a wall of silence – no one would disclose any information about prices.

On the brink of giving up, Jamie called one more laboratory and obtained the information he was after. He was amazed to learn that the cost of making a pair of glasses was £3–£7, takes approximately 20 minutes and is mostly done by a machine.

Spurred on by his findings, Jamie continued to make enquiries. He realized that, once a customer's eyes had been tested and they had obtained an accurate prescription, there was no further need for them to visit a high street optician. And so Glasses Direct was born with the premise of putting the customer directly in contact with the dispensing laboratory.

On 1 July 2004, at the age of 21, and with no formal business training, Jamie opened Glasses Direct for business from the playroom in his parents' home in Wiltshire, selling glasses from £15.

'I put a notice up on the university noticeboard advertising for a web designer, and we built the website over the holidays', says Jamie. 'It was just the two of us managing on the last instalment of our student loan, so we somehow scraped together a website on a small budget.'

'Our first customer was the delivery guy who delivered my first desk', remembers Jamie. 'And that's one of the reasons I knew the business would take off, because the first person ever to come into contact with the business wanted to buy a pair of glasses then and there.'

'Within eight weeks we'd had 8000 calls, so outsourced the calls to a call centre.'

Word spread about this company that could supply glasses cheaper than the high street and the business grew. What had begun as a sideline became a fully blown business, generating thousands of pounds a week.

However, Glasses Direct has had to deal with fierce opposition in going up against an established industry and exposing their margins.

In fact, the company's main frame supplier stopped supplying them with glasses after being pressured by High Street opticians to stop selling to Glasses Direct.

'That was a huge challenge for us', says Jamie. 'We had to restock and redesign our catalogue within a week.'

The decision was made to approach the big frame suppliers that supply independent stores.

'People use us because they can save money. That value proposition and our combined belief have driven the success, because this creates word of mouth, the best marketing tool any business can have.'

Jamie maintains his competitive edge by removing any potential objections to buying glasses over the web instead of in store. He's created a virtual augmented-reality mirror so customers can try glasses on. He also offers a no-quibble, seven-day, money-back guarantee.

The market for spectacles is £4 bn. Until Jamie established his market-driving disruptive business, spectacles were expensive. Since launching in 2004, Glasses Direct has saved consumers over £30 m. His tenacious research proved his point. Jamie found a gap in a growing market. Can you find one in yours?

One area that Jamie had no problem with is pricing. Price is his key differentiator. For most new digital enterprises, it's important to assess current competing prices to ensure that you price your product/service appropriately.

Exercise

Determining value

Note down the brand name and prices of products you feel that your product is better than.

Define:
- What does that product have in terms of functionality (this is how retailers generally display products) and the core benefits it offers to consumers?
- How does your product outperform those functions and benefits?

Consider:
- How much more might customers be willing to pay, based on their understanding of how much added value your superior offering provides?
- How are you going to convince them that you have something better?

(Don't forget to bear in mind the retailer's mark-up and VAT).

There are a variety of tools you can use to keep your eye on competitor activity and continually assess their value proposition (and, importantly, how yours compares).

- Set up Google Alerts using your competitors' business names or website addresses to track each time they are mentioned in Google News.
- Access real-time social media searches using Social Mention, a tool which pulls information from blogs, audio and video. Include your competitors' details as search terms and receive alerts whenever they are mentioned positively or negatively on social sites.
- Search industry forums for information or comments about your competitors.
- Approach competitors directly (either openly or covertly on an undisclosed basis) to uncover how they operate. It can be worth posing as a customer or as someone from head office to ask questions about stock, packaging or even about how much warehouse space is allocated to certain items.

• Attend trade shows as a punter and network. Pose as a customer. Get your finger firmly on the pulse of what people are excited by and why.

> **!** **Top Tips for Assessing the Viability of your Business Idea**
>
> 1. **Define your mousetrap.** Uncover your value proposition and what makes you and your products/services exceptional, memorable and differentiated. Do this early on. Then test, listen, tweak, build and improve on that proposition.
> 2. **Ascertain demand.** Speak to potential customers to see if they'd support you, buy from you and use your products; examine the status quo in terms of how people currently find products such as yours.
> 3. **Ascertain market size.** Assess how big the market is and decide what slice of that market you aim to gain.
> 4. **Talk to your competitors.** 'I went out to see our competitors to get an idea about how to set prices and how to sell advertising', admits Hugh Chappell, founder of TrustedReviews.com. 'I didn't want to divulge the DNA of the business, but I wasn't asking them to give away things that might compromise them either.'
> 5. **Discover how your competitors are perceived by consumers.** Read online reviews and examine their websites and marketing collateral in detail. How are they trying to differentiate themselves and what opportunity does that provide to you?
> 6. **Get feedback on your business plan.** 'Get your ideas down on paper and share it with as many people as possible who can assess how viable the idea is', advises Martha Lane Fox. For Lastminute. com Martha and Brent created a comprehensive business plan before showing it to people they trusted and respected to gather their input. It's vital to examine your business proposition from different angles. Speaking to people enables this.

Creating Your Business Plan and Action Plan

Business plans can become redundant when markets change. That is unless you:

• **Have a customer-centric enterprise and business plan.** For example, Made.com can react quickly to changes in its customers' tastes, making it more likely to succeed in the market. If you can create a customer-centric enterprise and supporting business plan you too will have your ears to the ground permanently and be able to tweak your plans accordingly. Agility is vital in the digital sphere.

- **Consider your plan to be a work in progress.** It's important to regularly evaluate whether your business is on track. Deviation is fine as long as it's in response to market conditions and the plan is accordingly updated to stay on top of those changing conditions.
- **Revisit your plan frequently.** 'We made sure that we were constantly revisiting our business plan, rewriting it and working on it with our board and later our shareholder base', says Martha Lane Fox.

Ultimately then, your plan must be written in such a way that it can not only benchmark and identify priorities as they stand at any given time, but it can also evolve. So, whether you write a detailed plan with supporting schedules and financial figures for investors, or a shorter document to help you improve performance; you'll need to structure your plan to include both internal analysis (your products, business model, operations and team) and external analysis (the market, competition, opportunities and threats) to make the plan flexible enough to deal with changing conditions.

Exercise

Summarize your unique selling points and value proposition

Review your research, your mousetrap exercise, your findings and customer feedback. Now write your elevator pitch. You should be able to summarize quickly who you are, what you do and what makes you differentiated and more attractive to customers than your competition. Aim to deliver this clear, concise summary in the length of a 'Tweet' (140 characters).

Your business plan should include:

- **An executive summary.** Highlights key points of your business including: your mission statement, track record of your company thus far, your business model, the market size, your current position and a definition of the investment opportunity (if that's your intended reason for writing a plan). Summarize with clarity. As Einstein said, 'If you can't explain it simply, you don't understand it well enough.'
- **The business opportunity/model, products and services.** Outlines your business (brand identity), what you sell (products/services), why you sell them (i.e. your USP and value proposition, e.g. low price, high quality,

exclusivity, wide choice, giving the best guarantee or the best customer service) and to whom (your target audience). Outlines your business model (where revenues come from) and your business opportunity. Defines the company's current position and structure of ownership.

- **The management team.** Details the credentials, competencies, experience and achievements of your management team and advisors. Lists key skills, potential plans to recruit further and planned training schemes.
- **Business operations.** Defines distribution channels to market and suppliers you use, along with where you run your business from. Lists assets, processes, IT and reporting systems to enable operational efficiency.
- **The market.** Specifies the size of your market plus your current and potential percentage of market share; details trends and opportunities to scale the business up. Explains the profit contribution of each part to the business overall. Includes profiles of your customers and defines your competitive advantage.
- **The marketing/customer plan.** Explains how you intend to get the right messages to the right people at the right time (methods/channels) and how you will create customer loyalty and referral. Outlines how you'll measure and analyze your marketing and sales methods to reap the best ROI. Includes information about any collaborative partnerships and strategic alliances. Expands on customer profiles and competitive advantage in terms of how you intend to continue to fulfil your customers' needs by providing something remarkable and uniquely differentiated plus how you intend to gather, retain and act on feedback to stay ahead of the competition.
- **SWOT analysis.** Lists key Strengths, Weaknesses, Opportunities and Threats in order to assess risk. Defines how you intend to deal with threats, seize opportunities, reduce weaknesses and harness your strengths.
- **Financial forecasts.** Details cash flow for the next 12–36 months and profit and loss account and forecasts for up to three years time. Plus balance sheet, sales revenue (by product/customer grouping) and margins. Summarizes how you have financed the business thus far. Banking facility arrangements are also useful along with repayment details included within any forecasts, plus credit terms. Also provides an investor profile (if you are seeking investment) including how much you'll need (adding up to 20% contingency) in order to scale up, plus an explanation of what you will spend the money on and why. Also outlines details of predicted ROI. As future financial assumptions involve a good deal of guesswork (particularly for start-ups) provide three different variations to cover all bases and achieve balance: 1. Realistic, 2. Optimistic and 3. Pessimistic.
- **The action plan.** Includes a summary of your vision, the long-term and short-term results you hope to achieve plus exactly what you intend to do

to implement your strategy and realize your vision. Goals should have deadlines and measurable outcomes with a prioritized list of actions that need to be undertaken in order to achieve those goals. Each action should strive to tick certain boxes. Does it serve the customer/deliver excellence? Is it a goal worthy of expenditure of both money and time?

• **Your exit plan summary.** Do you intend to sell your business at some point? (This is something most investors will push for, so that they may realize their ROI at exit stage). If so, in order to achieve the most preferable possible outcome for your business, it makes sense to know who your suitors are and groom your business for exit to suit their strategic needs. Address what your ideal exit route would be, consider how you will optimize the capital value of your company and have potential buyers in mind from day one.

• **Appendices.** May include market research reports, Curriculum Vitaes, marketing and product literature, and so on.

Numbers are not everything. In fact, it's actually the *narrative* behind the numbers, the *opportunity* itself in terms of the market size, strategy and action plan; the *people* involved . . . all of these count as much as historical and forecasted financial figures. Good business planning is about proving an opportunity is real using evidence to justify what you are saying, then fleshing out what you aim to achieve and how so.

Exercise

Revisit your vision

• Write down your destination – where you are headed (e.g. to become the market leading widget company with 35 per cent share of the total online widget market within four years, with the aim of selling to Widgets R Us or similar in year five).
• Write down your strategy/tactics – how you intend to get there (e.g. targeting young professional men who live and work primarily in cities via word of mouth – create amazing widgets, generate PR, partner with Widget & Co or similar, create a high quality content strategy and sharable online widget tool).
• Map out the milestones that you intend to reach on the way to your destination (e.g. 100,000 customers by the end of year one, generating 50 sales per day/week).
• Use this exercise to populate the Action Plan part of your Business Plan.

> ## ❗ Top Tips For Creating an Effective Business Plan
>
> 1. **Instil a culture of planning into the business.** This will help you to gather knowledge, prioritize effectively, unite staff and move together in the right direction.
> 2. **Tailor the content of your business plan to suit whoever will be reading it.** Investors will require robust financial information and a clearly defined investment opportunity outlining future potential, strategy to reach that potential, management team credentials and a tight executive summary. Whereas, a plan designed as an internal roadmap tool would focus more on the business model, products, services, market, marketing/customer plan and action plan.
> 3. **Summarize your findings in a clear, compelling and concise manner.** Try not to waffle and keep data organized with clear subject headings and readable paragraphs.
> 4. **Have clarity on the financials.** Include three versions of assumptions: pessimistic, realistic and optimistic.
> 5. **Substantiate your vision with evidence.** Justify your assumptions with facts, market data, statistics, numbers and a clear narrative about the people, partners and products that will help you to achieve your strategic goals.

Make It Official: Business, Trademark and Domain Name Registration and Intellectual Property

Before you launch forth with your brand new digital enterprise, you need to make it official. You will need:

- To come up with a brand name (one that is not already taken, has an available domain name and does not conflict with others that already exist on the web).
- To register that as your domain name (web address i.e. URL).
- To register your business officially.
- To protect your intellectual property.

Choose your name wisely

You have two methodologies to choose from here. Either you choose a name which clearly defines what you do and 'says what it does on the tin', such as Cheapflights, GlassesDirect or AnythingLeftHanded. Or you can choose a simple, memorable word which has nothing obvious to do with what you are selling, such as Moonpig, Google, Innocent or Amazon. These may seem like words plucked from nowhere but they all have some relevance.

- Moonpig was Nick Jenkins's nickname at school and illustrates the fun and unobtrusive nature of his brand perfectly. 'Google' is a play on the word 'googol', the mathematical term for a 1 followed by 100 zeros. The name reflects the immense volume of information that exists, and the scope of Google's mission: to organize the world's information and make it universally accessible and useful. Innocent summarizes the drinks brand's ethos of being angelic/innocent and adding no bad stuff to its products, while AmaZon gets its products from A to Z.
- 'We wanted something that was two syllables.com and phonetic', explains Moonpig.com founder, Nick Jenkins. 'If you have a consumer brand you need it to be passed on by word of mouth and that's difficult if you use a word that is hard to spell.'
- Consider your personality and the desired brand persona of your business. Think about what you offer, your USP and consider implications of being listed alphabetically and potential different spellings. Define your customer experience and consider words which describe that experience and the benefits or solutions you provide.

Check the viability of your name before you register it

'Google for your new brand', suggests Nick Jenkins. 'What comes up? Make sure that there are no conflicting brands that already exist on the internet.'

'When I started Moonpig, if you entered "Moonpig" into Google nothing came up', says Nick Jenkins. That is the ideal case scenario.

'When you come up with the brand, make sure that you have a domain', adds Nick. 'There's no point in coming up with a brand that is already booked on the Internet. So when you're choosing a brand you need to make sure that you've got a domain and then make a brand out of that.'

'When people say that all the good names are gone, that's actually not true', says Hugh Chappell. 'If you take parkatmyhouse.com – that's four words and there are lots of good dot com names available that are four words.'

- Choose a name that is easy to remember and spell which suits your brand personality.
- 'Ask people how to spell your name to check it is how you are actually spelling it', says Hugh.
- Check domain name and company name availability, including variations of your company name. Register your name using a reputable domain name registrar and register your business at Companies House.

If the domain name of your chosen name is not available. Don't give up. Investigate further. 'Sometimes there are domains held by individuals. All it takes is a chat and you could secure a decent domain name without spending millions', advises Hugh Chappell.

That's what Martha Lane Fox and Brent Hoberman did with Lastminute.com. They bought the Lastminute.com domain name for £5000 in 1998. 'One of the best decisions we made was to acquire the name, which we didn't have initially', Brent Hoberman told me. The brand became one of the most well-known e-commerce brands of its time and, after floating on the stock market and making a number of strategic acquisitions, the site sold to Travelocity in 2005.

Protect your intellectual property

Once you have your name and are about to launch your business to the world, you need to make sure that your brand and assets are adequately protected. Here is an extract from an article I wrote for own-it.org, reprinted in this book with their kind permission.

Doing The Rights Thing

(Reprinted with the kind permission of www.Own-it.org)

What Can Be Protected And How So?

PATENTS: A patent is a legal document that grants the owner absolute rights (a monopoly) to produce, use or sell the patented product, and prevent anyone else using the invention. The document also describes the full technical workings of the invention in detail, so a patent protects ownership and usage, but not privacy).

Patent protection is granted for a period of 20 years from the date the patent application was filed. On expiration, the invention then enters the public domain and is available for others to exploit commercially. Patents provide recognition and financial reward and inspire future generations of inventors.

COPYRIGHT: Creators of original artistic, musical and literary works can protect their work with copyright. This covers all forms of creative works, from books, paintings and films, to choreography, sound recordings and computer code, software, graphics and other digital media.

Copyright gives creators the exclusive rights to use, or authorize others to use, their work. The author, or freelancer or employer owns the copyright, rather than the publisher or employee, unless agreed otherwise. And copyright protection gives the owners rights to prevent copying, publication, broadcasting, distribution or hiring.

There is no copyright registry. Rather, copyright exists automatically as soon as an original piece of qualifying work is created. So, as soon as you write, upload or create your work, it is instantly protected by copyright.

Literary, dramatic and artistic works have immediate copyright protection that lasts until 70 years after the death of the creator. Computer

(Continued)

generated works and performers rights last until 50 years after the creator's death, while typographical arrangements are given 25 years protection. This is currently a thorny issue as the first wave of rock 'n' roll recordings, starting with Elvis, is about to go out of copyright in Europe. Not surprisingly, the UK music industry wants the current 50-year time limit extended.

TRADEMARKS: A trademark is a 'badge of origin' by which the public can distinguish the products and services of one business from another. A trademark can be protected by registering it, and a registrable mark must be distinctive and can consist of words, letters, numbers, images, drawings, symbols, smells and sounds, or a combination of these.

To be registrable the mark must be distinctive and not identical or similar to a previously registered mark that applies to the same or similar goods or services. A trademark registration must be renewed after 10 years.

A trademark that is registered gives the owner the exclusive right to use it or authorize someone else to use it. Protection usually lasts for 7–10 years or more and can be renewed.

Registered trademarks are enforceable under trademark law and use the ® symbol. Conversely, unregistered trademarks are not enforceable under trademark law and use the TM symbol.

Design Rights

Designs can be protected too. Design rights can be registered or unregistered and rights exist for 2D and 3D designs but don't protect the functionality of a design, only the 'ornamental or aesthetic aspect', i.e. the appearance of a product resulting from its features, lines, contours, colours, shape, texture, materials or ornamentation.

The design must be novel and have individual character. If successful, protection can potentially last for up to 25 years, renewable ever 5 years.

Unregistered design rights exist automatically, as with copyright. This lasts 15 years, but must not be a common-place design.

Two important points for any budding designer to remember are:

1. Employers own design rights, employees do not own rights to anything they've created in accordance with employment.
2. If pitching for a commission, it is the commissioner who owns the rights to the designs.

Important to know if you are thinking of taking a concept from your employment to market.

Moral Rights

These are your rights to be identified as an author or creator of intellectual property. You can waive your moral rights via a release form. Some entrepreneurs using research students to help them develop products may ask that they waive their moral rights, or broadcasters using footage of performances.

Managing your IP and Unlocking The Value Of Your Creativity

1. **Identify your intellectual property**
   - List any creative 'assets' – your intellectual property, from your logo and company name/brand, to your packaging design, products and software.
   - Check that your designs, expressed ideas and concepts and creative works are new and original.

2. **Protect your intellectual property**
   - Put in place a simple confidentiality agreement with a client, potential manufacturers or investors BEFORE you start negotiations. (You can download free sample contracts from www.own-it.org.) A well-drafted agreement will specify the type of information to be protected, how long the duty of confidentiality is to last and to whom the information may be disclosed.
   - Register designs, patents and trademarks, visit www.patent.gov.
   - Secure domain names to safeguard your brand.
   - Agree terms and get everything in writing. When approaching manufacturers you should strive to get various agreements in place, such as a confidentiality agreement, prototype agreement (whereby the factory agrees to make a sample to your specifications), heads of agreement and manufacturing agreement.
   - Catalogue everything that you have. Keep good records, including your sketches, notes, drafts, diagrams, contracts, letters and e-mail communications. Strive to keep all work-in-progress and a 'design' or working story. You can store these using a service such as www.designprotect.com.
   - Assert your rights. Mark the author/publisher or creators name on all copies of your work, along with the date and country. © (Name of owner) (Year of creation).
   - Put registered design rights and other IP renewal dates in your diary. Never forget IP rights or domain name renewals. Put them in your diary!

3. **Exploit your intellectual property**
   - Ensure any designs, trademarks and patents you register or apply for are the same as those you intend to market.
   - Inform people that you have a registered design or trademark to increase your credibility and make people aware of your rights. For example, you should put your design rights number on any packaging and R if you have a registered trademark.
   - Maximize returns by licensing your rights either as a while or separately to exploit your IP in different territories or different forms.

(Continued)

- Assign your IP (transfer ownership and relinquish your rights) if you'd rather make a one off fee than retain any future rights in your IP.
- License your IP (either exclusively or non-exclusively). You can license your rights exclusively to the licensee only, or non-exclusively to the licensee and anyone else you choose to license to. You can license reproduction or distribution rights, rental or lending rights. Consider what you are licensing (e.g. your trademark, copyright, design rights) in what format (exclusively or non-exclusively) and how long for (e.g. are the terms of the licence for a fixed term, perpetual or terminal?) and finally, where in the world you are licensing to.
- Figure out whether you require royalties, licence fees or both. (Royalty payments generally vary between 4 and 14%, dependent on the type of creative work/industry).
- Negotiate fair terms. This is the period where you spend time bargaining to work out a deal. Next comes the contracting part, which involves formulating the details to create a binding agreement.
- Look into franchising your business once you have a strong and effective business model.
- Use a Creative Commons licence to control and share your IP. You can choose to allow reproductions of your work but not for commercial purposes or other methods of use, so some rights are reserved instead of all. Visit http://creativecommons.org/ for more information.
- Make sure you are given equitable renumeration for your work. For example if you produce sound recordings, you should be paid royalties by the MCPS PRS alliance. And, if you have written a book, you should receive lending royalties as well as royalties from your publisher.

4. **Enforce your intellectual property**
   Even the big boys can experience problems enforcing their IP. DVD piracy costs the film industry hugely, just as illegal music downloading costs the music industry. So how can you enforce your IP effectively?
   - Monitor what competitors and new entrants to your market are doing. Get news alerts, subscribe to industry news, keep an eye on the patent.gov.uk sites and pay attention to new trademarks being advertised. If any infringe yours you are able to contest them once they've been advertised.
   - Send standard cease and desist letters if you find anyone infringing your IP rights. A lawyer can help draw up an effective letter to send out and advise you on the best course of action.

© Own-It (www.own-it.org)

Taking IP enforcement action

So what can you do if someone uses your brand name, trademark (registered or unregistered) without your permission?

If you have registered your brand name as a trademark and notice someone else using it, you can claim for a breach of trademark under the trademark law and potentially claim compensation in the form of 'damages', an injunction to stop someone using your mark, account of profits which enables you to recover profits that the other party may have earned as a direct result of using your mark or enabling products which infringe your mark to be delivered to you. However, if the other party can prove that your trademark should not have been granted to you (even if it has been) because it is, for example, their own name, or that they have not been using your registered trademark in relation to a business, they may have a reasonable defence. As IP law can be complex it is always advisable to seek expert advice.

Alternatively, if you don't have a registered trademark but have been using your unregistered trademark in business and have, as such, established 'goodwill' in that name in association with your business, you can use the law of 'passing off'. If you can show that the goodwill may be damaged by another party's use of your name or that, in using your name, they are guilty of misrepresentation, you may have a case.

If someone has registered a domain name using your name, there are various dispute resolution procedures in existence that you can pursue via organizations which maintain domain registrations.

All efforts would incur some level of cost however.

The key is to protect what you have for peace of mind. Without protection you cannot hope to enforce or exploit your intellectual property as you grow.

So far you've embarked on developing the concept part of your entrepreneurial journey which has led you from having and evolving your idea to validating it. Now it's time for the commercialization part of the journey.

Because once you have a firm grasp of who your customers and competition are, have defined your value proposition and planned your route map towards digital business success – you need to take your idea to fruition and put your ideas into revenue-generating, mouse-clicking action. To do so you will need time and money. So about that...

Step Four

Fund Your Venture

'If I have seen farther than others, it is because I was standing on the shoulders of giants.'
Isaac Newton

To put your plans into action and bring your vision to fruition you will need to spend money. The question is how will you access the financial resources you need to get your products/services to market?

The best time to raise money is when you are making money. Not when you are losing money or before you have made a single penny. However, it is not impossible for start-ups to raise the cash they need, particularly if they've done their homework and can demonstrate proof of concept or, better still, the much-sought-after traction.

By the end of this chapter you should be well-versed in:

- **the types of finance available to you and which sources of capital, if any, best suit your requirements;**
- **the pros and cons of giving away equity;**
- **how to find and secure the right investor 'match' for your business who will add value;**
- **how to deliver a pitch that will have financiers financing like there's no tomorrow; and**
- **how to develop a strong, mutually productive relationship with an investor once the deal is done.**

So first, let's explore what kind of financial help is on offer and what it'll cost you . . .

Suitable Sources of Finance

It's important for fledgling and growing businesses to apply the right type(s) of funds from the right source(s) in the right way, at the right time, in order to finance their plans and generate a good return on investment (ROI) for the founders, investors and other stakeholders.

So, once you have researched your idea and gained clarity about why anyone would be willing to part with their hard-earned cash to back your business, you can assess the available funding options to determine which are most applicable and accessible to you. The suitability of each source of finance will be determined by what you are funding and why so.

Those who are building or growing a business will probably need to use a blend of both short-term and long-term finance sources. Some sources of finance aren't as applicable to new businesses with zero track-record and no assets as they are to existing growing businesses. In general, financing through sales, retained profit, asset-based financing, invoice discounting or via flotation on the stock exchange are options for growth businesses rather than start-ups. So, for the purpose of this book, we'll omit those options. Rather, new businesses generally finance their budding enterprises via a combination of debt and equity finance.

Spreading the fundraising and raising small amounts from a number of different sources is a worthy consideration and is something that Moonpig's Nick Jenkins is an advocate of:

'Raising money from several different parties is worthwhile, so that you don't end up with one dominant investor, which can be problematic', advises Nick.

'Try to avoid having a single investor who owns more than 24% of your shares, or who can block a special resolution', he adds. 'You want to get advice [from investors] but not dictation.'

Not only can dominant investors gain more control than you may wish to give up, it can be easier to use a range of sources, from friends and family to business angels and the bank, to provide seed capital for a fledgling venture. That said, while a higher quantity of investors can provide additional added value, the more parties involved, the more (possibly contradictory) voices to listen to.

There's certainly a lot to consider as a cash-strapped start-up. Debt financing means you'll need to find the cash flow to pay back the debt, but you won't be giving away any of your business. Equity finance will cost you in a different way as you are giving away shares in your business for the privilege of a cash injection. There's a constant dichotomy between giving away the crown jewels and having something that's worth giving away in the first place. If you do give away equity in your enterprise, remember that 50% of a big pie is better than 100% of a small pie. If a source of finance is likely to enable you to create a greater pie, it may be worth giving away a slice.

The prevailing types and sources of debt and equity finance are as follows.

Friends and family

Debt. Apart from your own capital or profits you make from the business once launched, funding from friends and family tends to be the cheapest method of fundraising, as they may lend you money on an interest-free or low-interest basis. (Tax implications apply to both parties should you choose to pay interest.)

Equity. Alternatively, friends or family may consider joining your business as a sleeping partner to gain equity in return for risking their cash. If they do so they should invest only what they can afford to lose, as there are no guarantees of a return on their investment. It's worth considering too that both debt and equity financing via friends and family can affect personal relationships, particularly if the business fails and the loan or equity investment is not repaid.

Mr Bank Manager

Banks are worth approaching if only to set a benchmark in terms of what kind of financing is available.

Debt. If you opt to take out a bank loan and/or open an overdraft facility, consider the amount and rate of interest, along with the repayment period. In general, the rate of interest is higher for an overdraft, while both loans and overdrafts will incur arrangement fees. However, these are flexible financing options. Should you only require small amounts of cash at specific times during the year, the overdraft option may be preferable as you'll only be charged interest on the amount used rather than on the amount of the facility itself (whereas interest on a loan applies to the entire loan amount). Both loans and overdraft finance options make cash available relatively quickly.

Credit card companies

Debt. It's best to only finance short-term expenditure using a credit card as initial interest rates which appear attractive at first, often become much higher than overdrafts and loans over the longer-term. So, unless you can pay off your credit card balance in full every month and therefore accrue no interest, you should aim only to fund 'emergency' purchases in this way.

Asset financiers

Debt. Asset financing works by the lender securing a loan on the capital equipment asset that you are acquiring or hiring, such as a vehicle or a piece of machinery. If you want to own the asset at the end of your payment schedule, when you've paid off your loan, you would choose the hire purchase (HP) option. If you are happy not to own the asset, you can opt to lease it instead. Both options require you to pay fixed amounts each month. While opting for hire purchase means you can sell the asset once you own it, (and therefore get a return on your overall investment) leases tend to be more flexible and, as ownership is not part of the contract, the lending company is responsible for the maintenance of the asset, which can save money.

Government grants

A portion of taxpayers' money is made available by the Government in the form of grants in order to encourage enterprise. Most grants require the applicant company to pay for half of the cost of a project while the grant will cover the other half of the cost. There are a number of grants and loans available from the Government. Visit 'Solutions for Business' which is the Government's streamlined portfolio of business support products accessible via Business Link.

Grants typically do not need to be repaid, however there is often a lot of paperwork involved.

There are direct cash awards for training, employment, recruitment or capital investment; and there are repayable grants where payments come out of future revenues, unless the project fails, in which case the grant is written off.

There are also soft loan grants with preferable interest rates and repayment terms, as well as equity finance from providers of public funds. Shared cost schemes are another option whereby those embarking on research and development (R&D) projects can share the costs incurred and expertise gained with other small businesses.

Grants often depend on which sector and region you operate in, or which realm of expertise the grant provider is promoting at any given time. There are grant databases such as grantfinder.co.uk and businesslink.gov.uk plus initiatives such as Gateway2Investment (g2i.org) which list the availability and requirements of such grants.

Meanwhile, a scheme was launched by IC Tomorrow (ictomorrow.co.uk), a Technology Strategy Board programme, in Spring 2011 where UK digital entrepreneurs can apply for grants to test out their digital business models and products before taking them to market. The panel selects up to 20 six-month consumer trials to finance with £10,000 each.

Private equity: Business angels or venture capitalists

Equity. Private equity is money invested by a third party in return for an equity share, i.e. a percentage of ownership of the business. Private equity comes either from private investors, otherwise known as business angels, (for amounts typically between £10,000 and £500,000, with syndicates able to invest more) or from venture capital firms or trusts (for £1–2 m+ investments).

Typically, venture capitalists invest over a million in capital for a sizeable chunk of equity (and thus control). If you are looking to grow rapidly and need a large amount of cash injected into the business, VC can be the best route. If fast growth is not imperative to you and you don't wish to have too much pressure on meeting targets, business angels may be a preferable route. Attracting a sub-£2 m investment from a VC or private equity house can be very difficult. While VC is often provided to early-stage, high-potential/growth companies, including start-ups (particularly those with enabling technologies or disruptive business models); other private equity firms rarely invest in companies that are early-stage as the risks are generally greater the smaller the business is. In general, the higher the risk, the higher the equity stake sought. However, for companies unable to secure debt funding from banks or similar with limited operating history, private equity financing can be a viable option to give them the leg up to market.

Funding from a VCT (venture capital trust) comes from a listed company in which individuals have invested. They invest usually through a debt and equity mix, up to £1 m per year in each company.

When raising equity finance, viewing the bigger picture and considering the positive and negative impact of giving shareholding away is a must.

There are many benefits to equity funding. Investors can add considerable value, helping you to reach your goals and achieve your long-term vision. They are well aware of the risks in growing a business and are more prepared to take them on than a bank is. However, in giving away a proportion of ownership, you will be giving away some control and investors, particularly VCs, will keep pushing you towards generating a decent return on their investment.

You can source business angels via introductions through your own network, or by looking at business angel matching services, such as bbaa.org.uk, or by joining initiatives such as Angels' Den.

Venture capitalist firms can be sourced via your own network or via The British Private Equity, and VC Association (BVCA: www.bvca.co.uk) which publishes a list of member firms along with their preferred sectors and types of finance. Seek out those companies which specialize in investing in the space that you're in. Also take note of which companies have funded your competitors.

Also check out Seedcamp, an initiative which was established to 'jumpstart the entrepreneurial community in Europe by connecting next generation developers and entrepreneurs with over 1200 mentors from a top-tier network of company builders.' It enables early-stage companies from across the globe to compete for cash and advice from a number of investors via its global Mini Seedcamps throughout the year and its annual Seedcamp Week. Winning companies that are chosen to invest in, generally receive Seedcamp's standard terms of €50,000 for 8–10% per cent of the company.

Corporate venturing

Equity. It's not only high-net-worth individuals and private equity/VC firms who invest capital in exchange for equity. Large companies (often listed corporations) are also well-placed to help smaller enterprises to scale up. They can do this via a means of financing called corporate venturing (or corporate partnering) which involves them investing a combination of money and provision of their existing resources, from back office support and access to skills to use of their personal assistants to boost credibility and enable small businesses to create a perception of scale. This method of financing enables you to retain the agility and flexibility of a small business, yet have the weight and clout of the bigger business.

Crowdfunding

Equity. Enabling crowd-sourcing communities to back your project is a growing phenomenon. You pitch to thousands of individuals who make small pledges to help finance whatever you are working on. While the early days of crowdfunding predominantly focused on social ventures and creative industries, it has now become a mainstream funding option.

Crowdcube, for example, charges no upfront fees (unlike angel networks). It provides an alternative finance option for start-ups by connecting them to thousands of potential micro-investors (ordinary British people rather than high-net-worth individuals). The downside is that it can take a long time to secure enough pledges to cover all of the money originally requested. That said, having as many as 40 minor investors does mean that you'll potentially have access to the resources, contact networks and expertise of 40 people – a definite potential upside.

Darren Westlake, co-founder and managing director of Crowdcube says, 'We are democratising an age-old model for raising business finance by empowering the "crowd" to pool small amounts of investment money and give Britain's start-ups a much needed boost.'

Another company, Seedups, provides seed capital for new businesses by creating an investment 'crowd' of high-net-worth individuals, rather than the Joe Public investors involved in Crowdcube. The 2% 'finders fee' is only charged once the deal is done.

While Microventures allow investors to invest between $1,000 and $10,000 in startups online and Kickstart, the 'largest funding platform for creative projects in the world' enables its million members to fund creative projects.

Debt. Funding Circle offers an alternative crowd-sourcing option which provides loans to businesses ranging from £5,000 to £75,000. Some investors select the companies they wish to support while others simply place their loan capital into a central pot to be distributed among those applying for cash.

Evidently, the digital age has spawned new sources of seed capital that digital entrepreneurs can take full advantage of.

Exercise

Outline suitable sources of finance

1. Write a shopping list detailing exactly what you need money for – from software and supplies to staff and skills. Include intangible items, such as industry contacts and introductions to potential partners.
2. Write costs of expenditure next to each item on your shopping list.
3. Go through each source of finance above and note which could be appropriate to fund which expenditure.

Whichever means of money you strive to secure, it's vital to do your homework *before* pitching to anyone – be it your dad, your bank manager, a deep-pocketed angel investor or crowds within a crowdfunding community.

Raising Finance: Preparation

When it comes to fundraising, good preparation is vital.

One key piece of advice that anyone who has raised or provided finance will give is to raise money much earlier than you think you should. This applies whether you are a start-up or a growing enterprise. Existing businesses never want to be close to running out of cash when they're negotiating terms of finance. Similarly, start-ups need to allocate significant time prior to launch to find funds for the venture.

In keeping with the 'everything costs more and takes longer than you think it will in business' rule, Nick Jenkins of Moonpig says: 'Assume that it's going to take much longer and cost a lot more than you imagined at the beginning and, if you have the opportunity to, raise more money than you need, because you probably will need it.' Moonpig went from four years loss-making to £3m in 2005 to £21m in 2009 and £38m in 2011, before merging business with Photobox in a £120m deal.

There are five key steps that you should take before you pitch for finance:

1. Assess whether raising money is the right thing to do.
2. Beta-test or soft-launch your product/service on a shoestring.
3. Assess the level of investment required.
4. Assess your business valuation.
5. Provide persuasive proof to justify your valuation.

1. Assess whether raising money is the right thing to do

Before you ask anyone to invest in you, even the local bank, *you* will need to invest something. After all, why should anyone else invest in your idea if you're not prepared to? Whether that means using some personal savings, selling your car or your dusty collection of old vinyl, you'll need to stump up some cash in order to get your business off the starting blocks.

Nick Jenkins was fortunate to have a significant amount of his own money to invest in his digital enterprise and believes, had that not been the case, that the business 'may not have come through'.

'It took four years to make any money and lost £2.5m before it made any', admits Nick. 'And it was only the fact that I was able to raise that money that kept the business alive. I was lucky as every time we had a round of fundraising I was putting my own money in as well, which gave a lot of confidence to investors.'

Most financiers are reluctant to put money into a business where the entrepreneur has no pain in the game.

That said, many entrepreneurs will put in 'sweat equity' in the first year or two by working their proverbial socks off without paying themselves a salary (or taking only minimal remuneration). Nick Jenkins didn't take a salary for the first year and a half and didn't recoup his 'sweat equity' until year four, when the business started to generate a profit. If you decide not to take a salary at first, and invest sweat equity into your business, you should follow Nick Jenkin's important advice and do something that many entrepreneurs fail to do.

'Give yourself a notional salary of what it would cost to employ someone to do your job', advises Nick. 'You don't have to take it, but put it into the accounts/ P&L and then you can agree that it gets paid out of future profits, if that's the best thing for cash flow.'

'It's very easy to lose track of time contribution at the beginning', adds Nick. 'A lot of people starting out work for nothing for the first two or three years of the business; meanwhile someone else has maybe put in £100k, but they're neglecting the fact that the entrepreneur has effectively put in even more than £100k by working for nothing for three years, so the easiest way to solve that problem is to put it in the P&L as a notional salary. Then it recognizes the financial value of the input that you're putting in, in terms of time, and it gets paid when the company can afford it and, most importantly, it doesn't get forgotten.'

Regardless of whether you pay in sweat or savings, you need to decide whether to strive to secure outside investment or not.

Cash gives you the chance to:

- pursue opportunities you may otherwise miss out on;
- set the wheels in motion towards your desired destination; and
- reach that destination much quicker than you would without capital investment.

However, investment capital can also:

- restrict your freedom and flexibility to make strategic decisions or act fast without bureaucracy;
- place additional pressure on you to perform well in order to reach certain targets and generate a return on investment; and
- give you a false sense of security which can lead to spending too much on unnecessary items.

If you decide that raising money IS the right thing to do . . .

As a start-up early-stage business, you are at the beginning of your evolution. Many established enterprises leave fundraising until it is too late (i.e. they are

Keeping Growth Organic Rather Than Manic: iwantoneofthose.com

Tim Booth, co-founder of gadget site, iwantoneofthose.com is pleased to have grown organically. Tim and his two co-founders put in £5000 each to start. This created a total capital pot of £15,000 with which to fund organic growth.

> 'We decided very early on to build this as fast as we could without ever going overdrawn. So we built it purely on the growth of our sales and nothing else. What we didn't expect was the growth.'

The site, iwantoneofthose.com, doubled its first year revenue targets. The next year the founders thought they'd turnover £500,000 but quadrupled that projection and, in year three, the company turned over £6 million.

'Our competitive advantage when we started the business was that we could get a product to market within an hour of seeing it', explains Tim. 'But big companies slow you down like a dead weight. In the early days we did all of our own photography, we did everything in house. Yet the bigger we grew, the worse we became at that. We had to have special contracts signed with suppliers and so on', recalls Tim, who found the lack of agility when a big company took control through investment (or in their case acquisition) problematic.

'Growing organically was more exciting', Tim smiles. 'It was tremendously more stressful, as, while we got to £6m quickly, getting from £6m up was difficult. Yet, we were as excited about our brand as our customers were. I'm glad we did organic growth rather than VC-funded growth. We were offered funding at the beginning, but it was very expensive money and they wanted a lot of the pie, and it was money they could easily take away. So I'm glad we weren't tempted by it.

'If we'd have taken investment in the early days, when they were throwing money at start-ups before the bubble burst, we would have been put in a smart office and all of our focus would have come off of what made us great.'

Conversely, bootstrapping and doing everything on a shoestring budget helped maintain focus. 'You'd get a pen and you'd keep that pen until it ran out', says Tim. 'We used both sides of paper, we didn't waste anything. That made the brand much more honest. If we'd have been thrown a chunk of cash, we would have all gone and bought cars which would have detracted from the vision.'

running out of cash and face a period of dire necessity, have gone past the peak in their growth cycle or approach investors during periods when they're unable to meet targets or finance turnover). Far better to seek finance when you are in a strong rather than a weak bargaining position; to raise money when you don't need it – ahead of the curve.

! Top Tips for Bootstrapping

1. **Get online without breaking the bank.** You can create a website, communicate via e-mail and social networking and use a document collaboration platform for free or low-cost. You can get Gmail, use blogger.com, design your site using free template resources, or opt for a Drupal site (a free, open-source web development platform and content management system (CMS) for online content and user communities which powers some of the busiest and most popular sites on the web from MTV to WhiteHouse.gov). Then register your domain cheaply and use Google's free analytics package to track how your site is used and how your users behave. All of this can be done for as little as £10 in total.

2. **Test it out.** Use sites such as ictomorrow.co.uk to test your applications or products in front of a test-bed audience, or simply launch your offerings and collect feedback/measure response. Or, if you can afford to give stuff away for free in exchange for feedback, do so.

3. **Get busy.** Hire skilled students/interns who are seeking work experience or freelancers via sites such as elance.com or clickworker.com.

4. **Create a buzz.** Make yourself available for expert quotes by using free services such as MediaSync (mediasynconline.com) or Mediauk.com which can also be used to source editorial contact details, so you can email your story and expertise directly for free PR coverage. Use social networking to connect and engage with customers. Blog, share; just get out there.

Exercise

Question time

Ask yourself:

- Do I need non-monetary gains that come from equity investment (such as contacts, expertise, opportunities)?
- Am I prepared to share my shareholding with others, listen to their input and dilute my level of control over the business?
- Am I seeking rapid growth and exit (within say three to five years)?
- Can I build a profitable business at my own pace without outside investment?
- Do I have adequate capital of my own to invest in my digital business dreams?

However, generally, as a cash-strapped start-up, you have no proof of concept and no traction. Yet, if you have a strong, clearly differentiated value proposition and can demonstrate a strong brand, plan of action, growing market and untapped customer need – investors should be able to see and, crucially, value your potential.

If you have completed the exercises in Step 3 and created a customer-centric business plan which validates the commerciality of your concept, you are well on your way to making your proposition more attractive to investors. Furthermore, if you have set realistic achievable financial targets, you will be far better-equipped to persuade financiers to back you so you can reach those targets. Conversely, if you tell an investor that you're going to achieve xyz in month one and then fail to do so while they have their beady eyes on you during due diligence, they'll think twice about backing you. It is therefore critical to deliver on what you say you will, particularly when you are being watched. One of the best ways to gain some proof of concept is to get your offering out there, even before it is 100% market ready.

2. Beta-test or soft-launch your product/service on a shoestring

> '*Don't start until you've got your business off the ground because, once you've started, the clock is ticking and the overheads are racking up.*'
> **Nick Jenkins, Moonpig.com**

Saul Klein has founded and invested in many companies. He founded VideoIsland which became LoveFilm.com and founded Seedcamp, and, as a partner in Index Ventures and TAG, has invested in many successful digital businesses, from Last.fm and Moo.com to TweetDeck and GlassesDirect. As such he knows how important it is to prove the value of the opportunity before seeking investment finance.

'I would recommend that people don't even think about raising money until they've proven to themselves that there is a real business opportunity to be had', says Saul.

That is certainly what early-stage digital businesses which have no financial track record have done to command high valuations. They've demonstrated growth in a non-financial way to prove that their investment opportunity is viable.

> '*Twitter and FourSquare were started for very little money and, by the time they attracted further financing, it was clear that people really wanted to use those services. The business model may still have been unclear but the founders of those companies could point to a set of metrics that says every day more people are checking in, sending out tweets, signing up; every day more venues are being added.*'

Building a prototype and securing tangible feedback about whether there's a market for your idea is vital (see Step 3 on assessing viability). Saul suggests searching on Google for keywords most closely associated to your idea to see if people are searching for it; for the price of registering a domain name you can create a landing page containing an e-mail opt-in box, a Twitter 'follow button' and Facebook fan page. 'You can spend £50 on an Adwords campaign to drive people to that page to see how many visits you can drive and what your conversion rate will be... that's all without having written a line of code,' says Saul.

> 'Make sure you are validating your idea, otherwise you're going to waste your money and your time. And your time as an entrepreneur is the most valuable asset you have. Because it's your opportunity cost of not doing something else.'

Exercise

Using the bootstrapping ideas above, get your product to market and gain some traction and feedback before going cap in hand to seek investment.

Revisit page 56 for the exercise on getting your product into the marketplace to gain customer feedback.

- What areas need tweaking and improving?
- Which are the biggest selling points?
- What do detractors complain about?
- What do promoters praise your about?
- Can you gather testimonials and reviews from customers as well as revenue for purchases?

3. Assess the level of investment required

What do you need the money for and how soon do you need it? How much money do you need? Think long-term. Make sure that this figure is sufficient to deliver proposed targets and objectives without having to pause developments in order to go and secure more cash.

It is often difficult to assess exactly how much money you are going to need. Some say you should figure out a realistic number and then double it, while others confess to securing more finance than they needed. You should certainly allow for contingencies and ensure that the investment enables you to achieve your objectives as additional funding rounds can be dilutive (i.e. can dilute your shareholding down to a lower percentage).

Exercise

Be clear about what the money is for

Identify the purpose and benefits of the required investment and be specific about how the monies will be used.

1. Refer back to your shopping list on page 87. Now go into more detail. What will you spend the money on, why and when will you need it?

Expense	Why needed?	When needed? (Item/cost)?

2. Calculate how much you need in total.

    Next:

3. Create forecasts to cover the first two or three years with clear objectives and strategies. Ensure that the forecasts are based on realistic assumptions. This can be difficult as a start-up, and will need updating as soon as you start trading, however, if you test or soft-launch your business and research deeply, you should gain enough information to predict how much you can hope to bring in/spend while building your business. Double-check that you have included all expenditure from your shopping list in your outgoings and vice versa.
4. Decide how much equity you are prepared to give away.
5. Identify how investors will be rewarded and where their exit will come from.

    Clarity on what you need your investment for and when is critical to securing investment, as is clarity on what's in it for the investor, in terms of equity stake and reward.

Bear in mind that the amount of investment you secure will determine the post-investment valuation. (i.e. if you secured £250k for a 25% stake in your business, that would value your business at £1m) which should not only incentivize management, but will also enable investors to retain a sizeable enough stake following future funding rounds to generate a decent return on exit.

4. Assess your business valuation

How much is the business worth? With so many valuation methodologies and opinions, a business valuation is ultimately determined by whatever an investor is willing to invest and whatever an investee is willing to accept.

It is incredibly difficult to value a business that has yet to start trading. Most valuation methods are based on a multiplier of current profits or turnover figures. If you don't yet have these numbers, a multiplier of zero amounts to precisely nought.

All you can do is base your valuation on your potential. Anyone who has watched BBC *Dragons' Den* will know that many a hungry entrepreneur has been laughed out of the Den simply by overvaluing their early-stage enterprise and supplying overambitious financial assumptions with little factual justification.

So, what's an early-stage business to do? On the one hand, as a start-up you have no historical track-record. On the other, early-stage digital companies with minimal profitability but phenomenal traction (think Twitter, FourSquare, Groupon) are commanding incredibly high valuations. Foursquare's recent $20m injection of capital values it at $95m; Twitter's valuation is sailing high with the lowest valuation at $1bn and the highest around the $7.8 billion mark, despite having no income whatsoever for the first few years (capitalizing instead on the phenomenal cultural impact its micro-messaging service has had on a global scale), while the more profitable companies, such as Facebook (now valued at between $65–85 billion) is valued at around 30 times its forward profits.

Hence why most commentators and experts on the subject will state the two most common start-up valuation clichés, which are: 'your company is worth what the market will pay for it', and that 'start-up valuation is an art not a science'.

Vague yet true.

Challengingly, most of the traditional valuation methodologies don't apply to early-stage businesses.

- **Discounted cash flow.** This forecasts revenue and expenses over a few years and then works out an anticipated rate of return to discount the subsequent cash flow. However, simply by adjusting the rate of discount very slightly, a valuation can be doubled or halved, so this model is deemed as less worthy than it used to be. And, as start-ups have no historical financial data to use, it's entirely inappropriate to use this model to value a start-up.

- **Market multiple.** This model examines recent acquisitions of comparable businesses and adjusts the multiple depending on the characteristics of the company being valued.
- **Cost to duplicate.** This model estimates how much it might cost to recreate the business, thus figuring out whether it would be more cost-effective to start from scratch and create a company, or buy one that's already doing it. Start-ups shouldn't value their businesses at more than it would cost someone to build their own version of the company from scratch. However, intangible assets such as the brand and future potential aren't always given as much attention as they may deserve using this method.

Ultimately then, with minimal valuation methods at your disposal, the best way to maximize value as a start-up, is to create a market for it.

> **❗ Top Tips for Creating a Market and Heightening Perceived Value**
>
> 1. **Remove as much risk as possible from the business.** Present a product that is up and running as opposed to a mere idea; thus proving the concept works and the market exists; that people will buy/have bought. Test launch to get an initial base of customers and consequential metrics.
> 2. **Gain traction.** The more users you can get using your product/ service, the more investors you will attract. Traction validates your claims. It's as simple as that.
> 3. **Generate additional interest from other investors.** Having multiple interested parties leverages your ability to set a better price.
> 4. **Reveal a strong narrative, strategy, plan and management team.** Tick the investor's boxes as per the checklist below.
> 5. **Do your homework by crunching numbers.** Define how soon you will be profitable and examine the value of comparable companies once they reached profitability. Sites such as BizBuySell can tell you how much companies in your industry are selling for, as can accountants and lawyers, although start-ups need to consider that their value will be a fraction of that value at launch phase.

5. Provide persuasive proof to justify your valuation

To prove the value of your business as a sound investment opportunity and persuade gatekeepers of finance to risk their money and invest in your company, you need to know what they are looking for. Investors like to tick boxes.

For example, Hugh Chappell, like most angel investors, was looking to tick specific boxes when he invested in Parkatmyhouse.com. The key boxes he was seeking to tick were a) people b) uniquely differentiated product and c) scalability.

'Parkatmyhouse.com founder, Anthony Eskinazi, is a nice chap, intelligent, a hard worker and a true entrepreneur', says Hugh. 'His product, Parkatmyhouse. com, provides an alternative to commercial parking offering benefits to both parking space owners and drivers', he adds. 'The business is already successful, however I believe it will scale.'

And, as BMW has invested with Hugh, he is naturally 'incredibly excited about this combination'.

As someone seeking investment, a good grasp of typical criteria that investors are seeking from their investments is crucial. So let's examine these.

Do you have:

A strong value proposition, strategy and business/exit plan?

Investors look for companies with the right balance between risk and reward. This ratio needs to be attractive to them. As a start-up you may not have customers. You must therefore provide proof of concept and model via soft-launching/feedback, evidence of market appetite for what you are offering and validate the scalability of the business going forward.

Furthermore, in addition to proving your value proposition is attractive within the marketplace, you need to be able to communicate that value proposition clearly. For investor Saul Klein, this combination is a persuasive force. It is what persuaded The Accelerator Group (TAG), of which he is a partner to invest early in Moo.com (as well as Tweetdeck, Wonga, Moshi Monsters and bit.ly):

> *'Within two minutes of saying "hello," Richard [Moross] took a small plastic box out of his pocket with this funny looking little card and said, "business cards have been around for 300 years, I'm going to reinvent the business card." You were sold within two minutes because, firstly it was a big idea, secondly he could communicate it concisely and thirdly, because he'd actually made something.'*

Hugh Chappell and BMW invested in Parkatmyhouse.com five years after it was launched, but Anthony believes (and Hugh illustrates above) that building up a great product and loyal customer base during that launch phase was critical to securing investment.

'We've got a feedback system and 98.5% of drivers who park in a Parkatmyhouse space have a "positive" or "very positive" experience', Anthony explains. 'By providing statistics from that and increasing the brand awareness you build up a profile. I guess that's what attracted the investment', says Anthony.

Private equity investors also want to know about any planned exit strategy and at least that there is one. They don't merely want dividend income, they want capital gains. They require an increase in the capital value of the business at exit and hence a return that compensates their risk. Typically they'll be seeking to double their money within three to five years. We shall explore the process of selling a business and the importance of having an exit plan in Step 12. However, it is a point worth considering from the outset.

A quality likeable management team?

While many investors will back individuals i.e. sole traders, a small team will give them more confidence. As such, during the preparation phase it may be worth seeking someone to join you, to come on board as a confidante and/or co-founder. Certainly, you should assess whether you are credible on your own or whether you need to make further hires to create a strong management team.

As Anthony Eskinazi says, 'Sole founders can find it difficult to raise money. Investors aren't just investing in the product, they're investing in the team and, if you're a team of one and you get hit by a bus, the risk for them is vastly increased. My advice is to find a co-founder, not necessarily a full-time person (it could be an advisor) but someone who is willing to be that confidante to bounce ideas off, someone who can come with you to pitch meetings, someone for you to interact with. Running your own business can be lonely. If I were to do it again I'd definitely have a co-founder. Ideally someone who can do things that you can't.'

Having said that, investors themselves can often bring key people to the team, to bolster its strength going forwards.

If you already have your own management team in place: can you clearly demonstrate that you have a suitably supportive, skilled, experienced and impressive team with a balanced blend of competencies? Can you easily define everyone's role? Your management/leadership team must be skilled in core areas such as general management, sales, finance, operations and licensing and provide investors with peace of mind.

Most investors see the quality of management as the most vital intangible when it comes to assessing future potential of an enterprise they are investing in. In a start-up, you cannot demonstrate what business your team members have brought in, however you can mention track record in previous roles; including past accolades and achievements, outlining how key individuals have made things happen, have demonstrable knowledge and expertise within the industry and have set clear action plans for growth of the business.

Yet, as well as proving the worth of your management team, leaders should also have the likeability factor. Fundamentally, as well as being able to believe in a person, a strategy, a team and/or a business's offerings, crucially, investors invest in people.

Able operations?

Essentially business performance must be tracked, measured, monitored and controlled to ensure that issues are identified and initiatives are implemented. For this reason, investors are fans of robust procedures and reporting systems. Clear processes inspire confidence that those running the business are in control and that performance and organizational capacity is being optimized, measured and continuously improved upon, thus enabling a heightened growth potential and likelihood of a healthy ROI.

> 'A well designed organisational structure can speed up the flow of work and deliver better value.'
>
> **James Caan**

Transparency?

Investors like to invest in honest people with transparent businesses to avoid nasty surprises from skeletons in the closet. They would rather be made fully aware of any potential weaknesses and threats and how you intend to deal with them, than be kept in the dark. They are likely to be able to help you if they know what you are facing. If you can assure investors that you have adequately protected your intellectual property, they will have peace of mind. Investors with peace of mind are more likely to invest. Fact! Anything other than total transparency kills investment deals.

Exercise

Use this investment criteria checklist to ensure that you are ready to persuade investors to invest

Do you have in place:

- A strong value proposition, strategy and business/exit plan?
- A quality likeable management team?
- Able operations?
- Transparency?

❗ Top Tips for Preparing for Fundraising

- 1. **Allow yourself sufficient time to raise finances.** Commentators suggest you should give yourself at least six months to a year to source capital for your business.
- 2. **Beware of legal fees when considering how much finance you need.** They are generally deducted from the funds you raise, so you may end up with a less than you thought you would bank.
- 3. **Consider which sources of finance best suit you, your personality, your business model and vision for your company.** Assess how much involvement you want any financier to have and whether you will see investor input as a help or a hindrance.
- 4. **Be clear on how much equity you plan to give away (if opting for that route of fundraising).** Exactly how much will you need and why? How will the investor be rewarded? Or how will the debt-finance be repaid?

Exercise

Craft a pitch plan

Many entrepreneurs make the mistake of thinking they have to convince investors that they are practically perfect, with everything in place. But, if you were perfect, investors would ask you why you need investment in the first place. Investors want businesses in dynamic, growing, scalable, cash-generative sectors, but that aren't necessarily the finished article. The business needs a good 'storyboard' for future growth – a strong proposition that the investor can assist in achieving by providing a new perspective and adding value in multiple areas to accelerate growth and profitability.

Use a deck of presentation cards to summarize key points to draft a pitch of approximately 20 minutes

1. How will you seduce investors with your incredibly attractive investment opportunity? What will you need to tell them? How can you spell out the benefits and give them insight into your offering? Jot down your story in brief here. Define the problem you are solving, the pain you are healing and outline your strengths and opportunities. Write down your USP, your uniquely differentiated value proposition and milestones you have reached or intend to hit, such as securing a partnership deal with a certain company, or acquiring 500 customers by such and such a date. Quantify the potential of the

opportunities to the business. Summarize your background and what makes your team a winning one. Outline how you might demonstrate your product or service visually and any case studies/feedback you might mention. Summarize your price point and your financial projections and clearly define your business model in terms of revenue streams and timeline. Finally, describe how you have financed your enterprise so far, what you have achieved, how much money you are seeking and what you intend to spend invested capital on.

2. Consider how you will *maintain* that initial investor attraction. Demonstrate that you have already acknowledged what could go wrong and have plans in place to minimize risk and optimize opportunity. Identify your weaknesses and threats here and provide solutions as to how any weaknesses will be addressed. Summarize who the competition is, what they offer and why your offering is superior. If competitors have been acquired, note down how much for and by whom. Also jot down your snapshot of the market, its size and your proposed share of it; a brief customer profile and customer acquisition costs along with a summary of how you intend to engage your customers in order to retain them.

3. Consider how you will clinch the deal by demonstrating exactly what you will do to execute your plans. List the actions from your action plan that define that implementation. Show that you have considered an exit plan and potential suitors.

It's Not All About The Money

You cannot underplay the value of human capital. Successful investments go far beyond the money. Contacts, introductions to opportunities and partnerships, industry knowledge and credibility of individual investors can fuel success and growth as much, if not more, than an injection of capital. An investor's little black book can hold way more value than their cash. Smart investments (where deep-pocketed investors become partners rather than mere cash points) create immense added value, whether that's operational value or marketing value.

You might need, for instance, to achieve larger contracts in order to bolster your balance sheet or maybe you need to create structure; to harness corporate experience and gain introductions to chairmen and non-execs in order to mould a more professional management team. If your investor is a well-respected figurehead in your industry he or she will not only bring fantastic credibility to your offering, but may also play golf with the head buyer of a leading supermarket chain or the digital director of a major retailer.

'A lot of entrepreneurs are just chasing the money', says Hugh Chappell. 'What they don't think about is who the people are who are giving them the money. If you can find investors who understand your business, have experience in your market, or can provide assistance and help you with running your business, surely that'd be better than having investors who haven't got a clue, people who put money in and just expect a return?'

Furthermore, added value doesn't merely equate to achieving more sales or opening more doors. While investors are likely to have a network of influential contacts, the value added also comes from their knowledge, experience and fresh perspective. Entrepreneurs running their first company don't know what they don't know. Often decisions made are based on first principles rather than from experience.

Business angels and venture capitalists are often experienced business people who come with a whole repertoire of mistakes and errors. As such, they know what works and what doesn't; what to try first. Being able to learn from their mistakes and avoid making mistakes that they've already made is incredibly valuable. They've already lived through the growing pains of another company's growth. In having been there and done that, they are valuable people to have on board.

So, when seeking an investment partner who can provide added value to help you succeed, think seriously about what you want from that partnership and commit the same importance to finding that partner as you might to finding your life partner. Seriously! Take your time to get to know your potential investment partner, because there will be good times and bad times during your relationship. Indeed, many marriages don't last as long as partnerships between investors and businesses in which they invest.

Says Saul Klein, 'We were the earliest investors in Moo.com, Moshi Monsters, Wonga and Tweetdeck… and in all of those cases, it was important for the entrepreneurs and us to feel like this was a long term partnership. You may be working with these people for five or ten years and you don't want to rush into that decision in the course of two weeks, going from pitch to pitch.'

The Added Value Investor: Lovestruck.com

Internet dating services use increasingly sophisticated techniques to help their users find their perfect partner. Similarly, Lovestruck, 'where busy people click', the dating service for single professionals in and around London, found the perfect investment partner who could add value in Hugh Chappell.

'When I invest, I know what it's like to start, run and sell a business', says Hugh Chappell. 'I put myself in those entrepreneurs' shoes and I like to feel that I can provide added value.'

Brett Harding, founder of Lovestruck.com in which Hugh Chappell has invested, couldn't agree more.

The company has grown from turning over a few thousand pounds a month pre-investment to turning over £100 k a month post-investment. Asked what it's like to have someone like Hugh investing in his business, Brett replied, 'Extremely reassuring. Although a substantial return on investment is fundamentally important to how angels operate, I've no doubt that Hugh's proactive, regular and sustained mentoring and support has contributed to Lovestruck's current situation. In summary, Hugh's "got my back." And as an entrepreneur who is building a business in an incredibly competitive industry against leviathan organisations, his unwavering support is worth its weight in gold.'

'The two areas that I have absorbed the most from Hugh are, without doubt, financial control and sales', adds Brett, 'The most critical "double act" for a successful company.'

'He has also brought numerous deals and partnerships to the table that would have been otherwise "out of reach." He is refreshingly candid and has a work ethic like no other. I simply cannot see a business failing under his watchful eye and stewardship, unless it's fundamentally flawed.'

Exercise

Describe your perfect investor. What expert knowledge do they have? Who might they ideally have in their little black book? What skills and experience might they bring to the table? Do you want them to help you negotiate deals? Make introductions? Mentor you and your team? Play devil's advocate? How could they help you to achieve your vision? What added value are you seeking? Contacts and corporate experience? A fresh perspective? Specific knowledge that would help you strategically?

My perfect investor is _____

Has _____

Knows _____

Can help _____

Able to provide _____

The Right Match

There needs to be a common wavelength between you and your investor(s) in order to create an ongoing workable relationship and a strong foundation for trust. You need to see eye-to-eye. You need to want the same thing, to work toward the same results and be headed in the same direction. Compatibility is critical.

Also, remember, you may get on brilliantly with the team you are pitching to, but the team making the investment may not be the same team as the one that manages that investment. Some private equity houses have a new business team and a portfolio team.

> *'Compatibility is more important than a good deal.'*
> **Rowan Gormley, founder of NakedWines.com**

Exercise

Assess your prospective investor's ability to support and contribute to your business and uncover what they want to achieve. What's motivating them? They've grilled you, now it's your turn to grill them back.

Do your homework

1. Ask questions: On what basis will they invest? Are you on the same path? Do you want to exit at the same time? How do they propose to create value? And what level of participation do they want in terms of managing the business? What are their expectations? Do they match yours?
2. Read up on which sectors prospective investors invest in and what their investment criteria are. Gain as much background information as you can.
3. Ask your investor if you can talk to other people/companies whom they've invested in. Speak to those people to assess how the investment has been managed by the investor and what added value has been gained.
4. See whether they have any other businesses of a similar size in their portfolio and try to grasp whether they are likely to be interested in what you do. Ideally, you don't want to be an investor's smallest or biggest investment, but somewhere in the middle. You want to matter enough in order to be a significant part of their portfolio, but not too big to be able to cope with.
5. Uncover what their core skills, experience and knowledge-base are. They may have a big presence in India and a wealth of experience in offshoring, or they might be powerful in Buy and Build strategies, or in improving the operational side of a business, building in board-level discipline and driving profit performance.

Jot down everything you have found out about your potential investors. Assess whether you are compatible or not.

Pitching Do's and Don'ts

Do

✓ **Create a journey.** Make it compelling so the investor wants to buy into what you are selling as a customer and an investor. 'Carve out a captivating story, intelligently explaining the pain consumers are currently experiencing and your solution to cure that pain', recommends Brett Harding, co-founder of Lovestruck.com. Outline the problem you intend to solve and explain how you came up with the idea to solve it. 'Make sure the person you are pitching to understands very quickly what it is you are trying to create and whether they would be a customer', advises Brent Hoberman. 'It's a good idea to sell the idea to them as a consumer first; it's that much easier to get them interested as an investor afterwards.' Although give equal air time to the revenue model and team as to the product itself. An investor wants to know the whole story, the bigger picture.

✓ **Practice.** 'Rehearse in front of friends and family as 70% of a presentation is delivery and body language', advises Brett. 'The investment circuit is close-knit and word gets around quick, so there are no second chances.' Martha Lane Fox agrees. 'It comes down to having a really good business plan around a really clear vision, and then practising communicating it. If there are two of you, who's going to take which role? How are you going to answer questions? Test yourself on different bits of what you're doing and ensure that you've gone through it in a coherent way', advises Martha.

✓ **Show your passion, drive, belief and enthusiasm.** Give investors a reason to back YOU.

✓ **Put a figure on the added value that the investor might bring with him/her** in terms of contacts, expertise and experience. If you give this added value an actual valuation you will be better placed to decide whether to take or leave any offer that may be made and negotiate accordingly.

✓ **Be transparent and be yourself.** 'Be true to yourself, be the person that you really are', advises Richard Moross of Moo.com who raised $5 million from Atlas Ventures and Index Ventures in 2006. 'They see through you it if that's not the case. Be very straight with them. It's hard to go wrong with that approach.'

✓ **Be concise and engage investors immediately.** Simon Dolan asked for pitches for his £5 m investment through Twitter, as pitching in 140 characters disciplines entrepreneurs seeking capital. 'All really good ideas can be summed up in that length, and it means I can look at a lot of ideas in a short period', says Simon, who invited a handful of people for more information and shortlisted a few candidates to meet.

✓ **'Elaborate on any traction gained to date.** This is proof of concept, so critical', suggests Brett.

✓ **Ask questions** to assess compatibility and value-add that an investor can provide you with.

✓ **Seek professional advice when securing investment.** 'It's very easy when you're small and the business isn't worth that much to give a lot away', says Nick Jenkins 'Over the years, I've given bits away that I shouldn't have done. If you're raising angel funding you've got to be careful not to do anything that will be difficult to unravel when it comes to a VC round later on', says Nick who also advises that entrepreneurs should avoid investors requests to include anti-dilution causes, having had to buy-out an investor in Moonpig.com who had instigated such a clause.

Don't

✗ **Oversell.** 'Investors are very savvy', says Richard. 'They've done it more than you have. They've seen every different type of pitch.'

✗ **'Go into a presentation without knowing your finances back to front'**, warns Brett. 'This is normally the reason that most angels decline on investments.' Be accurate. Know your turnover, sales figures, break-even points, gross and net profit margins, actual and/or forecasted, inside out.

✗ **Make a bad first impression.** Dress for the occasion. If you're asking someone to hand you a stack of cash, at least do the investor the honour of dressing smartly. Wear a suit. Polish your shoes. Brush your teeth.

✗ **Be vague.** Investors need to know how much you need, why and when you need it, so be specific.

✗ **Be scared to negotiate or walk away.** Create a sense of them losing an incredible investment opportunity if they can't give you better terms or a better deal and make them aware that you are presenting the opportunity to others. Only walk away if the added value is not enough to justify being below your walk-away point and you feel you are compromising too much.

✗ **Argue.** Avoid getting overly defensive or arrogant. Listen to advice given and respond professionally to any inaccurate remarks, backing up your case with facts. Remain calm. In doing so, negotiations are far more likely to go your way.

✗ **'Give up'**, says Brett. 'Unless explicitly advised to. Tenacity and perseverance are key traits of successful entrepreneurs.'

When the Ink Has Dried

As outlined above, it's vital to agree future involvement before signing a deal so that the investor shows the right amount of interest in the business; not too much or too little.

It's also crucial to agree goals going forward.

Exercise

Get on the same page

Sit down with your investment team and draft a 90 day plan.

Define specific actions to be taken by whom in order to execute and deliver on that plan.

Revisit the plan frequently.

Keep investors in the loop. 'Keep them involved and up to date with information, whether it's good or bad news', says Martha Lane Fox. 'There should be no nasty surprises. Make sure you have a relationship where you can pick up the phone and say "well actually this has gone a bit wrong" as much as you can say "this is going a bit right."'

Keep information flowing and everyone aware of when targets are hit or missed and why so. This enables all involved to take necessary action to rectify things if the business is going off course and bolsters belief when the business in on target.

Communicate regularly and openly. 'Listen, absorb and act on investors' advice where prudent', recommends Brett Harding of Lovestruck.com. 'Hold regular monthly management meetings, with a comprehensive deck for perusal.'

Remember this is a partnership. Everyone wants the business to work so it is in everyone's interest to be transparent and open in order to take the business in the right direction towards a shared vision. Only then can you really launch forth with the backing you need; with the support from your investors.

Once you have developed your idea, written it down in a plan, tested it, validated it and have secured the financial resources you need to launch forth, it's time to get building. It's time to build your website, your team and your brand . . . because everything moves fast in the digital sphere and the website you present to the world, the content you choose to fill its pages, how you design it, how you enable users to navigate their way around it; the words you use to persuade people to take the actions you want them to take – all of these decisions could mean the difference between success or failure. It's time to implement your idea, put your plans into action and build a digital presence that will help you to achieve your goals.

Part 2

Building

Your

Business

Step Five

Build Your Website

'If it doesn't sell, it isn't creative.'
David Ogilvy

Setting Up Your Website

The web population are a fickle bunch. And yet, they don't really ask for all that much. All the average web user wants to do is browse websites which are fresh, useful and fast; that's it. If you can enable them to access information and perform tasks as quickly and easily as they possibly can, they'll most likely stick around and revisit.

By the end of this chapter you will be able to:

- **Understand the value of content, why it should be at the heart of your web presence and how to ensure it is high quality, engaging and shareable.**
- **Create a logical, usable, intuitive navigational structure for your website to guide visitors seamlessly through their journey.**
- **Create a wire-frame so that you and/or your developers know how content, functionality and structure will work together on each page.**
- **Write persuasive, clickable, readable web copy to convert visitors into customers.**
- **Decide how best to manage your website and its development to suit your exact needs: in-house, outsourced, or off-the-shelf?**
- **Ensure that your site is aesthetically pleasing, securely-hosted, multi-browser compatible and accessible to all.**
- **Ensure that your site is logistically ready to operate in terms of fulfilling orders via supply, payment and delivery.**

To meet the relatively simple needs of web users, webmasters have lots of work to do. For you must ensure that your website fulfils each of the following eight crucial criteria in order for it to be successful:

Your website must have or be:

1. **Content-rich to attract and retain website visitors.** Useful, fresh and engaging content engenders trust; builds user confidence and encourages visitors to dwell for long periods of time, revisit and invite their friends. Remember, content is king.
2. **User-friendly navigation.** An intuitive navigational structure with a well-considered hierarchy of information so that users can find what they are looking for effortlessly, without frustration. Good usability is vital.
3. **Persuasive, clickable and indexable web copy to convert visitors into customers.** Your site must be clear and easy-to-digest in order to get your message across succinctly. It must be search-engine friendly so it can be

indexed and ranked in search engine listings; wording, therefore, should be clear, concise and relevant.

4. **Aesthetically pleasing design and well-managed development.** Clean and simple design to frame content and attract users; well-managed development to ensure that changes can be made quickly and easily.

5. **Accessible to all.** All users including disabled and blind users who might be using screen readers or similar technologies must be able to access the site, as must those using a range of devices, not only via a computer/web browser, but also via handheld devices such as mobile phones and tablets.

6. **Reliable and fast-loading.** Always available, quick to load, with zero downtime.

7. **Secure and customer-friendly logistics.** Respond to questions and orders quickly, take payments securely, deliver goods promptly. Users' details and privacy must be protected by maintaining a secure site where transactions are restricted to a secure interface only. Supply and delivery logistics and payment and service processes must be in place to satisfy, enthral and take care of customers from point of sale to delivery.

8. **Analytical.** Has metrics in place to measure what users do once they arrive and when/why they leave.

Every single variable on this checklist must be considered. If you miss one out, your digital success will be hampered. For instance, if you tick all of the boxes, but fail to make your website search engine friendly, few people will visit this amazing site you have built. If you have a high-ranking and accessible site which gains high volumes of traffic through search engines and via smartphones; but have poor design, navigation or wording (copy), you will end up with lots of visitors to your site, but minimal orders and no repeat traffic.

1. Content-Rich to Attract and Retain Website Visitors

Fact: great content attracts customers and boosts user adoption. Unique content creation is the new Search Engine Optimization (SEO). Consequently, digital entrepreneurs today can tweet, blog and post their way to success, not only by raising brand awareness, but also by generating in-bound links, and engaging their audience directly.

Content that connects

Useful, up-to-date content is the most vital ingredient of a good website and should be at the very heart of it. It is essentially the glue that makes your visitors stick around long enough to take the desired action and convince them to revisit. It is content which users interact with, 'like' and 'share'. Yet, in order to be effective, content must CONNECT with the audience.

If content connects with them you can encourage your web visitors on a journey, which they will happily go on. If content fails to connect, they will stop in their tracks, and click away to another destination. Once a visitor lands on your page, you can persuade them to stay by keeping them interested, building your credibility (with testimonials/reviews/expert tips) and convincing them you are worth dealing with by answering their questions (with FAQ and product video) and inviting them to interact (via your blog and other content types).

'Most of our traffic comes in for the content rather than the products', says Keith Milsom of AnythingLeftHanded.co.uk. 'So people visit to find out about teaching children to write left-handed and why they can't cut bread with a bread knife normally, and how left-handers think and what sort of careers they take up. And they then get soft-sold on from that into our shop.'

'Once they're in the shop we try to encourage them to put things in their basket, and once things are in the basket, we encourage them to checkout and complete the order', says Keith – your choices about the content you use on which pages and the way you enable people to navigate around your site are therefore vital considerations.

What the website actually looks like, while important, is actually secondary to what is actually on the site; it's substance. It is the content which encourages visitors to return and refer others to visit you. It is the content which builds your credibility and gives your visitors confidence to trust you. Not the design. For a fickle crowd where trust is imperative, credibility-boosting web content should be valued.

The trust factor

To create trust, you need to deepen relationships with your users. To deepen relationships with your users, you need to listen to their needs and problems, meet those needs and solve those problems for free, at no cost to the user. Help people and users will value you and, in valuing you, they are far more likely to trust you and, crucially, buy from you.

In his book *Launch*, Michael A. Stelzner spells out his 'elevation principle formula' which aims to elevate those who implement the formula above their competition. The formula is:

> 'Great Content' plus 'Other People' minus 'Marketing Messages'
> equals 'Growth'.

It essentially suggests that people should stop pitching and start fixing. If you fix a problem by sharing your expertise, by answering questions, by offering helpful solutions, you will *connect* with your audience, engender trust and turn them into loyal advocates of your brand.

Exercise

Elevate your content to maximize connection

1. Write down problems that you, via your content and products, are able to fix. List the questions that your target audience might ask you in terms of fixing a problem.
2. Consider which methods you might use to answer those questions and provide advice and expertise to help solve problems (from articles and blogs to FAQs, user reviews and instructional videos).
3. Contact people you know internally (within your contact network) and externally (through searching for relevant experts online) who might also be able to answer these questions/provide relevant problem-solving advice to see if they'd be interested in supplying you with content (via a guest edit, guest article, guest blog post, or Q&A/interview).
4. Once you have completed the exercises below, have compiled your content and written your copy; check the balance between 'marketing messages' and 'genuinely helpful content'. Grade your content for usefulness.

How to use engaging content to connect with your audience and boost conversion rates

Content that connects, cuts through the marketing clutter and helps users to perform a task will outperform other content. For example, try:

1. User reviews and ratings.
2. Video.
3. Blogs, tips, guides and content showcasing your expertise.

1. User reviews and ratings

'We've gone from the 'power of the expert' to the 'power of the crowd' and now to the 'power of your friends.'
Rowan Gormley, founder of NakedWines.com

Giving users the opportunity to post their views (positive and negative) provides a mechanism for other users to trust you more, because you are being transparent. It also helps you to build a stock of fresh content to aid natural search (as search engines will send more visitors your way due to the increased amount of relevant keyword-rich content on your page) and thus drive more customers to you. User reviews are thus a win–win.

2. Video

Similarly, video is a useful tool for online retailers as well as being a great medium to help users understand something. It can be instructional; it can tell a story visually or explain key points quickly and easily. Scott Weavers-Wright, CEO of baby superstore, Kiddicare.com cites video as the number one conversion-rate boosting tool in his experience. Having pioneered the use of video in their sector five years ago, the company now has three studios, two presenters and two full-time producers.

'On average Kiddicare will convert at 5%. But any product that has video converts into just under double that conversion rate', says Scott. 'We've got 5000 products now with video and they nearly double in conversion.'

Thankfully you don't need a studio or full-time production staff to create impact with video content. Video production need not cost the earth.

! Top Tips for Harnessing the Power of Video Content

1. **Invite your customers to participate.** Get them to send in videos of themselves using your product. Not only will this save you production time and costs but, by enabling users to see other customers using your products, it will motivate them to buy.
2. **Make videos short, snappy and sweet.** Aim to make videos no longer than two and a half minutes. Entice viewers with a killer headline and exciting first 10 seconds.
3. **Reveal your passion and personality.** Video your team unpacking a new product that has just come in from a supplier. Tell stories to really connect with your audience. Create a story-so-far mini-documentary with memorable milestones and facts. Inviting users and 'fans' behind-the-scenes will make them feel like they're part of something bigger than themselves.
4. **Help customers solve a problem.** Create instructional how-to videos that are relevant to your products. For example, a wine retailer might post a 'how to host the perfect dinner party video'.
5. **Make yourself more approachable.** Give customers some 'digital face time' by using Skype to have one-to-one personal video chats.
6. **Include calls to action in your videos.** Ask viewers to share, comment, subscribe, visit or click to buy.
7. **Optimize the user experience.** Keep videos below the fold on web pages and ensure they load quickly without constant buffering.
8. **Provide text options to your videos.** Some visitors may not have the time to watch a two minute video but will happily scan through a bulleted list of key points summarizing the video.

Try out iMovie, Flip Camera, Vimeo to create your videos.

3. Blogs, tips, guides and content showcasing your expertise

Foster a community around a topic on your area of expertise, rather than around your brand. Then turn your expertise into timely and targeted content.

Have a dialogue with your target audience in order to identify topics and types of content they will find most relevant, engaging and, crucially, be most likely to share and interact with. 'It's a case of listening to what's come up recently', suggests Sarah Beeny. 'Looking at what others are talking about via trends on Twitter, and then crafting your solutions. Tepilo is very much designed to be educational as much as a platform to sell your property.'

Use your content to solve problems, answer questions and give advice on topics users have specified an interest in, through commenting on your blogs or engaging with you on social networks. 'A lot of our advice pages are the result of questions we get asked through the website. My advice would be to provide concise guides to common areas of related information or short topical news updates – top tips usually work very well', suggests Sarah.

Write a regularly updated blog. It's a great supplemental way to connect with customers and boost your search engine ranking as it enables users to interact and join in the conversation. Write about solutions to problems that your audience faces and on-trend industry topics they will be interested in. Use WordPress, Tumblr or Blogger to host your blog for free.

❗ Top Tips for Converting Readers and Viewers into Customers and Advocates via your Content

1. **Monitor your competitors' website and content strategies as well as your own.** While content is king, in order to be the King of the Castle, you must have a higher dwell time and higher percentage of users sharing your content than your competitors.
2. **Update content regularly.** 'TrustedReviews.com was updated several times every day', says Hugh Chappell who automated some of the weekend reviews publishing via his content management system using forward publishing dates.
3. **Define what your audience is using and where they are going.** Determine which social media platforms and tools will best enable your content to be viewed and shared.
4. **Remix content into different formats.** Turn blog posts into an e-book or podcast, turn poll results into an infographic or slide show, turn a video into a blog post.
5. **Follow the lead of software and app developers.** Measure what content works best and focus your efforts on those areas.
6. **Make your content findable, portable and shareable.** Ensure users can easily access, download, embed, or share it.

Customer-Created Content: MyDeco.com

'The content on MyDeco.com attracts traffic to the site and generates repeat visits, which impacts the bottom line through advertising and affiliate sales', says Brent Hoberman who also licenses the 3D Design Tool.

The site's 380,000 3D rooms have each been built by customers who can also create a mood board, clip an image, decorate a photo, enter a competition, comment on a blog, and so on.

Once a user has designed a room using a database of thousands of 3D objects or created a mood board, they are encouraged to share it with the community and write their own blog on the site.

As a consequence of enabling its users to create stuff on the site itself and share it, MyDeco has created some powerful active communities who can feedback into the creative process and rate/review the vast body of other people's user generated content (UGC).Pages of customer-created designs can see their rank change in real-time as they are voted on.

Furthermore, each item appearing in any room can be purchased. With 380,000 rooms now created by users, the site is 'democratising interior design' because, as their mission statement suggests, 'Most of our best ideas don't come from clever think tanks but from our community.'

Ask industry experts to contribute their valuable insight. Create a guest blog or interview luminaries. Promise cross-promotion to encourage guest experts to give up some time to contribute. 'We've written most of the content on Tepilo ourselves, but do get guest bloggers and writers to help out from time to time', says Sarah Beeny.

Shareable content

Today, the 'shareability' of your content is more critical than ever. In its bid to remain the most popular search engine generating the most relevant search results, Google's latest algorithm, Panda, assesses whether a page is relevant through a variety of means.

Nowadays, the higher the percentage of your visitors that share your content, the higher rank Google will award that page. So, while content must be engaging to increase dwell time (time spent on each page) and encourage return visits to minimize your bounce rate, content must also be *shared* as often as possible by as large number of your users as possible.

Ultimately, in creating engaging shareable content you will be optimizing your site for search engines and should generate more traffic from them as a result.

We shall look more at this in Step 9 on marketing, but creating content that people want to share is vital in this uber-connected digital landscape. Having foot soldiers sharing your content is a great way to build brand awareness around the web.

You can even implement a free site overlay to fit over the footer of your site, encouraging sharing and interaction of your pages. The Wibiya web toolbar (wibiya.com) provides a social bar that enables blogs and websites to integrate web apps and other interactive features onto their site. You can install the toolbar to overlay at the foot of your website and customize it accordingly. It's a great way to take content sharing to the next level and integrate social media onto your own site.

'People love to share interesting news; they want to be the first out of all their friends to do stuff', agrees Anthony Eskinazi. 'Make it engaging and then give them the tools to share it. Make sure it doesn't distract from the core purpose why they're there. But, after they've completed the booking or logged out, try and encourage your network to share.'

Aim to get people sharing, re-tweeting, liking, engaging and interacting with your content.

! Top Tips for Incentivizing People to Share your Content

1. **Give them the chance to save more money the more your content is shared.** Increase the value of a discount coupon or reduce the price of a product for every, say, 5000 people who share or like something.
2. **Provide them with something exclusive.** You might offer exclusive access to a free download or goody bag. For example, ilikemusic. com asked the pop stars it interviewed to doodle on a t-shirt. It filmed them doing so, for authenticity, then invited its users to share the video link and enter the competition to win the exclusive product themselves.
3. **Be ethical.** Donate an amount to a charitable campaign for every like or share.
4. **Involve them in decisions over incentives.** Enable them to vote on the products they want to see offered, the discounts or special offers they wish to receive, and so on. Then give them the tools to share their choices and selected discounts.
5. **Reward super-sharers for recruiting more fans and followers.** Give them and their friends freebies or preferential treatment. (You might even use tools such as Curebit by integrating its technology into your website to add social referrals to the purchasing process.)

Quality content: Create the best user experience possible

With millions of websites, emails, videos, text messages, voicemails, tweets, status updates, blogs and comments to wade through, there's a lot of content choice vying for attention.

As such, high quality content is crucial. Because trust (earned by providing high quality, helpful content) breaks through information overload. Content should not be seen as 'linkbait'. It should be high quality to satisfy user needs not low quality to satisfy search engine algorithms.

Use embedded podcasts and video, blogs and audioboos via audioboo.com (a mobile and web platform that effortlessly allows you to record and upload audio while on the move and add useful data to it, such as photos, tags and location), the more you can engage your visitors as they arrive on your site, the longer they are likely to stay put.

Dwell time has become an increasingly important metric for webmasters to strive for and use to assess the quality of their content. So much so that Google now uses dwell time as a factor when ranking sites in terms of relevance for search terms. If you have users spending a long time on your site, in comparison to competing/similar sites, you will be rewarded by Google and receive a better ranking on their search pages. If the reverse is true and people spend longer on other similar sites, you will be penalized and receive a lower ranking.

! Top Tips for Content Quality Control

1. **Choose topics based on the genuine interest of your users.** Ask of your content: does this piece of content add value? Ensure that your pages provide substantial value compared to other pages in search results.
2. **Assess every page.** Ensure that your pages are the kind people will want to bookmark, share with a friend, or recommend.
3. **Create authorship.** Include a brief author biography at the foot of content to reveal their expertise and credibility.
4. **Aim for originality.** Provide original research, reporting and analysis. Avoid mass-produced content spread across a network of sites.
5. **Aim to become a recognized authority on your topics.** Becoming known as an expert in your field will enable your content to be referenced and quoted and boost your search engine ranking.
6. **Be a stickler for accuracy.** Assess your content quality for spelling, grammatical, typographical and factual errors.
7. **Avoid repetition.** Check that you have not repeated terms and avoid duplicate, overlapping or redundant articles on similar topics.

Exercise

Create a content strategy

Achieving balance is critical. Offer a content-rich experience to attract and retain visitors to your website, but avoid creating too much clutter and noise that might confuse users or slow down load speed.

1. Consider your target audiences preferred methods of viewing information – on web pages, or blogs, as downloadable documents, in video or audio format?
2. List the stock of interesting content you wish to have on your site. Create a recipe of engaging sharable content from the following ingredients:
   - news, features, reports and white papers;
   - tips, checklists and link round-ups;
   - case studies of people implementing those tips;
   - blogs;
   - infographics;
   - slideshows;
   - podcasts and/or 'audioboos';
   - videos;
   - webinars;
   - e-books;
   - polls;
   - FAQs;
   - reviews, ratings and recommendations; and
   - customer testimonials.

   (Don't forget to include mandatory content inclusions such as a tagline explaining your uniquely differentiated value proposition, price details, contact details, a method of gathering data from customers, a privacy policy and security statement, returns policy and terms and conditions.)
3. Plan your content. 'We usually plan [our content] on a monthly basis and set out the articles we'd like to produce over the course of the month', says Sarah Beeny regarding Tepilo.com. Jot down how you will generate, access and manage such content, who will be responsible for doing so and how often you will need to update/how many pieces of content per day/week/month you will need to add. Will you need to hire freelance contributors and/or an in-house editorial team?
4. Note the objective for each piece of content and what visitors will ideally do in response to your content. What do you want them to do next? (e.g. comment, share it, contact you, place an order?) And how will you give them the guidance and means to respond accordingly? E.g.

(*Continued*)

Content	How Generate/Access/ Manage	Frequency	Objective	Action
Blog (web/ video)	CR to write/guest contributions from JS Hire freelance contributors and editorial team as experts	Daily	Build credibility Encourage debate	Comment
Articles	CR and interns to write and source	Weekly × 3	Inform/ engage	Share

5. Create or generate your content.
6. Use the checklist above to assess the quality of that content.
7. Publish it on your site (ensuring that you give users the tools to share it). There are 337 (and counting) social networks. Tools such as AddThis enable users to share across a multitude of them as does the Wibiya overlay.
8. Submit content yourself to social news sites such as Digg, Reddit and Mashable.com. Use social channels smartly. Use free browser-based solutions such as Publisha.com to import, format, and simultaneously publish your content across various digital platforms: to the web, Facebook, RSS, iPhone and iPad from a single dashboard.
9. Use feedback and user comments and questions to feed into your content strategy for the following month.
10. Repeat. If you manage to achieve a number one position on Google, you can no longer rest on your laurels. Nowadays, Google updates and refreshes its algorithms and indexing metadata every 40 days. So your content must be fresh and your content strategy must be rigorous and continuous.

That said, it is important not to focus merely on a specific algorithmic tweak, but to focus on delivering the best possible experience for your users.

Of course, before you publish and syndicate your content, you need to house that content: create a home for it, prioritize it and structure it…

2. User-Friendly Navigation

Once you have all of this incredibly engaging content and remarkable products or services to sell to people, how do you display it all on your web pages to generate the best possible results? How will the user navigate from page to page? How will you guide them?

Considering what people actually do when they arrive on your site is one of the most critical parts of the site building process, as it is this which will convert browsers into buyers, encouraging them to take the desired *action*, whether that is buying something, subscribing to a newsletter, downloading a file or sharing a piece of content.

Sadly, many webmasters fail to focus on what the visitor wants and how to guide them quickly and easily to achieve that aim. Instead they overload them with information without considering how that information is presented.

Creating a logical content hierarchy which considers the priority of information is a must. This will navigate the user on an intuitive and seamless journey, enabling them to reach their destination and take that all-important action, smoothly, logically and, most importantly, without getting lost or frustrated en route. If they don't find what they're looking for, they'll click off to a competing site, never to return. Fail!

> 'The key to navigation is simplicity. If it's complex, users won't use it and won't get to where you want them to get to.'
> **Neil Brooks, founder of Bluebit.co.uk**

Make every click relevant; otherwise the only place users will be clicking towards is your competitor's website.

To make it simple and guide visitors to whatever they landed on your site to find, you should know what they are seeking and what stage they are at in their buying process.

What they seek: Provide a smooth 'finding' process

The homepage should be divided into decision-making paths that quickly separate visitors by their interests and lead them to the information they are looking for. To pull users in and signpost exactly what they will find if they click a particular link, provide typographic 'scent trails'. 'Poor scent trails are a big fail', says Rob Walker, MD of web design firm, Xcite Digital. 'I just want my questions answered. If I can't find things easily and quickly then I will look elsewhere. Your job is to help people to sniff out the information they need.'

Other things to avoid are scrolling pages that scroll from left to right. All relevant information and main features should be visible without scrolling, not hidden from view.

Pagination is another big no-no, i.e. loading a top 10 list across 10 pages, merely to boost page impressions, when it could just as easily be displayed on one page. 'Pagination is a cheap trick to artificially inflate page impressions when publishers should be focusing on engagement', says Rob Walker.

In order to keep things visible, easy to find and easy to use, it's important to use common navigational techniques that the average web visitor expects to see. No surprises; keep it simple and logical.

> **❗ Top Tips for Creating a Usable Navigational Structure and 'Finding' Process**
>
> 1. Offer a clear search box in a prominent position to assist visitors.
> 2. Use visually appealing and easy to understand icons to aid navigation.
> 3. Use 'breadcrumb navigation' i.e. highlight or underline navigation text so that users know where they are/which page they are on currently and how best to proceed.
> 4. Include a link back to the home page on each web page so users can find their way home if necessary.
> 5. Ensure that navigation is the same on each page and consistent throughout the entire website. Ensure that link headings clearly suggest where the links lead to, that navigation links are grouped logically and the overall navigational structure is easy to grasp.
> 6. Provide a site map option including text links as an alternative browsing method.
> 7. Group the most important links on the top-level navigation bar (products, contacts, key content) and the more functional/legal links (account, settings, privacy) on a lower-level.

It's also worth reviewing how leading digital operations navigate their users around their sites.

For example, Play.com offers a diverse range of goods yet, what could be a complex journey is made easy because of its usable and intuitive navigation system. 'The use of mega-menus in Play.com's navigation are very powerful', says Neil Brooks of web design firm, Bluebit.co.uk 'Without detracting from the content on the page but still allowing the user to get anywhere they want as quickly as possible.'

Furthermore, the site provides clear methods of refining searches to help users find exactly what they seek. So, when you land on the DVD page, you can refine your search using the left-hand navigation by category, certificate, actor, director and price or, on the Toys page by 'sub category' from pre-school to puzzles, age range or price.

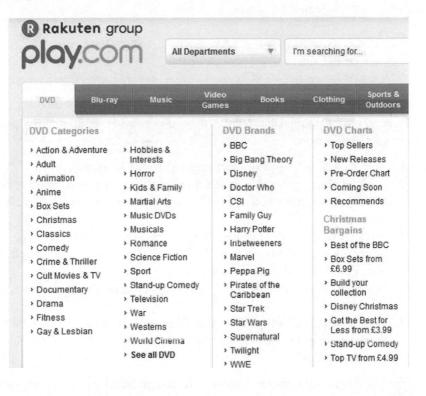

Alternatively, if you use the mega menu in the main navigation bar, DVDs are split up into categories (from animation and box sets to classics and comedy) brands (from BBC and Disney to Peppa Pig and Star Wars to DVD charts (from top sellers and new releases to coming soon and recommends) and DVD bargains (such as must-see kids films and TV) to sale items.

Similarly, on NakedWines.com, after clicking on Wines in the main navigation bar, a secondary navigation bar appears: 'See all/red wines/white wines/rose wines/champagne and fizz'. Once you've selected the type of wine you'd like to buy, you can filter your search results via type price, country, grape, style and are even given an option how to display your search results, opting either to view in rows or in blocks.

For sites with lots of skews and variations of products, such as Play.com, MyDeco.com or ASOS.com, it can be useful to enable users to refine or filter their search by price, colour, brand, material, size, and so on.

On Play.com you are also given the option to see what you have 'recently viewed' as images of your browsing history appear in the left-hand navigation bar.

Navigating deeper into these sites – whether on product pages or on results listings – the user can sort by a range of categories, providing choice for those with differing priorities.

- Play.com allows you to sort by bestselling, price, release date, A–Z or customer rating; and
- NakedWines.com allows you to sort by highest rated, price and popularity.

A review of leading sites reveals they also provide multiple navigational options to choose from:

1. Alphabetical listing of product categories on Play.com.
2. Horizontal navigation bar which displays the categories in order of popularity and thus priority (e.g. DVD is still Play.com's most popular product category).
3. A search engine with 'I'm searching for' makes the search more powerful and personal on Play.com with 'GO' being the call to action to search on both Play.com and Nakedwines.com.
4. Lower-level navigation options exist on Moo.com, Play.com and Naked-Wines.com.
5. You can search 'all wines' on NakedWines.com, use the site search engine or the site map and browse via types of wine from champagne to rosé and a 'go to top' option.

The point is that the user can browse the site and find what they are seeking quickly and easily using the route they feel most comfortable with. They are given a navigational choice.

What stage they are at: Provide a smooth 'buying' process

It can be useful to break down web users into the following:

a) browsing explorers,
b) hunters, who are seeking a specific type of product, service or information, and
c) trackers, those who know exactly what they want already and are ready to buy.

It's important to offer each type of user a smooth journey to accommodate where they are in the buying process and ensure that they find exactly what they need.

❗ Top Tips for Providing a Smooth 'Buying' Process

● 1. **Copy best practice.** 'Make the buying process really simple', advises Brent Hoberman. 'It sounds obvious. But if you're an online retailer you'd be amazed at how many times people don't copy best practice on the web and make it way too complicated. There are sites that have put hundreds of millions of pounds worth of investment into this stuff, whether it's Amazon or eBay or Expedia... copy the best of what's out there and don't make it a complex process.'

2. **Make it easy to set up an account, put items into the shopping cart and buy them.** 'Minimise the number of clicks it takes to get an item into the shopping basket', suggests Tim Booth, founder of iwantoneofthose.com and The Greenhouse Project, a company advising bricks-and-mortar businesses about getting online.

3. **Keep navigation consistent across all pages.** Remember, not every visitor will enter your site via the home page.

4. **Keep your cart process as short and quick as possible.** Don't tempt users with other offers or adverts. Don't slow down the cart process. Keep momentum going.

5. **'Make everything appropriate to the user, and remove everything else',** suggests Rob Walker, MD of Xcite Digital. 'For example, if you buy something from ebuyer.com the payment screens display nothing other than the checkout process, removing the main navigation.'

Smooth Operators Keep Things Simple: iwantoneofthose.com

Churning out hundreds of daily orders, the iwantoneofthose.com team did everything they could to provide a smooth buying process.

Focus on Each Order

'The second a product goes in the cart, look after that order, make sure there is nothing else on that page, just the cart', advises Tim Booth. 'Strip all your top banners away, don't try to upsell. Because the biggest drop off you're going to get will be once you've got it in the cart. It's a big deal to get something in the cart, then, once it's in there, the drop off out of the cart can be very harming.'

(Continued)

Keep the Cart Process Simple

'View every page of the cart process; watch that sales funnel', adds Tim who points out that the process is like an inverted triangle with fewer and fewer people reaching the final stage of entering their card details and confirming their order. 'The longer your cart process is; the more dramatic and terrifying that inverted triangle becomes.'

Think Like Your Customer

'We built our website as consumers not as retailers', says Tim who admits that none of the co-founders had retail experience. Rather than think 'how do we sell this', the IWOOT team considered 'how would we want to buy this. We examined: "What is confusing to us? Would that make us want to buy it? No, so lets try it another way." It was easier for us to think like our customers because we *are* our customers. Even our name is customer centric: the customer is saying "iwantoneofthose.com" rather than us saying "whydontiflogyouthis.com."'

Let your customer drive your navigation

'Create personas which describe your typical clients and then try to imagine how they navigate around the site with a view to completing a goal you set', suggests Rob Walker, from Xcite Digital.

Certainly, thinking like your customer, as Tim Booth suggests and understanding the motivations behind their buying decisions, is vital to creating an intuitive navigational structure.

That's exactly what Scott Weavers-Wright from Kiddicare.com did when he came up with his social tagging idea.

By asking customers reviewing Kiddicare products about the best uses and benefits of products they had recently purchased via e-mail, Scott decided to use the questions and answers provoked by that exercise in the site's navigation. As Scott explains: 'Say you bought a push chair, we'd ask, is it easy to fold, hard to fold, lightweight, heavy, durable? . . . What are the best uses for it? Is it good for air travel? What's your opinion?' explains Scott. 'Because we had development in-house, we put the results of that feedback into our navigation. So now, if you go into pushchairs you can navigate by "easy-to-fold" or "durable" or "best use air travel" . . . it means our customers are driving our navigation.'

Make your site easy, usable and intuitive to move around

'We humans do more of what's easy', says Jeff Bezos, founder of Amazon.com. 'When you lower friction, you always get more of what you just made easier.'

Lower friction; get more traction. Simple.

One way to ensure your site is usable and intuitive to move around is to use wire framing when creating the site's layout. A wire frame is essentially a visualization tool, a blueprint of your web pages which connects and prioritizes the information architecture (content and navigational structure) with the visual design and functionality of the website.

It presents the layout of the page in terms of:

a) what information will be displayed and how it will be prioritized and structured (content and navigational structure);

b) the location of key page elements, such as the header, footer, logo, content area, navigation bar, images, and so on; and functional interface elements, such as action/radio buttons, drop-down menus, check-boxes, and so on (visual design and functionality).

If you are using an open-source framework tool to develop your site, such as Drupal, you won't have to worry about the layout of visual interface elements as templates are provided which fit expected norms. You will still need to consider the flow of content and navigational structure though.

Exercise

Create a wire frame for your website

1. Examine existing websites and benchmark against them (including brand leaders and competing sites) to see how they display content and take users from page to page. Forget about fonts and typography, colours or graphics. Focus instead on location of content, what titles they use in their navigation bars and which content appears where.

2. Using a pencil sketch or software tools (such as Balsamiq, Keynote or Adobe Photoshop) to draw each area of your site (i.e. the visual interface elements). First draw where your header, logo, footer will be and write down what content will be displayed within those areas. Abide by certain rules such as positioning a sharp logo and strapline at the top of the page.

3. Draw in your text fields, i.e. where text will appear on your page.

4. Indicate where your functional interface elements should appear, from your navigation bars and drop-down menus to the positioning of call-to-action links, buttons, check boxes and so on. Stick to the rules regarding certain elements, i.e. keep call-to-action buttons in a consistent position above the fold; keep navigation at the top (with dropdown submenus if you feel these work well); keep shopping basket/account balance/sign-in information in the top right hand corner and logos to the left; keep advertising standard, relevant and non-obtrusive with no pop-ups.

   Again review how other sites do it. Many (Play.com, NakedWines.com, ilikemusic.com) house striking large images below their navigation bars, followed by between two and four content blocks revealing key offers and

(Continued)

content of interest, which are all above the fold. Privacy policies, copyright notices, and terms & conditions belong in the footer.

5. Write down each piece of content you need to include and every single call to action. Grade each piece of content on relevance asking what specific purpose each piece of content serves and whether it adds value.

6. Create your navigational structure. List all content onto a site map which links each piece of content to the next and groups content together. Which pieces of information should be in which order and why? Write your text links, put them in order and create the visitor journey. Can you navigate easily to every section on the site from the home page? Remember the three click rule: that useful content should be no more than three clicks away from the home page. Google's own recommendation is that 'every page should be reachable from at least one static text link'. Use your map to check you are abiding by these rules. 'Try not to double up on links (apart from the footer navigation and calls to action)', advises Rob Walker, MD of web design firm, XciteDigital, 'visitors can become confused otherwise'.

7. Map out how you wish to direct your users through their buying decision via the positioning of information within your website navigation (the hierarchy of information). Write down the titles you wish to include in your navigation bar. Keep these to ideally no more than seven, but definitely no more than nine. 'Make sure that you are displaying your products in an easy way, not just the buying process but the display function is absolutely fundamental', advises Brent Hoberman.

8. Test whether a complete novice could navigate their way round your website. 'If my mum can use it then you're onto a winner', laughs Anthony Eskinazi, founder of Parkatmyhouse.com. 'If someone who doesn't know the difference between a browser bar and a search engine is able to use your site then 98% of the audience will understand.'

3. Persuasive, Clickable and Indexable Web Copy to Convert Visitors into Customers

Many moons ago, the Poynter Institute established with eye-tracking studies that web visitors look at text first, at photographs next, followed by graphics.

You only have a few seconds to convince visitors why they should stick around and buy what you are selling. As such, the words you choose to use could make or break a potential sale. Words persuade. If you spend the first few sentences telling visitors 'Welcome to so and so, we do this and that, aren't we great', you will lose them.

The copy you use on your site – what you say (the message/language) and how you say it (the technique/readability) performs the same function as your navigation and content. It must **engage** users to stimulate interest, **connect** with them, **drive** them through their visitor journey and **persuade** them to click and take the desired action you wish them to take.

As well as being well-targeted, relevant, jargon-free and accurate, your copy must be clear, concise and compelling. When writing for the web, you must also ensure that your words are:

1. **Clickable.** Use benefit-rich compelling copy which addresses 'you' the reader. Include clear calls to action. Essentially answer the questions: What's in it for me? What do I do next?
2. **Readable.** Include headlines, signposts, highlighting in bold to break up the text and enable scanning.

To make your copy both clickable and readable, there are five key 'Message Rules' to follow so that what you say has maximum impact.

Message Rule 1 – Focus on what's in it for your visitors. What benefits will your visitors gain? How precisely can you help solve their problem?

Your website visitors care not about your story and that of your product. They do care about: what's in it for them? Many websites woefully underestimate the importance of answering this question in their copy. It's not about you, it's all about them. You can tell your story on a lower-level for those who wish to know more (i.e. on the About Us page). But, to compel action, don't talk about yourself as soon as they enter your site; instead focus on your user.

The benefits your product will provide, the experience they will enjoy, the problems you can help them solve, that's what they care about. They care not for product features (whether a vacuum moves rounds corners and has better suction power), but for benefits instead (faster and more effective vacuuming; more free time). Their experience is the deal clincher, i.e. that those benefits will enable them to be more effective, get promoted, admired, free up their time to spend doing stuff they enjoy doing, and so on.

By focusing on the end-result experience you focus on the target audience's genuine needs. But avoid extravagant claims which will undermine your credibility. According to Abtests.com, (where you can view and learn from other people's test results, upload and share your own) replacing feature-rich copy with benefit-rich copy achieved a 200% conversion rate increase.

Often you need to convince people to change from their existing provider to buy from you. People don't much like change. It's risky. Your perceived benefits must outweigh the perceived risk to persuade them to make that change.

Exercise

Generate benefit-rich copy

1. Revisit all the feedback you have gathered from customers/potential custom-
    ers since you started on your journey to become a digital business owner.
    Why do/will people buy from you?
    How has/will buying your product affected/helped them?
    What has been their end-result experience? What has buying your product
    enabled them to do?
2. Write down all the features of your product. Next to the product feature,
    write down the core benefits that feature provides i.e. 'what's in it for them?'.
    Flesh it out. Write down the experience that gaining those benefits creates.

Message Rule 2 – Use the right, relevant, targeted language

Of course, in order to understand what's in it for them, you must have a firm
grasp of who they are.

*   Refer back to your customer-focused business plan and customer profile
    exercises on page 59 and, later, once your site is launched, use your site logs
    to understand who your web visitors are and what they are seeking. In order
    to relate to your users, you need to understand their needs and target your
    words at them effectively.
*   Speak plainly and directly. Use customer language and not jargon.
*   Avoid CAPITALS and multiple exclamation points. Online it's the equiva-
    lent of SHOUTING!!!

Message Rule 3 – Speak to an individual and refer to them as 'you' rather than 'we'; leave 'about us' information for the 'about us' page

Use 'you' rather than 'we' copy (e.g. 'You can do this', rather than 'we provide
that'). Instead of 'We are Widgetsrus and we are Widget specialists', write 'If
you want to do XYZ faster with minimal fuss, you can solve your problems by
using such and such a Widget. Learn how.'

Some webmasters go the other way and avoid any 'we' copy at all and forfeit
any kind of About Us page. This does little for their credibility. Housing 'about
us' information on a specific page, enables those who do wish to find out more
about you, to do so. It enables you to add your brand personality to the site,
briefly share your story and it allows your users to meet the team via brief team

biographies (in reverse chronological order). About us information can make you more approachable. But keep that information for a specific page.

Your background story can help establish your credibility/longevity and, alongside testimonials, awards and accreditation, can prove to your prospects that you will deliver the benefits you say you will.

Adding the Personal Touch to Your Story: NakedWines.com

While NakedWines.com focus on outlining the benefits of 'what you get' as an Angel on their home page (half price bottles, cash back and better wine), they include their 'story so far' which is a letter from their founder, Rowan Gormley. And it makes compelling reading indeed. It explains the narrative behind the business idea and model, but also provides a perfect example of how founders of digital businesses should communicate what they do, how they do it and why they do it to their customers and, in doing so, clearly explain what makes them different (and better) than the competition. This founder's letter is engaging, inviting and personal.

> 'Naked Wines was set up by me and 17 deranged and passionate friends, who left sensible safe jobs, slap bang in the middle of the biggest recession since the Great Crash.
>
> **What's the big idea?**
>
> We set up Naked Wines because we could see one thing about the wine business that needed to change. And that was this... most of the expensive famous wines we were tasting were mediocre. And some of the unknown winemakers were producing stunning wines... but nobody had ever heard of them.
>
> The wine business is a bit like celebrity chefs. When you eat at a Gordon Ramsay restaurant, you don't get the great man cooking for you... but you do pay for the name. So our idea was to hire the people who actually do the cooking. Give them the finest ingredients – and sell them on to you without the huge celeb chef price tag. The exact OPPOSITE of everyone else.
>
> **We don't just buy wines. We make them happen.**
>
> Every talented winemaker wants to make wines their way... without compromise. But to do that someone needs to give them a break. Their first order. So that is what we do. We order the wine before it is made, so that our winemakers can get their heads down and do what we both want them to do... make their wines delicious!
>
> We can only do this because 62,411 normal wine drinkers, people just like you, have become Naked Wine Angels. Wine Angels, like theatre angels and business angels, sponsor winemakers and in return get preferential prices, an open invitation to visit, free tastings and the lovely warm feeling of having done something good.

(Continued)

> *It works. Ask our 62,411 Angels*
> In the words of Stephen Rapoport – 'You guys are utterly effing brilliant. Fact.'
> **But wait! There's more . . .**
> We only want you to pay for wines you love. So we will refund in full for the ones you don't.
> And if you tell us which wines you did like we will recommend new wines to you that we guarantee will blow your socks off.
> We deliver next (business) day for £4.99. Most of our competitors take about a week and charge £6.99.
> If you want to taste the wines before you buy, no problem. Sign up for one of our tastings.
> And finally, we are called Naked because we have nothing to hide. You can see exactly what our customers think of the wines for yourself.
> Regards
> Rowan Gormley, Founder
> rowan@nakedwines.com
> p.s. please do come back and tell me what you thought of the wines, the delivery and the website.'

Now it's your turn . . .

Exercise

Practice writing with the user in mind

Find some paragraphs of copy about a product, in a brochure or on a company's product page (perhaps your competitors).

Rewrite the copy ensuring that you allocate just 25 words to the product features, 100 words to the product benefits and 150 or more to the subsequent experience.

Make sure you use the word 'you' instead of 'we'.

Message Rule 4 – Include compelling calls to action

On the web, you need to lead people by the hand until they confirm their purchase.

So, once you've informed visitors 'what's in it for them', tell them precisely 'what to do next'. A strong call to action (CTA) on every web page is vital.

Consider how much commitment you want from your user at any given stage in their journey. In ascending level of commitment, you may wish for them to:

- learn more or why (request information);
- get a quote or request a call back;

- register, subscribe or enter a new section, such as your shop;
- place an order (order now); and
- checkout and confirm that order.

Different pages will require different calls to action. Detailed product pages will require hard/primary CTAs such as 'buy now'; whereas introductory category pages will require a softer/secondary CTA, such as 'learn why'. That said; it can be worthwhile to have two kinds of CTA for those who are not quite ready to buy but are happy to download a white paper, which could convert them into a buyer another time.

Whether you want someone to download or sign-up, avoid words such as 'click here', 'submit' or 'register now'. Each CTA must compel the visitor to take that action. Start with a verb, and clearly explain the value behind the action. You can further strengthen CTAs with testimonials, a guarantee and urgency.

The most successful websites all have clear and direct calls to action with every piece of content, whether that's an invitation to 'Shop for DVDs' on Play.com, 'Start Making' on Moo.com or a call to 'Read More' or 'Add to Basket' on NakedWines.com.

NakedWines.com is a great example of a site using compelling calls to action:

'The very obvious call to action on NakedWines.com is the timer at the top which tells you how long you have to get next day delivery', says Neil. 'This sense of urgency works very well.'

Individual product pages display an image of the wine label, the name of the wine with clear bullet points outlining reasons to buy. A box is displayed next to this information saying '83% of 2063 people would buy this again', and listing the price, 'NOW £7.99' before the green call-to-action box invites users to 'add to basket,' and displays how much 'cash back' Angels will receive on purchase. This is a clever way to use customer feedback at point of purchase to convince others to buy. Additional calls to action invite the user to 'review' or 'add to wishlist' with user comments and ratings displayed below.

The site also features images with headlines and call-to-action buttons down the right hand side of the site, from 'Got a voucher from one of our lovely partners – claim now' to 'Are you a winemaker? Pitch your wines directly to our 175,000 customers – tell me more'.

Additionally the site features an engaging real-time section entitled 'What's happening right now' which displays five text boxes with arrows indicating users can scroll left or right to view more. For example, 'John just bought Rimbaldi Monetpulciano 2009, 14 minutes ago', with 'John' being a text link to his profile and the name of the wine, a text link to that product. Or 'Kathy reviewed Klein Riesling S Trocken 2009, 20 minutes ago'. Showing what other customers are buying at that very moment is a clever call to action in itself.

Message Rule 5 – Make sure your words and 'meta tags' are relevant and indexable

If you want your visitors to stay, click and do, your words (and content) must be relevant. As Google's webmaster guidelines advise: 'Think about the words users would type to find your pages, and make sure that your site actually includes those words within it.'

These days, due to keyword 'spamming' and meta tag abuse, the importance of 'meta tags' has diminished greatly in the search engines algorithm. However, they are still used by secondary search engines, such as Bing and Yahoo! And the words you include in your <title> tag and <description> tag are still displayed in your search results on Google and all other search engines to describe the subject matter of your web page. Furthermore, your title tag appears in your visitors' browser tab and is what will appear if your page is tweeted or shared on social networks. As such, relevant word choice is a must.

- Keep your meta title tag to 65 characters or less and your description tag to 155 characters or less.
- Ensure that both tags are descriptive, relevant and accurate.
- Don't overuse keywords. While keyword density (the number of relevant keywords on your page compared to other words) used to be important, it

is more valid to write your copy for users rather than search engines to avoid being penalized.

The readability factor: How you say it

According to usability guru, Jakob Nielsen, it takes people 20% longer to read text from a screen than from a printed page, and 79% of website visitors scan web pages rather than read the entire page word for word. This makes writing for the web different to writing for print. While clarity is critical, so is the need to be concise.

To keep your copy web-friendly and scannable you should:

* Keep sentences and paragraphs short and succinct. Make just one point per paragraph, ensuring that the most important point is made first. Avoid large chunks of text and complex sentence structures.
* Create a compelling, meaningful strapline, which conveys your unique value proposition.
* Use magnetic, attention-grabbing headlines and sub-headings to pull the reader in and act as directional signposts. Don't put full-stops after headlines. You want visitors to read further.
* Break up text with bullet points and numbered lists.
* Highlight key leading points that you want your visitors to take away after visiting in bold text. The scanning reader will pick out these points.
* Keep these key points above the fold in the first sentences of each paragraph.
* Make line height, spacing and margins large enough to enable the reader to scan.

Exercise

Evaluate your word choice and give your copy a final check

* Could you replace any words to encourage action, increase credibility, give advice?
* Do your words convey your tone of voice/brand personality and create the right 'vibe'? E.g. quirky, serious, formal, informal?
* If your web visitor read your headlines, highlighted points/keywords and bullet points and nothing else, would they get the overall gist of your message and take action?
* Is your text accurate? If copy is littered with typos and poor grammar, you are sending the wrong signals to your visitor. Attention to detail is vital.

4. Aesthetically-Pleasing Design and Well-Managed Development

Outsourced or open-source?

How you intend to manage your website is an important decision – will you update your own content, using a Content Management System? Or will all changes be managed by your design and development team? Will that team work for you in-house or will you outsource development of your website to a web design company? Alternatively, as is increasingly the case these days, will you use an off-the-shelf content management solution (perhaps open-source) to build and manage your site?

'With Tepilo we used an agency to build the website we designed and developed', explains Sarah Beeny. 'They still have some equity in the company so we worked very closely with them. For mysinglefriend we have an in-house team, and have re-launched a site that we built internally. Both methods can work well', says Sarah.

Whether you have your own in-house team or outsource to a development firm, you'll need to create a detailed site specification outlining exactly what you want.

Most digital businesses which have been around a while will have at least one horror story to tell about the programming of their website.

Nick Jenkins, founder of Moonpig.com was particularly burned by outsourcing development to an agency. 'We spent £70,000 on developing the first site. But it never really worked.' Frustrated, Nick hired someone to write a new version of the site. 'After that we've only ever done [our development] in-house.'

Despite being a huge dot com success story, Brent Hoberman, co-founder of Lastminute.com says that his worst decisions were: 'a) to underestimate the technology cost, both financial cost and cost of time to build the site, because, initially when we launched the site it didn't work very well and b) having all our smartest people on the front-end of the site when the back-end was struggling to scale.'

It's important to take into consideration the complexity of your site as Richard Moross of Moo.com illustrates: 'We're not just a virtual website, we're a manufacturing business with a shop at the front end and a manufacturing business at the back end, all pulled together by an e-commerce platform. It's quite a complicated beast to manage, so you need really smart people to help drive it and we're really lucky to have such a great [in-house] team.'

Clearly, if you can get it right first time, you won't suffer the problem of wasted money or coding errors losing you traffic and your development team won't inherit poor code which cannot scale and have to start from scratch.

Get it right first time

'The biggest strength in Kiddicare's arsenal and an absolutely key success factor is that we develop our own website in-house so I can come up with ideas and bring them to market very quickly', says Scott Weavers-Wright of Kiddicare. com who didn't relish the lack of control that outsourcing development and programming brought.

Decide whether you wish to hire in your own team of programmers or trust an external agency to run your web development project. Consider the following questions:

- **How complex is your website?** Level of complexity will dictate how you manage your site and who you hire to do so.
- **How frequently do you intend to make changes** to the design (front-end appearance) and development (back-end programming)?
- **How much control do you wish to have over implementing ideas immediately?** If you need this to be instantaneous, in-house may be better, as you may have to join the queue behind another client if you outsource.
- **Do you intend to grow your business?** If so, will the core structure of your code be able to handle the growth? You need a solution that will scale. As such, you must have people on board, in-house or not, who understand technology and scale.
- **Have you at least tried out the current open-source offerings?** From Drupal and Joomla to Tumblr, WordPress and Blogger for blog-driven sites?

If you do choose to work with an external firm, ask them the following questions:

- **How will you demonstrate your commitment?** Ensure that your design and development team (in-house or outsourced) share your passion. 'I've always thought that the developers need to show some passion for the project – if it's just another site to them, that's probably what you'll end up with', says Sarah Beeny. Talk to their current clients to see how they measure up.
- **How often will we communicate about goals?** 'Communication is key and a well-written brief whether written by you (the client) or by the agency (on your behalf) is extremely important and should be in place before any work is carried out, unless you have bottomless pockets and unlimited time', says Neil Brooks, MD of web design firm, Bluebit.co.uk. 'We all work best when we have a shared goal and understanding.'

It may also be wise to hire in someone technical to join your own team and help you brief external designers and developers. It can be difficult to make decisions about technology if you don't have some rudimentary knowledge in-house. If you don't know what you don't know, then you can't make informed decisions, even if you are given external advice.

Off-the-shelf

While having a bespoke, professionally designed website is worthwhile, there are a number of tools for start-ups to build a website off-the-shelf, quickly, easily and for minimal or no cost. From Weebly and Drupal to monthly subscription services such as Squarespace, SnapPages and Jigsy, these sites enable you to get your business online and garner direct visitor feedback sooner rather than later.

'Drupal has grown to become a very comprehensive framework which allows you to build any number of Content Managed Solutions', advises Neil Brooks. 'Using PHP and MySQL and with 1000s of additional plugins, Drupal is one of the more powerful open source CMSs there is, but it comes with a steep learning curve. Fortunately there is a huge community of developers and a raft of documentation available.'

Strikingly simple: Minimalist design

The entire World Wide Web is vying for users' attention. While content attracts people, and well-crafted copy encourages them to stay and take action, an attractively designed site will make their experience more positive.

In 17 years of the commercial Internet, the biggest lesson that webmasters have learned is that simplicity is vital to design.

> *'Design your websites like people are driving by at 60 miles an hour.'*
> **Steve Krug, *Don't Make Me Think***

Essentially, modern, fresh minimalist design streamlines. It reduces confusion and aids concentration. It enables your users to *focus* on the meaningful content, key messages, signposts and calls to action, while still getting a flavour of your brand. A clean, uncluttered and stylish design interface prunes away unnecessary elements, uses bold imagery and typography, distinctive icons and call-to-action buttons and, crucially, plenty of white space to frame elements and aid the scanning reader.

'Play.com recently redesigned their website and also updated their branding and, in both cases, what is strong is the simplicity', says Neil Brooks from Bluebit. co.uk. The addition of the full width banner in the home page and the simplification from three columns to two in subsequent pages makes this website much less cluttered.

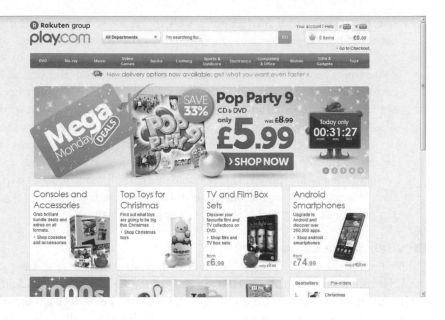

For a simple clean site design

- **Use a minimal colour scheme.** Give thought to colour combinations. Colours should be consistent and well-contrasted to maximize readability, define the flow of content and direct users' attention. For example, Play. com uses orange for headings, prices and CTA buttons. For Moo.com, the colour green in varying shades is used for the logo and CTA buttons, highlighting navigational buttons and carried through into each page for headings and bullet points. On both sites call-to-action buttons are all white text on a striking colour (either orange, green or purple) with BUY buttons being big, clear and well-contrasted.
- **Compress and optimize images and avoid bulky files.** Nobody wants to wait; indeed, nobody will.
- **Consider imagery carefully.** Does it serve a purpose and is it of high enough quality? Are you able to use unique custom photography or artwork rather than stock photography? If you do use stock photography avoid tired clichés such as smiling ladies, suited groups of people and handshakes; select instead images which serve a purpose and reinforce your brand message and personality. Don't shy away from imaginative abstract imagery if it empowers your message.

  On sites like Play.com and Nakedwines.com large, bright, engaging, high quality images span the page, most of which dynamically change between various special offers or product ranges with radio buttons highlighting which image/offer you are currently viewing out of four or five.

. **Use typography and font choices well to create strong branding.** Try oversized bold typography to grab attention, drive the flow and create contrast. Use it to place emphasis on the single most important message to avoid confusion. Typography used to give designers headaches until free and low-cost services such as Google Web Fonts, Fonts.com and TypeKit became available. These help designers to avoid Flash which, although latest versions work on tablets and Android smartphones, is not accessible on many mobile devices in its entirety. While some elements of Flash work fine, others aren't reliably supported and you don't want users to be unable to view a navigation menu on their smartphone. It is possible to use flash detection to 'swap out' flash elements with regular images, but there are languages, such as JQuery, HTML5, JavaScript and CSS3 that can replace Flash.

Browser/device compatibility

People browse the web, access and interact with content in different ways today than they did even five years ago. The mass adoption of smartphones and tablets such as the iPad has made the need for cross browser and cross device compatibility even more critical. So your site must not only look good in all of the different major browsers (Mozilla Firefox, Safari, Google Chrome, Internet Explorer, Opera), it must also be small-screen friendly and look good on all mobile devices.

The good news is that there is a growing adoption of standards-compliant browsers. Furthermore, coding languages, such as HTML5, CSS3 and Javascript are now supported by all of these browsers, making it slightly easier to optimize your site for each one. There are various tools to help you test your site on the different browsers.

Crucially though, to continue with the core aim of minimizing areas of frustration, you need to make sure your site is accessible on any browser and any device.

So test your site on all the mainstream browsers and older ones too. Additionally, Google's webmaster guidelines suggest that you use a text browser such as Lynx to examine your site, as 'most search engine spiders see your site much as Lynx would'.

Exercise

Keep design minimal and accessible

Seek out minimalist sites and note down any particular design elements you like.

Look at how major sites, such as Amazon and eBay use colour and contrast to highlight content and where they position their call-to-action buttons, and so on.

Check contrast on your website using a free colour contrast tool such as www.accesskeys.org/tools/color-contrast.html

5. Accessible to All

Your site must adhere to certain design standards (WC3) to make it accessible to the visually impaired. Not merely because Google penalizes sites not built to these standards, or even because it is only fair and ethical to ensure that everyone can view your site, but also because millions of people across the globe (53.2 million Americans and over two million Brits) are visually impaired, and the Internet is a platform which has revolutionized the way that they shop and find information.

! **Top Tips For Design and Development**

1. Decide how to manage your site based on its complexity, frequency of updates, necessity for control and planned scalability.
2. 'Do a search for award winning websites and see what they are doing well', suggests Rob Walker of Xcite Digital.
3. Use plenty of white space and well-contrasted colour schemes to aid readability. Don't over design.
4. 'Start off with simple wire frames and functional notes which allow the designer to know confines they are working too', advises Rob.
5. Keep call-to-action buttons in a consistent position above the fold, and test different formats (colours/text/shape/size and so on). Use the one that achieves the best conversion rate. (More on improving conversion rates in Step 10).
6. Consider each image you use to ensure it matches your branding messages. Compress and optimize them for load speed purposes. 'Design around your brand and market position', advises Rob. 'Think about fitting nicely into the box your client will put you in'.
7. Use typography cleverly to guide the reader to key points.
8. Ensure your design is responsive, compatible and optimized, i.e. will adapt to whichever screen size and look good on whichever device is being used to view it. Find out which are your customers' main browsers of choice.

However, as well as making your site accessible to blind users who use screen readers to read websites, you also need to make it accessible to those who don't use or need such software, but simply can't see as clearly as the average person.

To make your site more 'visible' you should:

1. Make font size larger by providing alternate stylesheets, particularly if you are targeting 'silver surfers' aged over 50 years old.

2. Ensure your layout remains to scale even when text zoom is enabled and ensure the site has a machine readable font.
3. Offer text-only versions of your site. Remember, not all users have Javascript enabled.
4. Use highly contrasted colours next to each other rather than similar shades to make text legible and graphics easy to see. Avoid patterned backgrounds. 'Make sure the colours are easy to read for the visually impaired', advises Rob Walker from Xcite Digital who is building a site for the UK's largest prosthetic limb company. 'A large portion of their users are diabetic with visual impairment, so it's important to build with good structured code that is cross browser compatible and follow the standard procedures as outlined here.'
5. Enable users to highlight text with their mouse (which some CSS and Javascript techniques can disable) as this is a method that some people use to improve readability.
6. Avoid colour combinations, particularly on call-to-action buttons, which colour-blind people will struggle to see. Colour blind users will confuse or be unable to see red and green, blue and yellow. For example, having a red button next to a green button or green text on a red button may visually confuse someone affected by colour blindness.
7. Give all users access to your mobile-specific site, so that anyone can browse your mobile site, even if they are using a desktop machine to do so. The minimalist layout and easier to scale elements are useful to those with visual impairment.
8. Enable keyboard shortcuts so that users can use their arrow keys rather than having to follow their mouse cursor across the screen.
9. Give every image 'alt-text' (alternative text) attributes to provide a voiced description of the image for people accessing the site via speech synthesis software. All images must have alt-text (even if the alt-text simply reads '*' to indicate that the image conveys no information). This enables search engine spiders, and visually impaired people to see what the images are.
10. Ensure that graphical links are supported by text links so the destination of each link is obvious.
11. Visit www.w3.org/WAI/eval/Overview.html to test your site for accessibility. A list of tools can be viewed here: www.w3.org/WAI/RC/tools/complete
12. Read Google's Webmaster Guidelines for using Flash and other rich media.

6. Reliable and Fast-Loading

There's little point having a brilliant website if your users can't reach it. You want uptime not downtime. 'The site has gone down', are words that no digital entrepreneur wants to hear, even if it is due to popularity, i.e. a spike in traffic creating server overload. You want to ensure that your site can handle any volume of traffic and make the most of traffic spikes rather than have a site that is unavailable or incredibly slow during busy periods. Having a site which is fast-loading and reliable is a must.

Allocate enough 'web space' to scale up, add new pages and rich media and enough bandwidth to attract more visitors to view more pages.

These days there are a number of hosted web platforms that enable you to perform tasks and establish a web presence without even having to consider web hosting. From WordPress's blog platform to Flickr's photo gallery platform and YouTube's video hosting platform. Hosting is just there. However, for those wanting to design, build and launch their own websites, hosting is still a necessary consideration.

Apart from using tools such as Loadimpact.com to simulate and test how much traffic your site can handle, you should be prepared by asking a potential web hosting company the right questions:

1. Can they scale up quickly if necessary in order to meet traffic and bandwidth demands?
2. How so?
3. If you go over your bandwidth usage, how will you be charged?
4. If your site experiences avoidable downtime, how will they be charged? Will they issue a credit for downtime?
5. What happens if the site goes down or experiences a problem at 3am in the morning? How will you be able to find out why it's gone down and when it will be online again? Good, round-the-clock technical support is vital.

Read reviews to assess quality of service, uptime and potential issues before committing to any provider.

The good news is, in the past few years, hosting costs have plummeted from hundreds of pounds for a secure managed server to less than £50 for the same service. The choices have expanded too, from shared server solutions to dedicated server and managed hosting services from companies such as Rackspace, to cloud computing, from companies such as Amazon Web Services. Each of these are viable hosting solutions.

Sophisticated data centres providing the cloud model omit the need for business owners to own or rent servers to host their websites and data. Computing and web infrastructure is increasingly being shifted to the cloud. Amazon, Google and Microsoft have all hopped onboard. Certainly, when it comes to hosting, it's a buyers market.

7. Secure and Customer-Friendly Logistics

Selling stuff online means you need to take payments from customers securely and deliver goods to them professionally. And, before you have anything to sell to them, unless you are producing your goods in-house, you will need to find and build strong relationships with suppliers.

So let's examine these critical areas of supply, payment and delivery.

Supply

> 'Treat your suppliers with complete respect and realize it has to be a win–win situation.'
>
> **Scott Weavers-Wright, Kiddicare.com**

As a retailer, without your suppliers you have nothing to supply your customers. Vital then to treat suppliers well and spend effort on managing supplier relationships.

Here are two very different online retailers with very different models selling very different products. Yet both have realized that it makes commercial sense to treat suppliers fairly and ethically, and both are benefiting from this realization.

Kiddicare.com – Baby Products Retailer

Stocks 30,000 products in its warehouse
    Supply challenge: To create a win–win partnership in every eventuality

With well over 30,000 products stocked in its warehouse, strong supplier relationships makes that initial part of the sales cycle flow much more easily.

'It has to be win–win', says Scott Weavers-Wright, who admits to managing suppliers very differently to the way the site's high street competition does so.

'We will pay our suppliers historically within 30 days and, if we receive a settlement discount, we will pay them within seven days', explains Scott whose main competitors take as long as 120 days/four months to pay!

Kiddicare.com will get preferential treatment as a result. 'Because they know we pay very quickly, they can clear stock', explains Scott. 'So Brittax will say they've got 1000 car seats too many as they've over produced the fabric in Germany, and ask if we want them as a special deal. And the reason they'll come to us is because we'll pay them quickly.'

(Note: Big companies like to keep their money in their bank accounts for as long as possible as it is earning big interest for them, hence the slow payments. They know that suppliers are so desperate to supply them, that they can't do much about it. This works both ways so be wary of this if your digital business intends to supply big companies.)

Furthermore, the status quo punishes suppliers for supplying faulty stock. Kiddicare.com sought an alternative to keep everyone happy.

'When we sell a product and it's faulty and comes back to the shop, we will fix it. If the customer is happy with that, they go away happy; if not we refund them', explains Scott. 'Customers can return goods up to seven days online within the UK law, so if it can't go back into stock because it's got a damaged box or a wheel has come off, we'll put the wheel back on, put it back on the shop floor and sell it for £5 less.' But we won't necessarily send that product back to that supplier and hit them with a big stick.'

'Kiddcare's competitors will send that whole product back to the supplier, request a refund and hit them with a fine.'

'We treat suppliers as a key part of our business, have a very robust relationship with them and do not fight them on returns.'

Building credibility as a start-up

NakedWines.com

Ships 10,000 bottles of wine (a bus full) per day

Supply challenge: Convincing suppliers to embark on a new business model

If you are presenting a disruptive business model that a particular industry has not seen before, it can be problematic persuading suppliers to supply you. That was the case for NakedWines.com, who found getting winemakers to take them seriously to be the hardest thing, not helped by a competitor threatening suppliers that they'd be dropped, a common challenge faced by disruptive businesses.

'The problem initially is that it's too good to be true and "growers" kept wondering where the catch was', explains Rowan Gormley. 'We had to explain the concept to them very slowly and we had to keep hunting until we found winemakers who were more open to doing business in a different way.'

Fortunately, word-of-mouth works among suppliers as well as customers. 'When their wine-making neighbours saw a big truck going down the road and carting out a cellar load of wine . . . they wanted to do business too. Our words achieved nothing, but seeing your neighbour drive around in a smarter car and have an empty cellar was the catalyst.'

However, the disbelief of potential suppliers still goes on today. 'I'd say 19 out of 20 people who we approach simply don't get the fact that they can simultaneously reduce their prices *and* make more money doing business our way. They're so into the mindset of it being all about increasing prices, so it's a tough sell.'

(Continued)

One method that helped supplier buy-in has been to take suppliers on tour.

'What we've found is that traditional companies keep their suppliers and their customers far apart and get nervous about customers going direct to suppliers and vice versa. So we've tried to do exactly the opposite, we've tried to get them as close together as we can.'

In spring 2011 the NakedWines.com team invited 25 winemakers over to the UK and did a seven day 'rock n roll' bus trip around England, visiting 3000 customers. The effect was incredibly positive.

'The more the suppliers meet the customer, the more they realise how passionate our customers feel about helping another human being and that the wine tastes better than you get from the supermarket. The more the supplier sees that for themselves, the more bought into the model they get. Additionally, the more the customers see that these really are winemakers who are overjoyed as their lives have been transformed through the customers' support, the more customers feel proud about what they're doing,' explains Rowan.

'Part of the new way of doing business is relinquishing control. The historic way of doing business is you keep people apart, beat up suppliers, and see what you can get away with with the customers. By reversing those traditional laws of business one at a time it frees up more value in the chain.'

In the early days of business, Tim Booth from iwantoneofthose.com also found it difficult to persuade suppliers to supply them.

'Everyone thought we were idiots', recalls Tim. 'Nobody wanted to supply us, because they had the attitude back then of "what's online? We've got shops." The only way I'd get through to suppliers was by talking to people; picking up the phone instead of e-mailing, going to all the trade shows and saying "hello."'

Fortunately, as the IWOOT business proved itself, it got easier. 'We received supplies quick and got good deals because we constantly talked to them and sold what they supplied us with', says Tim who also ensured he kept suppliers on side by paying up quickly.

'We made a deal right at the very start that we would always pay our bills – on time or early, but never late', says Tim. 'We got some stuff at better prices and margin than some huge high street retailers because they knew they'd be paid. Someone like Argos might buy 10,000 of something and we'd be buying 1000 but we'd get a better price.'

MyDeco.com is another brand which has relationship-building at its core, bringing together more than five million homeware products, from over 2000 retailers it needs to develop strong supplier relationships with retailers, despite holding no stock.

However, as co-founder, Brent Hoberman, points out, how do you build strong relationships with suppliers when, as a start-up, your orders may be minimal? 'It's about building credibility', says Brent.

Your website, your management team, your partners, your investors and how innovative you are can all help establish and build your credibility, before you go on to sell lots of whatever your suppliers are supplying you with.

'You build credibility by getting good people on board either by attracting brand name investors, or by partnering with companies that you'd want your company to be in the presence of', suggests Brent. 'You build credibility by being

---

! Top Tips for Building Strong Supplier Relationships

1. **Pay suppliers as soon as possible.** You'll receive preferential treatment in doing so.
2. **Be on the same side as your suppliers.** Treat them with respect and empathy and they'll offer you stock deals, good prices and clearance opportunities that your competitors just won't get.
3. **Pick up the phone or visit them.** Human contact works well when dealing with suppliers, particularly if you have to convince them about your business model and prove your concept to them.
4. **Build credibility.** Do this by selling what you are supplied with to prove yourself, but also by creating a usable website, credible team with brand name partners and investors and by being innovative.
5. **Hire in people who have experience and contacts within the supply chains in which you wish to join.** Take Play.com which trades directly with suppliers, rather than through wholesalers. Knowing that they wanted to diversify from music and DVDs, they hired in experts who had years of experience in each field to head up each new category.

---

innovative so you can act as R&D for the suppliers to some extent, and become their future thinking area', he adds.

Payment providers

Selling goods online requires a credit card merchant account/payment gateway to take orders via credit card (connecting your customers' credit card account to your bank account) plus the option for customers to pay via PayPal. Bear in mind, ongoing transactional fees of between 1–5% and initial investment in a shopping cart/payment gateway system.

In choosing a payment provider to accept payments via your site you must:

- Consider your audience and their geographical location and age. For example, if you are selling to a global audience you will need to grasp which methods are favoured in those territories and whether your payment provider can support these options. Or, if your target audience is mainly teenagers, some of whom will be without a credit card, how might they pay for your wares? You have to be 18 to have a PayPal account (check) so mobile payments might be the answer.

- Discover how the provider handles things such as chargebacks (when a consumer disputes a credit card transaction appearing on their statement) and regional variant tax calculations. Also find out whether they support functionality such as Account Updater, which enables payment providers to update credit card numbers behind the scenes
- Find out the types of report that they will provide you with and how you might reconcile these with your own financial systems.
- Ensure that your payment provider is compliant as a Level 1 Services Provider under the PCI DSS standard, and verify that it's on the Visa website, so can provide the Verified from Visa option.

You will also need to consider data security and credit card protection and stay up-to-date on current legislation. In March 2011, new guidelines were provided by the Security Standards Council stating that customers' credit card data should not be accessible after purchase in order to avoid fraud. Cloud computing solutions offer an automated non-human transaction process, reducing fraud and secure services such as Verified from Visa should be used.

For more information, visit impartial directory and comparison site for online payments: www.electronic-payments.co.uk.

Delivery

Kiddicare.com processes approximately 40,000 orders a month and has invested millions into its hi-tech warehouse in Peterborough which uses smart automation to make it extremely efficient. However, as Scott Weavers-Wright admits, personalizing their packages is a big challenge for the big boys, like them. 'It's trying to figure out, how we can personalise our packaging so it doesn't just look like a box', says Scott. 'When I buy from a good small retailer; the box, the returns label, the package inside, it's all very neat and presentable and makes me feel like I've been sent it as an individual, not a mass mail from a warehouse.'

Being small can be advantageous in this sense, so harness the power of being small and add the personal touch when distributing your wares.

Scott also advises that you choose the right delivery firm. 'Find a delivery company or courier that is "you" on the road. When they give that parcel to the customer, they represent you. That last smile is key; as it's all about your reputation. They must live and breathe it', says Scott.

It's important to check that there are no mistakes with the order ahead of shipping it out. What Moo.com does is a nice touch: they have a final checklist near the end of an order which asks you questions such as 'have you checked your spelling for mistakes and missing digits?' And, once you've ordered, instead of the tired 'Thank you for your order', you are presented with 'Yay! Your order has been placed.'

❗ Top Tips for Order Fulfillment

● 1. Personalize with perfectly wrapped packaging and fulfill orders yourself when you are small as this enables you to retain control over how customers receive their goods.

2. Try free, open source based e-commerce web application software such as Magento (www.magentocommerce.com)

3. Ensure that your chosen delivery/courier firm represents you well. Speak to their other customers and get assurances from them about their ethos and how it fits yours. Assess their customer support.

4. Offer reasonable delivery slots and give the power to the customer to choose and change if they won't be at home. There are various ways of offering non-restrictive delivery slots and you should look into these options when choosing your delivery firm.

5. Keep delivery simple. NakedWines.com does this in two ways. Firstly, with pre-ordering it avoids warehousing costs and sends wine straight to customers on arrival in the UK. Also, instead of offering normal, five day special or next day delivery options it makes Next Day delivery its standard delivery option.

6. Document the fulfillment process on paper clearly so that everybody involved understands what they're supposed to be doing with deliveries and when they're supposed to be doing it, even if the key person responsible is unavailable. 'With processes being incorrect you can get bad financial figures, inaccurate stock figures and get into all sorts of trouble', advises Stuart Rowe, ex-MD of Play.com, which handles as many as 1000 orders per minute during peak periods, such as Christmas time.

---

8. Analytical

Your website must have metrics in place to measure user activity, so you can constantly improve your site and conversion rates and maximize your ROI (Return On Investment) as your business grows.

This vital step will be covered in detail in Part Three of the book in Step 10 on measuring and improving your marketing and website performance.

Once you've built your website – the core tool in your armoury as a digital enterprise – you need to make sure it is mobile-friendly and, to really take advantage of digital, build yourself a smartphone app too.

Step Six

Build Your Mobile App And Mobile-Friendly Site

'An iPod, a phone, an internet mobile communicator... these are NOT three separate devices! And we are calling it iPhone! Today Apple is going to reinvent the phone. And here it is.'
Steve Jobs

Digital enterprise is evolving. With the advent of smartphones, an increasingly relevant part of digital enterprise today is mobile. Furthermore, as smartphone ownership increases (IDC estimates that manufacturers will ship more 982 million smartphones by the end of 2015, double the number shipped in 2011), so too does demand for browsing and buying through handsets.

In the next few years, spending via mobile phones is expected to grow exponentially. M-commerce statistics vary from $119 to $630 billion, accounting for at least 10% of e-commerce activity. Some (like Gartner) say that, by 2013, more people will access websites through mobile phones than through desktop computers. Evidently, smart entrepreneurs know that they need to exploit this opportunity and embrace the critical mass favoured mobile.

You have three options here. These will depend on the level of demand from your specific target audience and the level of budget you have available. In this chapter we shall explore each to enable you to take full advantage of the mobile opportunity. So, by the end of this chapter you will know how to:

- **Optimize your existing site so it can be viewed and navigated easily on a mobile device.**
- **Develop a mobile-specific, mobile-commerce website which accepts mobile payments.**
- **Develop an appealing app as a stand-alone digital product and/or to use as a tool to drive traffic to your site and push information and discounts to your users.**
- **Make your value proposition well-suited to an app.**

Optimize your Existing Site for Mobile Across Multiple Platforms

Today, web content is increasingly being accessed via handheld devices. As such, digital enterprises should, as a matter of course, offer a site which is fully optimized for mobile usage.

However, with so many browsers and operating systems, it can be difficult to make your site accessible and compatible across multiple platforms and devices from iPhone and Android to Blackberry and Symbian. The jury is still out on whether you should use standard technologies and one common language, such as HTML 5 and Javscript or build specifically for individual devices, such as iPhone or Android. Having said that, as technology evolves and improves at an exponential rate, it is getting easier to optimize your site across all platforms and device type.

'I think over time it's getting easier', comments Brent Hoberman. 'With HTML 5 coming on, people can create great websites and align them to mobile and not have to do as much work as previously to get them to work well across various mobile platforms.'

Indeed, there are open source tools which allow you to convert your code into HTML5, such as PhoneGap and Appcelerator. And savvy developers can use various methods to serve content across multiple devices, such as using multiple mobile-specific stylesheets on a website to add or remove certain features, depending on the device being used.

Furthermore, if you are using an open-source content management system, such as Drupal or WordPress, you can use one of their own free or paid-for mobile plug-ins which work across a number of devices. These even enable you to select preferred devices to load full web pages and devices in which you want to use the mobile-specific stylesheet.

❗ Top Tips for Optimizing your Site for Mobile

With touching and swiping replacing pointing and clicking on many devices, you can take advantage of the various ways that mobile users interact with content, but you must first ensure that any potential areas of frustration are removed.

1. **Determine the level of demand and identify the type of phone penetration of your users by examining your website statistics.** Which devices are the majority of your users and potential customers using to access your site? Focus on optimizing your site on this platform first before commencing work on the next most popular device, and so on. Some parts of the world favour Symbian devices; whereas Blackberry, iPhone and Android are the key devices in the UK.
2. **Consider users using tablet devices.** These users are open to a more immersive experience and will happily view videos and wider content than a rushed mobile-user who requires a more trimmed-down experience. That said, sites optimized for tablet users should still be simple, touch-friendly and easy to navigate.
3. **Check how your website appears and functions on your own mobile phone and other devices.** Jot down any areas of frustration, if any. Use an emulator if you don't have access to a particular type of device. From iBBDemo2 and Android SDK to Blackberry Web Development Page, Symbian S60 SDKs and Opera Mini Emulator – each will show you what your site looks like on each handset type.

(Continued)

4. **Strip away any unnecessary graphics or content.** Consider how to make the site easier to view and navigate. Have your development team make changes to your site accordingly.

5. **Check on multiple devices and across multiple browsers.** You can use tools within browsers to switch user agent to help you test your site. For example, you can go to 'Developer Mode' in Safari to change your user agent and download a User Agent Switcher for use in Firefox.

6. **Use free mobile plug-ins and mobile-specific stylesheets and conversion tools.** There are a variety of tools available to make your life easier.

7. **Avoid extensive use of Flash, complex navigation or fixed elements.** By doing so, you will minimize the risk of delaying page response or displaying error messages.

2. Develop a Mobile-Specific Mobile-Commerce Website Which Accepts Mobile-Payments

Millions of coffee-drinking consumers are already using Starbucks' mobile payment app to pay for their beverages. While more products are being purchased via mobile on Amazon than ever before ($1 billion in 2011). Shopping from the palm of your hand has never been easier for consumers. According to econsultancy.com, visits to ecommerce sites from mobile devices accounted for 7% of total traffic during the second quarter of 2011, up from an average of 1.4% the year before.

Mobile-commerce has major advantages for business owners too. By adding mobile payments to your armoury, you can really capitalize on the growth of on-the-move activities, such as peer recommendations, social media and geo-location functions.

With PayPal's two-click mobile payment system, Mobile Express Checkout, now available to those with a fully fledged PayPal account, and other technologies being developed to initiate and accept transactions using mobile devices, mobile-commerce is growing by enabling businesses to accept payments from anyone, anywhere. Whether you use micro-billing, short-codes, NFC (Near Field Communication) or m-commerce credit card processing solutions, consumers can instantly purchase products or services or subscribe to something using their mobile rather than their desktop. I shall explain these options in more detail shortly.

Not only is PayPal's mobile option easy to use for merchants already using PayPal Express Checkout on their web-commerce platforms, it also gives merchants the ability to accept credit card payments as well as PayPal, thanks to a partnership with VeriFone.

Principally there are three main methods of mobile payment in terms of how transactions are processed by merchants and paid for by consumers:

1. Paying using a mobile phone itself instead of a credit card via a mobile network which will authorize or initiate a transaction (while on the go). E.g. using micro-billing, Payforit or short-codes.
2. Paying using the mobile phone itself instead of a credit card (while in-store or on the go). E.g. using NFC (Near Field Communication) applications such as Google Wallet.
3. Using a mobile phone to browse and buy direct from e-commerce stores or via apps which have been m-commerce enabled by integrating with a credit card gateway. e.g. using m-commerce credit card processing apps or services which integrate with an existing merchant account such as Square or SagePay.

OPTION 1: Take boxPAY, an SMS-based micro-billing payment platform with which your customers can make a web purchase for digital goods, services and currency without a credit card; they simply enter their mobile phone number at the point-of-sale. The transaction charge appears on a customer's mobile phone bill or is deducted from their pre-paid balance.

Payforit (www.payforit.org) is another payment service, supported by all licensed UK mobile operators, designed to make it easy, trustworthy and consistent to pay for low cost micro-payment services (generally under £10) on the mobile phone. With Payforit, consumers don't need a credit card or bank account to use the service – they don't even need to sign up or register any details. All they need is their mobile phone. Visit payforit.org for a list of Accredited Payment Intermediaries, such as Oxygen8 Communications (oxygen8.com) who can help you set up this type of m-commerce.

Short-codes provide another m-commerce payment method. By texting a message to a short-code, customers can be billed at a premium rate and/or subscribe to a recurring monthly service that is then added to their mobile phone bill until they text "STOP" or similar to stop the service and charge.

OPTION 2: The alternative method of using your phone to pay for items directly uses Near Field Communication (NFC). This essentially enables consumers to wave their mobile phone at a payment terminal instead of using their credit card, by enabling them to store credit card information in a virtual wallet. Over the course of the next few years more and more NFC-enabled mobile and tablet devices are predicted to be shipped.

Most NFC solutions are predominantly for physical in-store use, where consumers tap their phones on the reader. Some, such as Google Wallet (Google.com/wallet) can also be used online by merchants that support Google Checkout. That said, it is still early days and NFC is not yet ubiquitous.

Deloitte predicts that in 2012 shipments of decices equipped with near filed communications capabilities will likely grow about 100 percent to almost 200 million and in 2013 as many 300 million NFC smartphones, tablets and eReaders are likely to be sold.

As Alexander Svensson from leading mobile innovation and development agency GrappleMobile.com, says, "It is possible to do it via digital, it doesn't have to be a physical NFC tag, (i.e. having to bump your phone to some kind of terminal) it depends on how that NFC tag is integrated."

OPTION 3: If you already have an e-commerce solution and merchant account, as well as optimising your e-commerce website for mobile usage, it is certainly worth adding m-commerce by integrating with the credit card gateway via your merchant, so that mobile payments can be taken 'in app' or 'online'. "Adding m-commerce provides consumers with a quicker way of entering in details and making that transaction happen." So says As Alexander Svensson from GrappleMobile.com. So, instead of tying m-commerce into a mobile operator and taking payments via a consumer's mobile phone bill you can go straight through the merchant by integrating with the credit card gateway, 'in app' or online, using a solution such as SagePay. "Once a consumer enters the payment process within an app, for example, they will either be redirected to an optimised mobile e-commerce website or it will all be done 'in-app' and integrated with the credit card gateway," explains Alex.

This option enables consumers to enter their credit card details using their mobile instead of via their desktop, either by visiting your optimised store or 'in app'.

Alternatively, you could use a specific app/solution for processing credit cards using *your* own mobile phone. Square is is a credit card processing app, founded by Twitter co-founder Jack Dorsey. It provides a free app for iPhone and Android along with a small, portable, square-shaped card reader which is plugged into the *merchant's* mobile device. Square charges 2.75% transaction fee with no other costs.

Online merchants can use the service as it is possible to accept payments without a card reader. However, for every new Square user, there is an initial $1,000 weekly limit applied to manually-entered transactions (payments for which the card is not swiped).

Square is a device-independent service as it can be plugged into any device with an audio jack. While Intuit Go Payment and Verifone's PAYware Mobile are iPhone-dependent services. The latter two services provide all-in-one hardware and charge monthly service costs and transaction fees; all three services require a merchant account, and give you the option to either use your phone to swipe a card (for physical retail) or enter transactions manually (for online retail).

Which service you choose will generally depend on:

- the transaction amount (micro-payments);
- volume of transactions you intend to process; and
- the type of business you run (traditional retail or e-tail).

Whatever solution you choose, the market is growing as consumers start to buy more tangible goods instead of using their phones purely to buy applications and ringtones or to claim discounts and use coupons. While m-commerce fraud and security issues are less well understood than e-commerce, strategies are being put in place to tackle these.

! **Top Tips for Mobile-Commerce**

● To convert transaction-oriented mobile users into buyers, help them reach their objective:

- **Prioritize information.** Focus users' attention on essential content by limiting what appears on the first screen to only the most necessary information and key points. According to usability guru, Jakob Nielsen, 'it is 108% harder to understand information when reading from a mobile screen'. He advises 'defer secondary information to secondary screens'. Don't cram irrelevant promotions and images into a small space. Keep it relevant and focused.
- **Think minimal.** As Jakob Nielsen says, 'short is too long for mobile'. So keep text ultra-concise and use large buttons with nothing close to them that may be mistakenly tapped. 'Keep it simple, light and quick (remember you're on 2 or 3G) if you're outside', adds Scott.
- **Keep it convenient.** Make your mobile-specific checkout experience as seamless as your online one.
- **Keep it fast.** Aim to minimize the number of clicks to checkout in order to retain shopper engagement. (Avoid taking your user to a third-party site to checkout or forcing your shopper to re-enter information, scroll or resize; as with e-commerce, if they face any frustrations en route, they will abandon their purchase.)

---

3. Develop a Mobile App

As outlined earlier, the mobile web generally offers up a minimalist version of regular websites, whereas native apps provide more of a tailored yet limited experience. Ultimately, an app's shelf life is as long as it can hold a users' attention – not a problem if you intend to create novelty one-off apps, but, if you intend to build a following and generate revenue from your app, it's a difficult environment to compete in. You need to ensure that your app's content/functionality is useful or engaging enough to go the distance; make apps for each platform and keep on giving users more of what they want.

The good news is that you can harness the power of open-source and free/low-cost services to develop, test and get your app to market. And, with almost a billion smartphone and tablet owners by 2015, that's a huge captive market to target.

As Martha Lane Fox suggests, 'You can now develop an app at a relatively low cost to see if it works. So that's what we've done with Lucky Voice. We've got a Lucky Voice iPad app and a Lucky Voice mobile app. With not too much investment we've got it out there to see who's using it and we've done the same with MyDeco.com. This app driven culture is the quickest way to go. It's worth having a think and giving it a whirl.'

There are many incredibly useful free tools to take advantage of. Check out Conduit.com – a network of web and mobile app publishers which enables you to create quality custom mobile and tablet apps with no OS or device hassles and deploy on all platforms, then develop, publish, promote, monetize, exchange and distribute your app without any coding required. Or use ictomorrow.co.uk which allows app creators to test their apps in front of a live focus group/panel of real customers.

Furthermore, there are no major barriers to entry because, taking the Apple AppStore as an example, Apple does everything from distribution and currency exchange to payment processing and internationalization. Apple takes a mere 30% slice of your gross revenue for doing so.

The bad news is, while you can create and test apps relatively simply, creating a truly successful app which has longevity within the burgeoning app market can be a little more complex than that.

Making your value proposition well-suited to an app

Just like any product available in the digital world, in order to generate serious returns on the investment of developing an app, it must be memorable, interactive, and/or solve a problem and serve a niche. As well as being suitably brilliant and useful, your app must also be intelligently priced, heavily marketed and regularly updated.

What makes an app appealing?

An appealing app must tick at least one of these boxes. It should be one or more of the following:

- entertaining and interactive;
- unique or better than the rest;
- well-designed and usable in terms of its aesthetics, navigational structure and functionality;
- community-driven with viral potential;
- well-suited to one of the most popular app genres;
- helpful, useful and meaningful;
- able to harness the power of location.

Your app should ideally be unique or, if not unique, better than existing alternatives. If it is not useful it should be entertaining. Take the Plane Finder AR app taking the world by storm. You no longer have to wonder where the plane flying overhead is headed; with this app you simply point your phone at the plane and are informed of its destination on-screen – a simple and incredibly viral idea.

Your app must also look good and function well with fluid navigation. As is the case with mobile-optimized or mobile-specific websites, apps must avoid bulky elements, keeping the user interface touch-friendly, intuitive, unobtrusive and minimal. First impressions count on mobile as much as any other medium, particularly with free apps where the 'churn' rate is high.

> *'Design is not just what it looks like and feels like. Design is how it works.'*
> **Steve Jobs**

If your app can harness the power of established social networks, so much the better. For instance, apps which pool community-driven reviews are particularly sustainable as repeat usage is high, and you can simply plug your app into those networks where millions of people are already having conversations.

In general your app should also fit into the more profitable of genres. Games account for half of the most profitable apps and are the most popular in terms of downloads, followed by social networking, books and entertainment. However, as trends shift, the popularity of other genres may increase.

The most successful apps outside of the entertainment market (which require constant fresh content) provide functional tools which enable users to reduce the time it takes to perform certain tasks. So, apps which help people to organize themselves or their information, such as expense trackers, calendars and to-do lists, work well. As do task-based utilities such as instant messaging, weather forecasts and barcode scanning.

Useful and Meaningful Apps Create a Positive User Experience: Kiddicare.com

Kiddicare.com's iPhone app lets its customers scan barcodes. 'Users scan the product and it comes back with Kiddicare's price, which is hopefully more competitive', explains CEO, Scott Weavers-Wright. However, the Kiddicare team took the app further than mere price-comparison to tell users whether the site has any of that product in stock and, if it doesn't, presents comparable items. It works quickly and intuitively to provide the user with something meaningful within a matter of seconds and enhance their experience as a Kiddicare.com customer.

(Continued)

'We took it further because we wondered, what happens if the system can't find the barcode or Kiddicare doesn't sell the product?' says Scott. 'We didn't want it to come back with nothing, that would be a negative customer experience.'

So instead, behind the scenes in a matter of seconds, the app resolves the barcode to a name, finds out what product that is via an online search and feeds it back into Kiddcare.com. It then locates either that it has the item in a different colour to the one scanned or has a different model. 'So our system says, "we can't find the product but we have got these,"' explains Scott. Simply by scanning a barcode, a user can find out what their options are and receive a positive customer experience as a result.

eBay is another company providing a positive customer experience to its users who are out and about. They are selling hundreds of millions of dollars worth of goods via their mobile app (with one item purchased every two seconds) thanks in part due to their push alerts and SMS notifications which inform users when they have been outbid, encouraging them to bid again via mobile. Their app ticks the boxes of being interactive, being useful and solving a problem (of being outbid and able to resolve that by bidding and buying via the app wherever they are).

Music-discovery app Shazam also serves a purpose. It helps people to identify songs they might hear in a public place or on the radio. It is memorable and useful and objective-based, enabling people to tag a track quickly. It invites users to tap the screen to begin the track-identification and tagging process, focusing primarily on the users primary task. It then gives users the chance to buy, listen to or share a track via social networks which encourages repeat usage.

Dating site, Lovestruck.com, has a value proposition particularly suited to mobile users. Theirs was the first mainstream dating website to provide iPhone and Android apps enabling dating on-the-move. The app enables users to see who's nearby. So, on a Friday evening, you can find out who is in proximity to you and may be available for a date. It's useful and interactive and harnesses the power of location.

Lastminute.com founders, Martha Lane Fox and Brent Hoberman also had a site perfect for mobile. Yet their ideas around location-based services and enabling people to access their site from wherever they were, were a little ahead of their time.

'We had a big vision for mobile because Lastminute.com on mobile makes complete sense', says Martha. 'If you're looking for a good deal and you're on the move, of course on your mobile phone is where you want to look at it. But, to be honest, it was a bit too early in the mobile cycle for us to really get the business income. Sadly, smartphones were not commonplace in 1997 nor were any kind of device that would be easier to use than carrying a computer around.'

Exercise

Creating an appealing app

1. Look at the top existing successful well-designed apps within each category to understand how they generate value and solve a problem, how they organize and present information to their users and what actions users need to take in order to achieve their goals within the application. Also use this opportunity to assess what's missing in the app market.
2. Figure out which types of people are most likely to use your app, why and where they'll use it (for example if using an app in a car to find a location, you don't want to include the need for too much reading). Considering the environment that an app is viewed in as well as how it is viewed is vital.
3. Focus on the primary task and elevate content that people care about. Display the main feature of your app and a call to action prominently. For example, place emphasis on a specific icon to enable content sharing.

'Try not to pack too much into an app', advises Sarah Beeny whose Tepilo app helps you find properties for sale and to rent privately. Users type in a postcode, use the integrated map or search in their current location using their mobile phone's GPS. They can then use buttons to contact the seller or save the property to their favourites list. 'Think about what features you really need and what will actually work on the go', adds Sarah.

Going app: How it works

Revenue comes from selling apps themselves, from ads served within apps or, in the case of free and paid-for apps, from in-app purchases where creators provide a free version and then generate revenue by charging consumers for additional (premium) features or content. For example, Tapulous sells in-game avatars as well as reaping revenues from game sales and in-game advertising.

It's important to research your market and, if building apps across different platforms, understand how users interact with apps. Take creators of the uber-successful Angry Birds app, Rovio. Their research revealed that owners of Android phones were, in general, less spend-happy than iPhone users. Consequently it launched a free port for Android owners integrating an advertising model instead of the download for a fee model it presented to iPhone users.

In terms of pricing, unless you are a well known brand or big publisher, you'll need to charge no more than £1 for your app. If you offer your app for free, you can make money from in-app purchases.

If you do decide to take advantage of this high growth yet fiercely competitive marketplace, you'll need to sign up as an official Apple iPhone developer, if opting to develop an iPhone-specific app or ensure that anyone you outsource development to has done so. In that instance, you or your provider will also need to know the iPhone programming language, Objective C. You can download a free Software Development Kit via the iPhone Dev Centre (http:// developer.apple.com/iphone). You'd also be well advised to get yourself an iPhone, iPod Touch or iPad and create an Non-Disclosure Agreement (NDA) to protect your idea.

You'll need to do the same for app stores on Blackberry and Google's Android phones plus the Nintendo Wii Virtual Console Store and digital pen maker, Livescribe. Facebook also provides an opportunity for creators to build app brand awareness but only accepts free apps. Amazon has opened its Kindle reader service to third party applications, while Yahoo too has plans to bring apps to the web at large.

App building

Be aware, too, that creating an app will take a good deal of effort, a minimum of one month of full-time coding, not including the time it takes to work on improvements and upgrades to sustain success. Most of the teams developing the top selling apps spend as much time developing updates (to introduce new features, streamline functionality and submit fixes) as they do on the original applications.

The cost of developing an app can be anything from a few hundred to many thousands of pounds (although you can use the free/low-cost services such as Conduit.com to test the market for your app before investing fully). Plus there'll be costs for developing updates and promoting the app. If you don't have the technical know-how or financial resources to create an application, but *do* have a killer idea, there are alternative methods of making it happen.

For example, you could submit your idea to App Incubator (MedlMobile. com) which offers a revenue share deal in exchange for developing great app ideas. However, while there are no upfront fees, you'd have to share 75% of the profits with App Incubator, taking only 25% for yourself.

Alternatively you might post your project on iPhonefreelancer.com or Odesk. com, which matches those who have ideas with developers and programmers. Alternatively, you could use a company such as Umee (Umee.tv), which provides a comparatively lower cost development option by running much of its development offshore out of Bulgaria without sacrificing quality.

So, while becoming an app millionaire from the bustling App Store goldmine may not be as easy as we are often led to believe, it is still a viable digital opportunity for entrepreneurs out there who have a great idea backed up with strong skills, effective marketing, and competitive pricing. Analysts valued the app market as worth $1 billion in 2011, and estimate it will be worth $4 billion by the end of 2012.

If you do wish to launch forth into the world of apps, consider these seven tips:

> **Top Tips for Designing, Developing and Launching a Successful Application**
>
> 1. Examine each app store's User Interface Guidelines to maximize your app's chances of success.
> 2. Consider screen-by-screen what you need to present to users in order to take them on their journey and connect screens. Think sequentially and focus on each feature, screen and action to provide users with a logical path to follow. Also consider planning for multiple releases by listing all features you'd like your app to have and making the first version incorporate only a proportion of these.
> 3. Use standard buttons, icons and menu structures that users are already familiar with. Annotate options within a toolbar. Your aim is to make usage as easy and obvious as possible, so don't over-design and ensure that you give users the chance to cancel, go back, forward and home.
> 4. Start building. Hand your information to a designer or start the design process yourself and get a developer on board to programme your application. Set a timeline.
> 5. Have your developer assist you in compiling your application to the various app stores and submit them.
> 6. Market your application. Create an early buzz and sustain it by communicating with bloggers, reviewers and journalists. Enable users to post on social media sites and set up your own fan pages on Twitter and Facebook. Gather feedback on your app's quality and capability and tweak accordingly.
> 7. Boost sales by launching new versions of the app periodically. For that reason, ensure that your app is easy to change and update to stay up to speed with users' needs.

Once you have built your website/mobile site and your app, it's time to build your team and your brand. These are the core foundations for your business. Without a strong website, app, team and brand, you will struggle to compete in the digital realm. So it's time to fill the gaps in your skillset and knowledge base, recruit and retain the best possible talent you can find and create a brand that people will relate to, believe in and trust.

Step Seven

Build Your Team

'Enchant your employees; they will work harder, longer, and smarter for you.'
Guy Kawasaki

People deliver value, drive growth and make things happen. They enable success. Your team is essential to help you develop your idea and execute your vision, because an idea is merely an idea, and one that is in limbo, until it is executed by a team of carefully selected talented people. And, because 'people buy from people', they also represent your brand and sell the product, in many cases more than the product itself does. As such, the people you choose to work with you are your most essential asset.

On the flip-side, ineffective people who fail to do their jobs properly can cause massive problems, sapping morale and resources. So, while productive talent is valuable; conversely, non-productive talent is expensive. This means that you must get the right people 'on the bus'. The wrong people will simply hinder your growth. Start-ups simply cannot afford to make the wrong hires.

> *'Only ever employ a tiny number of very good people. Mediocre people actually create work.'*
>
> **Rowan Gormley, NakedWines.com**

By the end of this chapter you will understand how to:

- **Source the very best talent that you can afford.**
- **Find the right match for your company culture.**
- **Become an attractive company to work for.**
- **Provide a stable and secure environment for people to work in.**
- **Motivate and retain people, unlock potential and enable talent to shine.**
- **Unite teams, both domestic and offshore, in-house and remote.**

First things first; in order to grow and run an effective and successful business, entrepreneurs must realize that they need help. You can't do everything. You need to let go and hire people who are smarter than you in various areas. The classic entrepreneurial mistake is to control everything and delegate nothing. Conversely, those who learn to bring people in to plug the gaps in their own experience and hire people who are better than them at certain things, prosper.

However, sourcing and developing talent, then motivating and retaining it, is one of the most difficult jobs an entrepreneur faces, particularly in the digital sector where a talent shortage makes it more likely for top talent to be lured away.

'The digital space has been a challenging area to recruit in since day one', comments Nick O'Connor, Divisional Director at Xchangeteam.com, a recruitment company specializing in marketing, media and communications recruitment. 'The reasons are very straightforward. Digital platforms, markets and companies have grown so rapidly in the last 15 years that demand has outstripped supply in all areas, resulting in inflated salaries. In addition a large percentage of companies are SMEs. The industry has also been through two recessions which have resulted in recruitment freezes that have further reduced new blood coming into the industry.'

Certain trends apply against this backdrop. From a lack of sufficient graduate schemes and junior staff training, to a prevalent culture of headhunting which leads to employees staying in each job for shorter time periods.

'Getting out of this cycle can be very hard for young companies', says Nick. 'The key is a robust talent acquisition and retention strategy.'

As such, in order to build a dream team of truly remarkable people, you need to pull out all the stops to first hire promising people and then earn their trust and loyalty so that they will stay.

In order to do so, you need to allocate significant effort because, just as securing cash resources to fund your business takes time, so does securing human resources. So you need to factor in sufficient lead time of how long it takes to build up a team. From deciding which types of staff to get on board and drafting an accurate job description, to sourcing, interviewing and hiring candidates, recruitment is a time-consuming process.

Staffing Options

Digital start-ups need not commit to hiring a bunch of full-time staff however. As well as using technology to automate some processes, you can also opt to hire freelancers via the crowd-sourcing or outsourcing models. This enables you to create a team of remote workers and subcontract specific roles, tasks and projects to an outside source while keeping your costs down in the process.

Exercise

Considering the type of staff you need

1. Align your recruitment efforts with your business objectives. Consider your long-term goals and strategies and what kinds of skills gaps you wish to fill in order to reach those goals.
2. Consider workload and how you wish to build your team – what kind of hours do you think certain roles will require? Think about the tasks that will need to be completed and decide whether roles should be part-time or full-time, in-house or outsourced.
3. Consider how much obligation you want to have to people and vice versa. Again, this will help you to determine whether you should hire permanent staff (full-time or part-time) , self-employed freelancers, temporary staff or zero-hours contracted on-call staff.

Crowd-sourcing and freelancing

The emergent crowd-sourcing model affords you the opportunity to outsource tasks and projects that might have once been carried out by a single freelance contractor or employee, to a community of people, rather than outsourcing to an individual. Typical projects include data input or analysis and community-based design, to new technology development, or human-based algorithm computation. Crowd-sourcing is essentially a way to leverage mass collaboration at the forefront of Web 2.0, to connect collaborators and skilled communities with enterprises who are striving to reach specific goals.

There are a number of crowd-sourcing portals available. For example, Click-worker.com provides a workspace platform for its 115,000 registered freelance internet workers (or 'clickworkers') to carry out digital tasks for business owners; from SEO text creation and translation to web research and opinion polling. Additionally, there are a variety of online directories where freelancers bid for projects, such as Freelancer.com and Elance.com, giving digital entrepreneurs 'immediate access to the talent they need, when they need it.'

As well as hiring a team of full-time journalists to create original content, Hugh Chappell outsourced content to professional freelancers. 'The nice thing about freelance is you pay on result, you pay someone to do something and they do it', says Hugh. 'Freelancing work out is more cost effective than putting it through the machine of employees, because employees need desks and so on.'

Hugh also kept his staffing costs down by offering long-term freelance contracts for one or two reviews per week over 52 weeks, enabling him to negotiate. He always committed to paying promptly, which was refreshing for journalists who were used to writing a piece and in some cases not being paid for three months.

Hiring offshore

Many people outsource tasks offshore and hire teams of skilled workers from countries such as India, Bulgaria or South Africa, particularly in the tech industry. Certainly, by casting your net wider and effectively knocking down the geographical barrier, you can open your doors to a wider talent pool and are consequently more likely to find the exact matches to the skills that you need at any given time.

However, as Neal Gandhi illustrates in his book, *Born Global*, there are issues to consider when outsourcing, at least offshore, and he warns small businesses to consider these before farming projects out overseas. Often there can be a lack of integration, says Neal: 'an outsourced team can't become part of your team as smaller companies often lack mature processes that make outsourcing easier (such as detailed specification processes, change control processes, etc.)'. There is also a limitation to the amount of flexibility and control you have. Neal suggests using freelance websites or outsourcing locally to a domestic company which has its own offshore team and can pass on the cost-savings.

Alternatively, if you intend to sell into different markets and, like Moo.com, are Born Global (defined as a company that, within three years of launch, gains at least a quarter of sales from overseas foreign markets) a model of offshore engagement worthy of consideration is to set up your own facility overseas. Moo.com opened up an office in the USA in 2009 and 40% of revenue comes from their US customers. If you choose that method and need to hire staff overseas, there's a lot to consider, and you really need to get to know the culture in order to create a unified cross-border team. Inclusion and cultural competence are especially vital to motivate and integrate offshore teams and remote workers. Richard Moross, founder of Moo.com says he has 'watched a lot of American TV', as it's important to understand the market you are selling into and be aware of what's going on there.

Of course, you might have no intention of selling to foreign markets but simply want to take advantage of the low cost yet high quality talent available from other countries, or you may simply wish to establish a remote workforce domestically. In either case you will need to foster an ethos of inclusion, and create a strong culture and purpose for them to buy into, which I shall cover in more detail later in the chapter.

If you do choose to outsource work to freelancers, domestically or offshore:

- ask for references and to view previous examples of their work;
- clearly communicate your vision, brand values and methods of working;
- keep remote workers informed, included and made to feel as much part of the team as possible;
- enable remote workers to contribute by asking them for their input and recommendations; and
- have remote workers meet in-house workers. Invite them to visit your office to create a connection with the business and other people working within it.

You can better integrate dispersed workers to create a close-knit albeit far-flung team by sharing personal team news such as birthdays and anecdotes from HQ. It's also worth suggesting that in-house and remote teams connect personally on social networks to get to know each other's interests, hobbies, family and passions. There are additional ways to replicate the social banter and buzz that geographically dispersed teams miss out on, such as using tools such as Yammer to keep conversations visible.

Regardless of the type of staff you recruit, they should fill the gaps in your existing knowledge base and skillset.

Specifying Talent: Filling the Gaps – Defining Strengths and Weaknesses

Variation = Value. A diverse blend of people with different personalities and complementary skillsets creates a truly dynamic and strong team. So define who you want and why you need them. Additionally, aim to hire aspirationally, for where you want to be in the future, rather than for where you are now.

Exercise

Assess strengths and weaknesses to fill the gaps

1. Consider your objectives as a company. Write them down.
2. What skills, knowledge, industry contacts, experience do you currently have within your existing team? What are your core strengths?
3. What skills, knowledge, industry contacts, experience are missing? Which areas are you weaker in, i.e. which gaps do you need to plug?
4. What roles do you therefore need to recruit for and which type of staffing option will apply to those roles (e.g. full time developer or freelance engineer)? In other words, what talent do you need to get the job done and reach your goals?

Remember, as a start-up, the first people you recruit will set the tone for your culture. Fundamentally, high quality hires will attract more high quality people to join your team. In order to attract the best quality talent that you can afford, you need to define the job role with absolute clarity, so that you can match each person with a position in which they will thrive. You only want to attract applicants that are suitable for the job at hand so a clear job description and person specification are a must, not only to attract the right candidates, but also to deter the wrong ones.

Exercise

Create a job description and person specification

1. Consider how the role you are wishing to fill will help you reach your objectives. Be transparent about the purpose of the role and how it will enable your business to step up to the next level.
2. Consider the role and responsibilities that the person you are seeking will need to undertake. Consider which job title best fits the role. List tasks, define duties, projects, objectives, expectations, milestones, and so on.
3. Search LinkedIn.com, Monster.com and other job sites for job and person descriptions using the job title or variations of it and note down the list of responsibilities and desired skills and experience that other companies request for similar roles. Have you missed anything out of your description that other companies are specifying? What kind of salary seems to be the going rate?
4. Note down general information such as hours, location and salary.
5. Pitch your vision. Create a summary outlining the company's mission/vision, culture, values and personality. Give people a reason to want to work with you.
6. Write a compelling and concise job description.
7. Based on this, define the necessary skills, abilities, knowledge, expertise and track record/experience you believe the right candidate will need in order to perform well in this role.
8. Define also the key characteristics and mindset that your ideal suitor would have, such as creative, analytical, reliable, confident, extroverted, introverted, focused, ambitious, persistent, tenacious, and so on.
9. Write a compelling and concise person specification based on these attributes.

Remember, as you grow, you'll need to find the time and space to step back from the day-to-day management of your business in order to work 'on' the business instead of 'in' it. Doing so will enable you to innovate and strategize; improve and create.

'If all you're doing is fighting fires, you don't have the time to think of new ideas', says Moonpig.com's Nick Jenkins who noticed that he was more concerned with tackling tasks on his to-do list rather than creating a what-we-should-be-doing list.

Consequently, Nick stepped back from the business to become chairman, installing as he did so a CEO to run the business. 'A lot of our innovations, like the way that we do our emails or mailing list functions, a lot of innovative functionality has come about as a result of taking time out to think about it.'

It's important for founders of digital start-ups to consider succession and keep their eye out for a person who might take over as CEO or MD, should the business grow. More on succession in Step 12.

❗ Top Tips for Plotting your Recruitment Plan

● 1. **Seek out missing diverse yet complementary skills.** Identify weaknesses and plug those gaps. You might be strong on sales and marketing but not so great at negotiating deals, in which case you need to find someone who is. 'Don't fall into the entrepreneur trap of trying to do everything yourself', advises Nick O'Connor.

2. **Optimize your business.** Don't constrain the company's growth by the abilities of its people. Ensure that you are constantly on the look out for people with the right level of skills and experience, who can take your business to the next level.

3. **Avoid owner-dependency.** If you plan to take your business to exit stage and sell the company in the future, you will need to put processes and people in place to ensure that the business is not reliant on you. Keep your eye out for people of MD stature who could help you to run the business and take over the day-to-day management.

Sourcing Talent: Finding People to Fill Those Gaps

Once duties have been defined, the scope of work and the type of person carefully considered, you need to contemplate *where* and *how* you'll find the right person.

Allocate time to get your recruitment right and allow a long lead time. Don't simply pass the task to a recruiter. You are best positioned to sell the opportunity and find the right fit for your company. Nobody else.

'A classic mistake is engaging a recruitment drive when the hire is mission critical', says Nick O'Connor. 'This may result in hiring the "best available now" rather than the best available in the market. With massive shortages in all digital disciplines, recruiting the best staff is a challenge so engaging with the best talent over a period of time will give you competitive edge.'

Talent acquisition methods

1. Use your network

Get networking. Seek introductions to top talent. That's what Sarah Beeny has done when employing staff: 'We've never had to advertise much for people, I've been lucky to have some great introductions from others along the way.' Nick O'Connor of XChangeTeam agrees: 'Build a personal network of potential hires or industry experts who can refer the best talent to you.'

Invest in your own talent pipelines and networks. It's no good merely posting a job online and hoping that amazing people apply. You need to go the extra mile. You can do this by:

- Building relationships externally and networking. Connect with talented people within relevant sectors and stay in touch with them until you need to hire.
- Building relationships internally and engaging your existing workforce. Give them a sense of ownership. A strong team will certainly want to be involved in placing matching candidates who fit the bill (and the company culture).

2. Use an agency

Only when you have exhausted your connections, seek help from a recruitment company to help generate leads and source candidates on your behalf. There are over 10,000 recruitment agencies within the UK. Research to find market specialists rather than generalists. If you work with contingency agencies there is no upfront fee. Some agencies base fees on successful placement; others accept an hourly rate, with a cash incentive for a high quality or fast hire.

'Key recruitment agencies often have access to talent that is tough to find if you recruit direct', says Nick O'Connor. 'Good recruitment partners will be able to advise you on salary, options, available skillsets, interview process, provide job specs, take feedback, help with second stage briefs and manage the process from start to finish.'

Before you commission an agency:

- Examine their client testimonials, track record/time in the market, level of control over the process, size of the team resourcing directly for you, terms and conditions and accreditation (they should ideally be members of regulatory bodies REC or APSCo).
- Ask if they interview all of the candidates face to face. This is essential if you are going to be hiring a team where team fit or client skills are relevant.
- Check whether they headhunt from clients. Ethical recruiters do not place with you on one hand and headhunt out on the other. You must make sure that this is an agreement when engaging the agency.
- Find out what their candidate generation strategy is. It should include advertising, referral schemes, social media and industry events.

- 'Ask who they work with as clients', advises Nick O'Connor. 'Ask to see a list of successes in the immediate space. A black book of clients that a recruiter has been successful with is gold dust. A good recruiter can turn to their network to find candidates who are actively looking.'

3. Use social media

Social media has essentially made the world smaller and networking smarter. As well as enabling you to source and evaluate prospective talent via Twitter, LinkedIn, Facebook and via blogs, you can also follow talent-producing companies to see who joins and leaves. You should also select people who are connected to your connections who might fit within your company, then ask your contacts directly about those people. You can also use social media to make yourself accessible as the founder of your start-up. This will better enable prospective candidates to connect with you and have conversations with you directly, enabling you to get to know them and vice versa.

Other sourcing methods to try

- Host a get-together for skilled professionals. It'll cost you a couple of hundred quid in pizza or curry, but you could attract a number of candidates worthy of an interview.
- Visit universities, job fairs, start-up events and social communities. BitTech, the business acquired by Hugh Chappell, was started by 13 students while they were still at school, college or university. One of the programmers was just 13 years old when he started working on the business. Many programmers start programming as a hobby. They are passionate about development.
- Visit relevant communities online such as Mediabistro, Elance, Clickworkers.com or Freelancers.com if you are seeking freelancers.
- Subscribe to technological tools for a monthly fee and cast your net wider to tap into social networks. Try LinkedIn Talent Pro which provides extra access to everyone on the world's largest professional network, as well as handy tools such as a candidate matcher, daily notifications of potential matches, expanded profiles and premium talent filters. Or try The Resumator: an automated job listings poster to social networks which includes a job listings tracker, applicant tracker and e-mailer which has an in-built 'What Makes You Unique' feature which applicants must fill out in 150 characters or less. Try more expensive but very impressive end-to-end social web recruiting and tracking tool, Jobvite, which enables your own employees to invite suitable friends and followers to apply for specific roles and matches prospective 'passive' candidates based on their profiles and your job listings.

Recruiting Talent

Whether you are head-hunting passive candidates or interviewing job applicants, once you have sourced a bunch of talented people, the next step in the recruitment process is to get to know those people as well as you possibly can.

Because, in order to maximize loyalty and retain key talent, recruitment is as much about finding the right job for the person as it is finding the right person for the job.

It's critical that you uncover what a person wants out of the role you are offering. For a person to have longevity within an organization, the job you are offering needs to be their dream job, not just something to tide them over until they find their dream job. The role must therefore satisfy their current and future needs and ambitions, as much as their qualifications, experience and abilities must satisfy your candidate criteria. Ultimately, the person/role fit must be a two-way mutual match.

To match sufficiently the person to the role both ways, you should examine the bigger picture. During the interview process:

- Find out what makes them tick. Uncover exactly what motivates them. Are money and security their key motivational factors or are they motivated more by recognition, responsibility, being part of a unified team, or independence? Find out where they want to be and what they want to be doing five years from now. What drives them? Scratch under the surface. Dig deep.
- Assess how they have dealt with problems, mistakes and crises in their previous positions and what they have learned with the benefit of hindsight about what they might do differently. Ask them about specific results they have achieved, why they want to work for your company and why you should hire them?
- Discover insights into their personalities by using psychometric testing which involves their selection of words which best or least describe them.
- Find out what they like to do in their spare time. What are they passionate about? What side projects or other work experience have they been involved in? Do they blog? What about and why?
- Set tasks for subsequent interviews to gain insight into the interviewee, such as asking them to load information into your CMS (Content Management System); create a presentation, write a one page marketing plan or carry out specific IT-based tasks.

As much as your candidates need to persuade you that they are the right person for the job, (and the job is the right one for them) you and your company need to persuade your candidates that your company is one they really want to work for. So, as well as selling the position and the package, you must also sell the company vision, brand identity and culture.

> **!** **Top Tips for Creating a Good Impression**
>
> ● 1. **Greet and treat the candidates well.** From the moment they have
>   their application acknowledged to the moment they walk out of
>   the door following the interview process and beyond, make sure
>   they are looked after throughout the whole recruitment process.
> 2. **Create a good vibe.** Make sure the office environment which they
>   step into is welcoming and inspirational.
> 3. **Keep them informed.** It's important that the person the inter-
>   viewee would report to shows them out and lets them know about
>   exactly what will happen next.
> 4. **Fulfil that promise and keep in touch.** Don't go cold for too long
>   in between interview rounds (if you carry out more than one
>   interview).

Choosing wisely: You're hired

Making the right decision when choosing who to take on is critical. Getting it
wrong at this stage will cost you dearly on a number of levels. So, once you've
shortlisted candidates, how do you pick the winner?

- Use your instinct.
- Evaluate their answers analytically to ensure that their competencies, expertise and personal characteristics correspond accurately with the duties,
  responsibilities and person specification you've outlined.
- Get input from people who'll be working with the person. Involve existing
  staff in the decision process to ensure the right chemistry exists. Teams
  must be on the same page to be effective. Ensure that everyone instinctively
  feels that they're going to work well within the team.
- Hold out for your hero. No matter how desperate you are to fill a position,
  don't take someone on just because you need someone immediately. Wait
  for the right person. Meet candidates more than once where possible as
  this gives both parties the chance to ask and answer additional questions
  that may not have been apparent at the first meeting; helping you to make
  a more informed well-rounded decision.
- Take up references. It's surprising how few businesses do this, but references
  are a great way to get another opinion on how an individual performs in
  the workplace and validate the candidate's claims.

Once you've chosen your stellar suitor, notify them and persuade them to
accept your formal job offer. Some recruiters have gone as far as inviting the

candidates and their 'significant other' to a dinner to make sure both are suitably impressed with the offer and that it fits their exact needs, or sending press kits to their home address for the whole family to peruse. Stellar candidates are worth their weight in gold, so it's worth investing in securing them to join your team.

Legally you must provide new employees with a written term sheet and employment contract within two months of them starting to work with you. This should include your name and address and theirs; the date they commence working with you, their job title and description, working hours, salary details, holiday entitlement, sick pay, notice periods, disciplinary procedure details, and contract duration.

Retaining Talent: Keeping Hold of Your Best People

'Look after the people who make your business work.'

Sarah Beeny

Cultivate and keep talent

Companies that do not engage their employees suffer the consequences. Staff turnover rises, along with re-recruitment and training costs, while productivity and morale decrease. Ultimately, such companies end up paying more to do less!

Conversely, companies which engage and motivate a happy workforce within an inspirational environment reap the rewards. Productivity and morale are boosted by energized staff. Turnover of staff decreases while turnover of revenue increases. Investing time, effort and money into a staff retention plan is clearly a win–win.

By tracking and rewarding performance, by engaging and empowering your brightest minds to participate, by unlocking potential and by creating a culture with a common purpose, you can build and retain a team who will take your business forward to achieve its vision. Understanding and appreciating people spearheads success. Caring about people's well-being and including them in the journey begets loyalty, builds confidence and empowers an organization to reach its destination.

So how do you keep hold of great people and get the best out of them? The simple answer is that you keep them happy, you keep them secure, you treat them well and you sufficiently reward them. Fundamentally, in order retain talented people you need to be an attractive company to work for and provide the right tools, attitude and environment to encourage each individual to flourish. You really don't want to lose the gems that you've sought so hard to find. So you need to motivate, cultivate, inform and inspire people. There are a number of ways to fulfil these requirements.

1. **Make people happy.**
   - Motivate people by understanding what makes them tick and providing them with those incentives, rewards and motivating factors, whether that's financial security, personal development or recognition.
   - Provide people with a happy, productive and fun environment to work in with an attractive work space and atmosphere.
2. **Make people feel secure.**
   - Communicate well. Share your vision. Keep your team informed.
   - Cultivate talent. Include them. Listen to people, nurture and nourish ideas.
   - Develop a cohesive culture and foster a united team spirit.
3. **Treat people and the wider world well.**
   - Be fair. Enable your staff to enjoy a healthy work–life balance.
   - Be kind. Attract good people by having an ethical stance to your wider environment, community and planet.

1. Make people happy

Motivate people based on their personal motivations

A motivated workforce is a happy one. If you really *know* each individual member of your team, you will know exactly what makes them tick and use those motivational factors to encourage, inspire and reward them. Don't muddy motivation with money. You want people who perform because they believe in your company and what you have to offer, not just because they like the pay-package.

People are motivated by a number of things: peer recognition, the level of interest they have in the work they do, the environment in which they work, the kinship they feel for their team, the appreciation of and reward for their efforts and their own personal career development and achievement, among other things.

Financial rewards

If someone is motivated by financial security, provide them with a generous remuneration package with a pension plus performance related bonuses and shares in the company.

'It's important to get your reward structure right', says Martha Lane Fox. 'Making sure you're generous with people and giving them enough of the company and the right to earn options and shares or, if not, helping them to understand why you're paying them what you're paying them.'

Richard Moross agrees, 'All of our full time employees are shareholders, so they all have a vested interest in the business. We treat them all with respect. We try to look after them.'

'Entrepreneurial employees in high growth markets will expect it and may be tempted to your competitors if you don't have a shares scheme. Budget for top notch practitioners in all the key roles', adds Nick O'Connor, of XChangeTeam. 'Having said that, digital is an entrepreneurial space, and offering stock can give you a negotiation position. Unlike most industries, digital is a sector that breeds entrepreneurs. There is a type of candidate who is looking for an exit just as there are businesses owners who are looking for an exit. If the company and product is strong enough and the stock on offer is high enough then some candidates will take less money.'

Ensure that any remote teams or workers are included in your reward structure. Their productivity and successes should be recognized. They too will provide better results and stick around if they are motivated, cultivated and rewarded.

Opportunities to achieve

If someone is motivated by personal achievement, getting results and recognition for those achievements, give them awards, bonuses and incentives for reaching targets and provide them with ample training and career development, opportunities for promotion, plus shares in the company they are working so hard to gain results for.

'Make sure that you're mapping out some kind of career opportunity for people as well', advises Martha. 'Make it very clear how they can progress. It's part of their responsibility to have their own career plans but it's also great to help someone feel that they can get to a point that they want to get to.'

Certainly, people are more likely to stay with you if they see their role as a long-term career opportunity because, in committing to a person's personal growth and career development, you are committing to their personal fulfilment.

The way in which you handle your top, middle and low achievers is important; it has a knock-on effect throughout the organization, particularly among those who are motivated by recognition for their achievements.

- Devote time to your best star players and most promising talent. Share your positive observations with them. Appreciate what you have. Reward their contribution. Boost their confidence. Allow them to shine. Flag them up as role models.
- Encourage and coach middling performers too. Tell them that they are wanted and valued. Find out how you might better motivate them to become star players. Talk to them and give them guidance, targets and incentives.
- Don't keep poor performers on. If you do they will affect the environment by bringing your star performers down, and result in the need to counsel peeved co-workers who have to carry the load of the underachievers.

Inclusion for team players

People are also more likely to stay with you if they genuinely feel part of a team. As such, your team must be united and cohesive. The more your people are on the same page, the more effective they and your company will be.

Create a culture of winning. Focus on the collective good of the team. Make tangible team results count. The best way to celebrate success is as a group. So focus on the group win over the individual win to ensure that 'getting credit' for something is not something that bugs people. In strong cohesive teams, team mates will give credit where it's due to idea-creators and idea-executors.

Celebrate successes, big 'end-result' ones and smaller 'en-route' ones. Order in pizza, take your team out for a pampering session at a local spa. In doing so you'll show people how great it feels to win. The resulting dynamic will be a team of people who want to win and will strive to do so again and again.

Paint a clear picture of what winning will mean for your team. Be honest and transparent about what you and they need to do in order to stay ahead of the competition. Be passionate but candid. Give clarity and direction. Reveal outcome and reward.

Trust is efficient

And be honest. Because truth breeds trust. Reward transparency as well as efficiency and productivity. Encourage people to ask questions, provide answers, say what they mean and freely share their ideas. Infuse your team with trust and they will deliver the results that you trust them to deliver. Trust empowers people. It empowers them to do more of the right thing well. Moreover, they will be less risk-averse as they know that it is better to try and fail than not try at all. Honesty creates security, which, in turn promotes a healthy environment of boldness and risk-taking. And it is those types of teams which win.

It's fine for team members to disagree about ideas and the execution of those ideas. It is far better to be open, disagree and engage in discussion, than be closed and dishonest, keeping opinions to yourself. With trust, everyone is open to listening to others' input. With trust, conflict is merely trying to get to the best outcome. With trust, there is accountability. Without trust, conflict is political.

Working at the right pace in the right space

People perform better in workplaces which have a good vibe and a well-considered infrastructure. The space, equipment, facilities and atmosphere all work together to create a happy working environment.

In terms of infrastructure, offices and equipment should be up-to-date, training and support should be structured. The atmosphere, too, should be optimal for staff to feel happy, included and valued. By tackling the physical environment and atmosphere, you'll retain people and optimize performance. Essentially, physical space matters. A playful and colourful space will have a far more positive impact on creativity and productivity than a dull grey one will.

While, as a start-up, you may not have the budget to create a Googleplex environment with free food, free scooters and volleyball courts, or do as Facebook does with its free laundry service and keyboard vending machines you can still create an environment to encourage, engage and inspire the people who work within it.

The first GlassesDirect office was situated in the middle of a beautiful park in a converted medieval barn with glass sides. 'I always want to make the environment a quality one', says founder and chairman, James Murray-Wells.

And, while the actual space should be welcoming, so should the atmosphere. Your people should want to come to work and enjoy it; not see it as a chore.

'iwantoneofthose.com was a great fun place to work', says co-founder Tim Booth, but not just because there were so many toys around. 'For eight months of the year staff were allowed to go home early on a Friday. We had camping trips every year. We'd get beers and pizzas in once a fortnight or month on a Friday', smiles Tim, who now runs web consultancy, The Glasshouse Project.

A flexible attitude to what people wear and the hours they work can also create a more productive vibe, because you trust your people to do the job they are paid to do without putting restrictions on them.

'If you wanted to come in at 10am and finish at 7pm then that was fine as long as your line manager knew what you were doing and you were producing the results. The few people who came in at 10am and finished at 5pm didn't stay with the business for very long', adds Tim.

'Having fun is important', agrees Martha Lane Fox who never had her own office, but hung out with the rest of the staff. Certainly, leading from an ivory tower doesn't tend to work. Open-plan offices where the management are accessible are common practice for leading digital enterprises, particularly those featured in this book.

'It's important that you know each other a bit beyond the working environment too', adds Martha. A team which socializes together creates alignment and that is something that the team at Moo.com are big on. 'We're very sociable as a company for those people who want to dip into that', says founder, Richard Moross. 'We all work together in an open-plan office, we all have a big sit down lunch together on a Friday. So it's a very interactive social business to be in and we're pretty non-corporate. There's no dress code or anything like that.'

❗ Top Tips to Motivate your Staff and Keep Them Happy

1. **Pay well if you can, certainly those for whom financial security is a motivational factor.** Consider offering performance-related bonuses on top of a generous basic salary, particularly for sales people and those directly instrumental in bringing revenue into the company. And benchmark your remuneration packages to stay competitive.

2. **Engage with your staff to uncover every single individual's self-actualization and motivational drivers.** Make them feel that they have a future with your company. Where do they see themselves in five years time and how can you help them realize their career aspirations within your company? Provide them with career progression and the opportunity to accomplish their goals and they will thrive.

3. **Commit to designing a long-term career structure for people.** In doing so they will commit to your business over the long-term. Invest in training and development to help people to unlock their talent potential and bolster their strengths. Regularly discuss people's training requirements via appraisals and one-to-ones. Look at actions and performance milestones to help them progress on their career journey and grow.

4. **Provide recognition for achievements and performance related incentives.** Tell people when they have done well. Praise them, thank them, reward them and promote them. Take staff to lunch to thank top performers. Stage an annual event where you take your team off for a mini-break. Celebrate every success your team achieves and treat them to something uplifting to celebrate, whether that's pizza and wine, gift vouchers, gym membership, air miles or discount cards, or something a bit different and inspirational, such as team away days or annual cash bursaries to learn something new (from dancing to cookery).

5. **Demolish the phrase, 'there's no such thing as a free lunch'.** Give your staff free lunch once or twice per week. Or provide free bowls of fruit to keep staff healthy as well as happy.

6. **Provide ownership.** Give key staff a vested interest in helping the business to reach its objectives and become successful. Offer stock via shares and share options.

7. **Trust in people.** Be transparent with your team, expect the same of them and reward honesty.

8. **Provide a welcoming environment.** Create a good infrastructure and fun atmosphere.

9. **Be fair but flexible in terms of working hours and dress code.** Trust that happy staff who enjoy their jobs will do them well.

Place Study: Moonpig.com

'You need to have a fun atmosphere', says Nick Jenkins. 'If you have a bunch of bored people who are dissatisfied, sitting around wearing suits in a dull stuffy office, you're not going to get a good end result. So we created an environment which is fresh and fun. It's a nice place to work.'

'The Moonpig.com office has one big open-plan area. It's light and bright and airy. We've got a big open-plan kitchen and dining area and a soft seating area where people can relax. It's just a very welcoming environment', Nick explains.

'Our second boardroom has a table tennis table rather than a boardroom table. So, when it's not being used for board meetings, we use that.'

Moonpig.com also has a company pig called Kew who visits the office from time to time.

'We don't keep her in the office', explains Nick. 'That would be a bit smelly and noisy. She does squeal quite a lot. She often comes down for the day and then we take her for a walk around the Tate Modern. And the rest of the time she visits primary schools and teaches kids about farming and livestock, so she has a useful purpose too. It's all good fun and everyone gets terribly excited when the pig comes in to the office.'

And, as well as creating a positive space for its people, (and its animals) the company has a relaxed and sociable vibe which enables staff to spontaneously organize a lot of social events, arrive late and stay late.

'We're not particularly strict about what time people come in. But they're not very strict about what time they leave', says Nick. 'We believe that if people are enjoying their job they will get on and be conscientious and do the job well.'

2. Make people feel secure

Strong communication and a shared vision

Essentially, an informed team which is kept in the loop outperforms a team which is kept in the dark. As such it's important to give people clear objectives and expectations about what they're going to get out of a role and what you expect of them. The overall vision of the company should also be communicated with every member of staff so they can help strive towards it. Additionally they should be made aware of opportunities and threats that the business is facing that could impact that vision. Inclusion is a powerful motivating factor and staff who feel included feel trusted. As trust begets loyalty, keeping staff up to speed on the goings on of the business within the wider market is vital.

'For me [retention] just comes back to communication, communication, communication', comments Martha Lane Fox. 'It's incredible how many organisations don't get this right. Err on the side of over-communication all the time. Set out your really clear vision, not just on paper, but ensure that you've communicated it to people and continue to involve them.'

Martha suggests weekly meetings are also mission critical, both in terms of assessing individual and team performance and to keep the core vision on track. 'Personally I like to make sure that people are able to ask lots of questions and get involved early on, and keep coming back to that vision', says Martha. 'I like working in this environment where you are getting that feedback and regularly know where you are. That's incredibly important.'

Enabling the team to know where you all are, what others are doing and how you are all working in harmony to create an end result is a continuous process. As well as the usual regular calls, emails, chat rooms, private networks, shared docs, Skype and video conferencing, there are some fantastic agile management tools and cloud based apps that can help keep teams on the same page and enable smoother collaboration and communication by providing a shared view.

From Basecamp, Dropbox and Yammer to Google Docs, Box.net and Wikis, you can access, coordinate and track ongoing projects, solve team management problems, share feeds and updates of what co-workers are currently working on, avoid duplication and review a continuous stream of banter and Q&A across multiple timezones if necessary. Communication has never been so zealous.

Using technology to communicate is particularly useful when managing remote teams. Beware however of misinterpretation and margin for error if the majority of your communications are typed. Tone and meaning are less easy to gauge via written word as opposed to via phone or video calling. And take cultural differences into consideration too. For example, just as us Brits might speak indirectly in comparison to other cultures by saying something like, 'I wouldn't do it that way if I were you', instead of 'don't do it like that'; there are similar ambiguities in foreign cultures. In India, for instance, it's regarded as rude to say 'no', so Indian people will often say 'yes, it'll be ready by then' and try to deliver, even if the answer should have been 'no, I'll need more time'. Hierarchy and job title are also of high importance to Indian staff. If you intend to hire or outsource offshore, it is worth getting to know the intricacies of people's expression and communication as well as their cultural mindset. Technological tools aside, good cultural competence is a must if you wish to communicate effectively across distance.

Furthermore, it's important to remember that your team extends beyond your staff members. There are other players to communicate with constantly, from supporting significant others, family and friends to investors, evangelical customers/fans, suppliers and partners. Keep people informed, be open and approachable, gather feedback, listen carefully, and your team will function at its optimal level.

> **❗ Top Tips for Smooth Communication**
>
> ● 1. **Share your vision with clarity and conviction.** Your team will subsequently be as excited about your mission as you are.
> 2. **Be precise and write everything down as a record.** Minimize the margin for misunderstanding errors.
> 3. **Harness the power of technology to keep everyone in the loop.** Make conversation threads and ongoing dialogue visible and accessible in real-time. This will enable transparency, mutual understanding and accountability.
> 4. **Be culturally competent.** Understand differences in mindset, attitudes, language, expression and communication.

Nurture ideas and foster an ethos of inclusion

The best companies show people they are valued by including them and listening to their ideas. Staff feel secure when they are valued, included and listened to. 'If you have an "inclusive" approach to sharing knowledge and information employees feel more engaged', says Nick O'Connor.

In *Drive: The Surprising Truth About What Motivates Us,* Daniel Pink explains what employees want from a boss: an opportunity to master new skills while working autonomously towards a high purpose. People like to develop, but they also like to feel a part of something, to feel like they are working towards that shared vision as part of a united team; to feel like they are participating in a team win. And, if they are going to contribute towards that vision, their ideas must be taken on board. They must be given the opportunity to shine.

Just as people need care and attention within an encouraging environment to thrive, so do their ideas, because ideas fuel growth; particularly in an economy that is changing at an exponential pace. Essentially, successful organizations with loyal and committed teams are those which allow the ideas of their people to flourish. They do this by:

a) Creating an environment of inclusion where staff are listened to and given the chance to contribute to the decision-making process.
b) Providing an environment and creating a culture which stimulates innovation and provides a platform for individual and team creativity.
c) Creating an environment that has the right blend of autonomy and connected team spirit; so that staff can make decisions independently and together as a team.

Conversely, if you don't listen to people and consider their ideas, your competitors will. You can prevent losing the best ideas by simply listening and fostering an environment which shares ideas, identifies opportunities and threats and enables each individual to contribute.

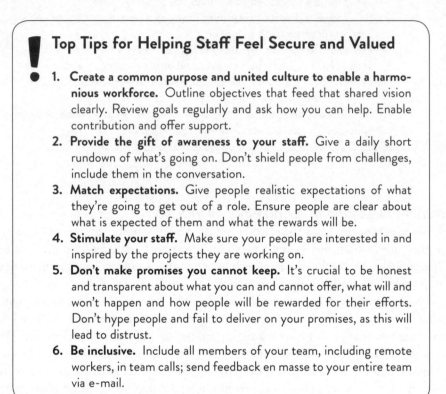

Top Tips for Helping Staff Feel Secure and Valued

1. **Create a common purpose and united culture to enable a harmonious workforce.** Outline objectives that feed that shared vision clearly. Review goals regularly and ask how you can help. Enable contribution and offer support.
2. **Provide the gift of awareness to your staff.** Give a daily short rundown of what's going on. Don't shield people from challenges, include them in the conversation.
3. **Match expectations.** Give people realistic expectations of what they're going to get out of a role. Ensure people are clear about what is expected of them and what the rewards will be.
4. **Stimulate your staff.** Make sure your people are interested in and inspired by the projects they are working on.
5. **Don't make promises you cannot keep.** It's crucial to be honest and transparent about what you can and cannot offer, what will and won't happen and how people will be rewarded for their efforts. Don't hype people and fail to deliver on your promises, as this will lead to distrust.
6. **Be inclusive.** Include all members of your team, including remote workers, in team calls; send feedback en masse to your entire team via e-mail.

3. Treat people and the wider world well

Being ethical in business not only makes the world (and your office) a better place, it also makes your company a more attractive one to work for. And, in the modern workplace, where your best people can easily be lured away by a competing company, you want to give them as many reasons as possible to join your business and stay there.

It is essentially your culture (your values and purpose) and how you treat people and the wider world that will magnetize people towards you and give them a reason to believe in you.

Cultural affinity

By creating a strong purpose-rich culture it becomes far easier to engage and motivate staff. Just as you should nurture camaraderie through creating a fun and appealing environment for people to work in; so should you instil a common purpose throughout the workforce. Doing so unites people, aligns them to your vision and provides a sense of loyal kinship that your competitors will find it hard to replicate. A united team is also better able to deal with change when necessary.

As such it's important to communicate the company vision and purpose regularly: at interview stage, when you make the job offer, throughout the probationary period and beyond.

Ethical practices

If you have work–life balance policies in place that enable your staff to enjoy their life as well as their work, to spend time with their families and take time out, they will appreciate that gesture and be happier, so will consequently be more productive during their working hours.

Employing a remote workforce also makes good financial sense as less admin is required and overheads are lower. Ultimately, it's greener and cheaper to hire remote workers, whether they are offshore or UK-based (or allow your existing office-based staff to work from home from time to time).

According to a survey by Opportunity Now, 78% of managers see flexible working which enables staff to work from home, 'helped to retain and motivate important members of staff', and made a team 'more responsive' to customers.

As well as treating your staff well and implementing supportive working practices, you should also show responsibility to the wider world. Corporate Responsibility (CR) spans a multitude of better-world building activities from saving the planet and working with local communities to treating employees and suppliers fairly and implementing transparency. Today, more than ever before, (thanks to years of marketing half-truths and the consequential erosion of public trust in corporations) it's important to consider and measure the three 'P's: Profit, People and Planet, rather than focusing merely on profit alone. If you can be financially, environmentally and socially responsible, you will gain respect from all stakeholders in your business. From being charitable, recycling, or enabling staff to take part in voluntary initiatives, there are a number of ways to make your business ethical.

'We have a Moonpig Foundation', explains Nick Jenkins, 'which is all about getting our staff involved in charitable projects. We have a project in Uganda where we've sponsored a child for every person in the company and we've sent a team over to Uganda every year to see the impact that has.'

Today, employees are demanding morality from their employers and voting with their feet. As such, how responsible a company is has become an essential element in the competition for recruiting and retaining talent.

The focus has become not only how you are doing but how you are doing *good*. Today, public companies are required by law to report on matters of a social and environmental nature. Indeed businesses can no longer afford to ignore the importance of having an ethical purpose. Subsequently business is becoming more responsible and responsive as corporate responsibility has become a valid cornerstone.

Being responsible enables:

- Better talent recruitment and retention. People want to work for companies with which they share the same values and which has goals beyond profits.
- Enhanced and protected reputation by generating positive PR and brand association which strengthens relationships with partners, customers, staff and the wider community.
- Competitive advantage as customers, suppliers and partners choose to work with you over your competition.

As such, a responsible purpose should be entrenched into the very core of operations. Here are some action-oriented ideas:

Donate resources

Donating time, services, goods and/or funds can have an incredibly positive and motivational effect on a workforce.

1. Allocate the role of CR (corporate responsibility) Champion to various members of staff.
2. Involve your staff, supplier and customers in setting up charitable projects, from funding the building of schools to quarterly fun-runs and fetes.
3. Create voluntary community schemes for staff so they can partake in local or overseas volunteering initiatives, ranging from skill sharing to regenerating wasteland. Not only will this help communities, it will instil a sense of pride in your workforce.
4. Create a 1-1-1 Model as Salesforce and Google have done, whereby 1% of equity is donated to a charitable foundation, 1% of pre-tax profits are given away and 1% of employees' time is given over to volunteering initiatives.
5. Fundraise for local communities or campaigns close to the heart of members of the workforce. Let people vote on the causes they'd most like to get involved with.

Protect the environment

Effective waste management not only helps companies to save the planet, it also saves the company money therefore boosting profits. NetRegs, the online environmental advice service and Greenbusiness.org.uk both report that UK businesses are losing at least 4.5 per cent of their revenue through poor waste management.

1. Save energy. Switch off unused lights, heaters and fans; use energy efficient light-bulbs and plant trees.
2. Establish recycling processes for staff to utilize so that water, paper, cans and plastics are recycled. Use packaging materials that are recyclable, fix leaks and compost food products.
3. Establish a paperless office policy where e-mails are forbidden from being printed and e-mail or other technologies are used in preference to printed communications.
4. Fix returned products and donate to charitable organizations.
5. Suggest that your staff cycle to work or get a lift with someone else.
6. Encourage litterless lunch days where possible, including the use of mugs over plastic cups.
7. Provide staff with stationery that has been recycled, such as recycled paper and products made from reclaimed materials. Do all that you can to reduce waste.

Produce and source ethically

Low cost supplies from overseas may help to increase profitability but suppliers should be thoroughly checked and monitored to ensure that nobody is being exploited down the supply chain. There must be an element of ethical due diligence in terms of what you buy, source, produce and sell.

1. Add sustainable products to your existing offerings sourced from fair trade, local or organic suppliers to ensure that what you sell is produced and traded fairly.
2. Use healthy, ethically sourced ingredients if you source or produce food or drink items.
3. Ensure that ethical standards are adhered to across your supply chain. Ask suppliers to sign a socially responsible trading policy, particularly in some overseas countries where labour markets are less regulated.
4. Innovate and create socially and environmentally responsible and sustainable products that create change for a better world.

Decent, virtuous, honest and dependable businesses which have a moral imperative are leading the way, profiting from their principles, winning custom and market share and reaping significant rewards. As a digital start-up you should endeavour to do the same.

> **❗ Top Tips for Being Kind, Ethical and Fair**
>
> ● 1. **Enable remote working.** Provide your increasingly mobile work-force with the chance to see more of their families, work flexibly, (for instance, they may collect their children from school but work for an hour in the evening to compensate) and reduce their carbon footprint from commuting. Zero commuting is a bonus for every-one, while freedom motivates people to do well.
>   2. **Lead by example.** Treat people well and they will afford you with the same courtesy.
>   3. **Give something back to the planet and local/global commu-nity.** Donate time or money, save energy and reduce waste and implement responsible sourcing and production methods.

If you create a workplace that people really want to work at, you will attract and retain staff. Take iwantoneofthose.com. 'We were in a really awful part of London, so anyone who wanted to come there really wanted to work for IWOOT', says Tim. 'We weren't great payers because we were a small company; people probably could have got more money going to a big corporate, but they didn't want to work for a big corporate, they wanted to work for us, a company that they loved.'

Creating a strong reputation as a company that people love to work for is a crucial part of the staff recruitment and retention process. People talk. If you treat people well, create a happy environment, word will spread... That's all part of your brand identity, part of who you are as a company. So, about that . . .

Step Eight

Build Your Brand

'People are immune to brands. They want something real. They want brands that are honest and moral.'
Dame Anita Roddick

Branding differentiates you from your competitors. It characterizes you and personifies your business. It puts your stamp on your offerings. Indeed the word 'brand' is derived from the Old Norse 'brandr' which means 'to burn' in reference to the practice of marking products with a branding iron. And yet branding isn't just about your 'mark'; what you look like or what you say; it's about *who* you are as a company and how you make your customers *feel*; it's about personality, purpose and promises. Frankly, it's emotional.

In this chapter we'll examine the essential ingredients that form a brand; from purpose, values and culture to logo, colour scheme and slogan. And we'll consider how these elements work together to attract customers and engage everyone connected to your brand.

By the end of the chapter, you will understand how to:

- **create a meaningful purposeful brand that people relate to, believe in and trust;**
- **define your core brand values and company culture;**
- **personify and package up your brand to create a strong brand personality that connects with people emotionally; and**
- **create a brand, logo and slogan which concisely summarizes your value proposition and brand identity.**

To create a strong competitive brand that has the longevity to survive and succeed within your marketplace, your company must be perceived as, not only providing a solution to a problem, but as the *only* solution to a problem. If you can do this, you will become known as a 'come to' company; one with such brand recognition that people will automatically 'come to' you if they want a specific product/service/solution. In order to make this happen you must:

1. Be passionate about your purpose; about what you stand for.
2. Focus on you strengths, on what you are really good at.
3. Package up your brand identity and image and then articulate and communicate it clearly and consistently.

Let's examine these three criteria one by one . . .

A Passionate Purpose: The Importance of Brand Values

Over-marketing and brand image overload has created a modern consumer landscape where, in order to cut through the marketing hype and stand out from the ever-expanding crowd, brands must have a genuine purpose; a cause that they believe in, a mission they strive to deliver upon. Just as singers who have amazing voices yet lack in personality are rejected from TV talent shows, companies with great products that don't have strong brand identities often fall by the wayside. To survive in business today, you really need to stand for something. To compel people to sit up and take notice of your brand and, in doing so, create brand longevity, you need a cause and a purpose that people, including your staff, will believe in and stay loyal to.

'You want loyalty beyond reason and loyalty beyond recession', says Kevin Roberts, author of *Lovemarks: The Future Beyond Brands*. 'For small-business owners, this is even more vital because they don't have the purchasing power that large corporations do.'

To create a brand with a buzz that people want to talk about, you need to zoom in on what contribution you make to people's lives (whether that's helping people to live more healthily, making a luxury item more affordable, making life easier or simplifying a complex way of doing something). Secondly, that contribution and cause must be on-trend and thus something that the media and blogosphere will want to write about.

Because purpose is the precursor for everything else, it doesn't only influence the amount of column inches (or pixels) that your brand generates and the consequential loyalty of those who believe in you. Purpose reaches deeper than that. Your purpose influences actions and decisions, principles and values, culture and behaviour. Your purpose is the pin holding every area of your business together – strategy, planning, raising finance, recruiting and retaining a dream team of people who'll go the extra mile. An organization's purpose and subsequent set of values should therefore be embedded into the very heart of the company in order to engage each stakeholder in the business: staff, customers, suppliers and partners.

A clear purpose and vision galvanizes an organization and provides focus. It connects with people on an emotive level. People need to relate to your brand and its emotional essence. So ask yourself:

- Why did you start the business? What need did you wish to fulfill? What problem did you wish to solve?
- What is your value proposition (the bit that makes you remarkable)? What are you good at?
- How does what you offer enable your customers to behave in a certain way? In aspirational terms, how does being your customer enable people to be who they wish to be? How does your purpose reflect theirs?

The answers to these questions are critical for reminding you of your core purpose.

Brent and Martha from Lastminute.com started their business with a long-term vision of 'building a global multi-lingual multi-category website'. The need they fulfilled and the problem they solved was providing access to last minute deals that had previously been unavailable in one place. This was what they were good at, this was their value proposition (the bit that made them remarkable) and it was this that informed their ethos: a five-star lifestyle for three-star cash, and their purpose: of enabling their customers to be 'spontaneous, romantic and adventurous'. This purpose or 'customer vision' as Martha calls it, informed everything they did. Their purpose created a brand with a certain attitude as it represented a feeling 'of romantic spontaneity and adventure'. And, in a crowded marketplace, this experiential element of brand creation is critical.

'You have a business vision but I think the customer vision has to come first', Martha told me. 'You must have a regular idea about what you're doing at the forefront (e.g. creating this site that allows people access to all kinds of deals and products at the last minute). And the emotional bit of that was the customer vision – "spontaneous, romantic, adventurous behaviour," which was always absolutely core. Then we built the business on the back of that, rather than the other way round.'

Exercise

Values are valuable: Define your purpose, values and point of being in existence

1. Define your point, your promise, your purpose. Revisit your vision and mission statement on pages 16 and 72. Then go deeper than that. What effect do you wish to have on your customers and the wider world? Do you want to put a smile on people's faces? Support sustainable and fair trade? Save the planet's resources? Take on the corporate giants in your space to save people money? Do you want to make something available to consumers that has previously been inaccessible? Do you want to empower people in a certain way or flag up a particular cause?

   Write it down here:

   _____

   As a business our purpose is to: _____

   Because we want to: _____

   What do you do well and why do you do it?

   We: _____

   Because: _____

   What is your mission? What are you passionate about? What are your customers passionate about?

   We aim to: _____

Because: _____

Our customers aim to: _____

Because they: _____

What does being your customer enable your customers to do and how does it enable them to behave?

How does your brand make people feel? _____

_____

Being our customer enables our customers to be: _____

And it makes them feel: _____

_____

2. Define your values, as a person and as a company.

   What do you stand for? What do you value (e.g. honesty, family values, good quality and service, high performance, value for money)?

   _____

   _____

   What do you preach as well as practice (e.g. integrity, fairness, good ethics)?

   _____

   _____

   What values do you/will you teach to your children (e.g. good manners, politeness, kindness)?

   _____

   _____

3. Consider all of the words you have used to describe your purpose, what you do and the values you hold dear. Use these to shape and infuse your brand personality and branding.

'[Successful brands] are the ones that don't need batteries of marketing consultants and over-sophisticated research to tell them what they need to be, because they know what they are.'

Dame Anita Roddick, Founder of The Body Shop

Your best behaviour

Your brand will permeate every single aspect of your organization, from the way you pick up the phone and communicate via e-mail, to the way you treat your staff and suppliers. You can only create a positive brand experience if the sum of all points of contact with your brand is positive. Aim therefore to enhance your brand rather than detract from it by ensuring that the way you and your staff behave echoes your ethos.

From how a travel firm deals with its stranded passengers to how environmentally responsible a company is with its packaging, it is the amalgamation of company-wide actions and behaviours which shape and actualize a brand identity. Your purpose, personality and the way you behave as an organization must inform your customer service methodologies, recruitment and selling policies.

Ultimately, the living and breathing corporate culture must capture the true soul of your brand identity and, in doing so, influence decisions around marketing, production, distribution and communication.

As such, consider everybody within the company to be a brand manager, because they are all representing you and your brand every time they communicate. Each staff member must therefore understand and embody your brand and behave accordingly. They should know your purpose, believe in your vision and feel the passion behind it.

'If you're passionate about what you're selling and are passionate about what you do, you will build a brand', says Tim Booth, co-founder of iwantoneofthose. com. 'As long as you can translate that passion through your website and through your communications. If you haven't got passion and are just doing a job, then the likelihood that you'll build a brand is pretty slim.'

Play To Your Strengths

MP3 players provide consumers with the same functionality and the chance to listen to music while on the move. Yet Apple's iPod has dominated the market having grabbed a whopping 73% market share, despite being more highly priced. Apple has a brand identity that is synonymous with innovation and 'insanely brilliant' design. Their products not only look fantastic, but they are highly intuitive and user friendly. Apple does what it does well. It plays to its strengths and has built its brand using its strengths as its foundations. The company has subsequently created a loyal tribe of fans.

While the company has its detractors, it also has a large base of evangelical followers who think very highly of the company and fiercely defend wholeheartedly any criticism levelled at it. Fundamentally, it almost doesn't matter how Apple pitches its products – the whole world, including detractors, know that they are pioneering and brilliant. Every product release has the Apple brand stamped on it, which encapsulates a lifestyle and whole host of attributes and aspirational connotations that go far beyond the logo. By building a true brand with such passion, Steve Jobs has left a legacy which the world perceives very highly.

'The really important thing is that a brand has to be true', comments Moonpig. com's Nick Jenkins. 'You have to live the brand and it has to come from the top.'

Apple is a case in point. Apple's 1998 "Think different" ad campaign, featuring Gandhi, Einstein and Picasso was described by Steve Jobs in Business Week as a way for the company to remember who the heroes are and who Apple is. In reminding the Apple team about the "think different" ethos, Steve Jobs renewed Apple's sense of its true brand identity, after it had lost it's way during his absence. The brand has since remained true to its origins, purpose and vision – of bringing the best experience to users of its products. It never attempts to be anything it isn't. It just is what it is: innovative, stylish and market-driving, because of the passion, focus and vision of its founder.

'easyJet doesn't try to be anything other than no-frills', says Nick. 'It doesn't try to be posh and smart and swanky. It isn't. That's not what people go there for. The same applies with Moonpig. Our brand is fun and it's efficient. We're good at what we do and we don't try to be anything else.'

'A brand is so much more than whatever a brand manager says', adds Nick. 'Your brand is basically the summary of what your customers think of you. It doesn't matter if you've got a brand manager who says "this is what the brand is," if people don't believe and feel it and if it isn't reflected in the product and by what the customers think, then that isn't your brand.'

Exercise

Focus on your strengths

1. Uncover what your customers really think of you. Survey your main advocates and detractors (customers and staff). Ask them to tell you frankly what you are doing right, wrong and could do better. How so? Where could improvements be made? Monitor your brand name using Google Alerts to see what others are saying about you. (More on reputation management in Step 11).

2. Define your key strengths. What are you really good at? What would you like yourself and your company to be best-known for? How do you wish to be seen? What do you think you do better than anyone else in the world? What do your customers think you do better than anyone else in the world? Do these characteristics and perceptions contrast? Do you need to do anything to ensure that your own perceptions of your brand and strengths and those of your customer base match? What can you do to ensure that people see you as you wish to be seen, whilst staying true to yourself?

_____

_____

_____

Package Up Your Brand Identity and Image

Your brand identity is the outward expression of your brand. It includes your name, visual appearance (logo/typography/style), personality and the way you communicate all of this (slogan). So, while clarity of purpose, integration of culture and definition of your core strengths are vital parts of the brand creation exercise, so too are how you choose to summarize this information visually in words and symbols (via your slogan and logo) and how you choose to personify your brand and relate to people (via the characteristics that your brand personality comprises).

Brands with strong identities have identifiable attributes that people have an affinity with. Whether it's the reliability of Rolls Royce, the creativity of Apple, or the caring characteristics of ethical fashion company, Hug; a strong purpose requires an equally strong persona. What's more, you need to be able to convey that personality through the way you represent your brand image visually.

Essentially, your name, slogan and logo should capture the essence of who you are, what you stand for, what you're good at, how you make customers feel and what you enable your customers to do.

Take Moonpig.com. Greetings cards are generally fun and engaging; the workplace culture Nick Jenkins created was a fun one. Naturally, the brand identity he chose had to be fun and unobtrusive. Nick also wanted a name that was phonetic, short and thus easy to remember. As well as being his school nickname, Moonpig.com ticked all of those boxes and was fun. The logo captures that fun-loving ethos and that purpose of wanting their customer to have the best card possible. 'First and foremost we take an enormous amount of joy and pride in producing our products', says Nick. 'We enjoy creating them, choosing them and we love the end result', he continues. 'And that enjoyment and pride is captured in the brand identity' (a grinning pig, smiling proudly from under his space-helmet).

Consequently, from the brand name evolved a catchy TV jingle which catapulted the site into the mainstream to achieve nationwide brand recognition. With all of these visual aids, Moonpig.com personified its brand and created a strong and vibrant personality.

Exercise

Brand characterization

Bland brands merely add to the mental clutter that the information age has presented consumers with. Via billboards and web pages to flat-screen TVs and phones, being sold to the whole time is annoying. That's why today's consumers want more from the brands they choose. As well as buying from brands which stand for something, consumers are opting for brands with strong personalities, brands which stand out.

So who are you as a company? What's your hallmark? What's your essence? What's your character?

1. Define your brand personality. Brainstorm words which epitomize the personality of your company. What characteristics do you, your team and your company possess? Write down words which summarize the characteristics of your brand identity. For example:
    *   Are you smart, serious and sleek?
    *   Are you reliable, logical and punctual?
    *   Are you sociable, bubbly and fun?
    *   Are you creative, edgy and witty?
    *   Are you warm, independent and cheeky?
    *   Are you confident, bold and sassy?
2. Consider how these words tie in to your list of values in the 'Values are valuable' exercise on page 196. Do they fit?

When my partner and I set up I Like Music, the name captured our reasons for starting up the business. We wanted to set up a business doing something that we liked, so my partner thought . . . 'what do I like? I like music.' Since the company merged, the redesigned logo captures the personality of the brand which is 'playful and strong'.

In fact, the new brand identity created for I Like Music was awarded the highest design accolade in the USA – an AIGA award. As a result our brand identity is published the *AIGA Annual* (the design bible), displayed at a public exhibition at the AIGA National Design Center in New York and is now housed at the Denver Art Museum.

I Like
Music

3. List keywords that evoke feelings, visual imagery or memories (such as Christmas holidays, family Sunday roast, falling in love, feeling free, strolling

along the beach, keeping fit and feeling strong and healthy). Emotive words and descriptions bring your brand to life and create a visual scene that will make your brand really mean something.

4. List the names of celebrities that your brand persona is most like. For instance, when I wrote my first book, *The Small Business Start-Up Workbook*, I suggested that ilikemusic.com might choose, for that list, an independent artist who packs a lot of good content into his music, such as Mike Skinner (aka The Streets). Today I might choose an artist such as Adele or Example. (Funnily enough, Adele won the award for Best Independent Artist at the 2011 BT Digital Music Awards, an award that was sponsored by I Like Music.)

5. Translate your name, purpose, slogan and attributes of your brand personality into an image. Create a logo that uses the right colours, shape and design to convey all of this with simplicity. Note down logos that are memorable to you.

6. Choose your colour scheme and typographic style with care. Your personality and purpose should inform the colours you choose to represent your brand via your logo and other visual aids. For example, bold primary colours may appeal well to a target audience of time-starved people who want things fast and cheap (think McDonalds or easyJet). Sleek clean lines and silver colouring might appeal more to those seeking quality and style (think Apple or Bang & Olufsen).

    Energetic and fast? Go for high-contrast, bold, primary colours such as red, orange or yellow.

    Calm and natural? Opt for neutral, earthy shades such as green, brown and blue.

    Feminine and light? Opt for pastel shades such as pink, lilac or peach.

    Make sure you opt for colours that exist within the web palette of 256 colours and, ideally, choose sans-serif fonts for your digital brand.

7. Create a style guide to ensure consistency when presenting your brand identity; a template which outlines the font faces and sizes and defines web colour values for logos and backgrounds.

Your slogan

Summarize your core purpose, personality, value proposition and values/aspirations of your target audience into a slogan. Consider your target audience's core needs alongside whatever it is that you want to help your audience to do or feel when writing a strapline for your business.

For example, traditional companies such as leading supermarket chains have carefully considered slogans which target their specific audiences. Sainsbury's 'makes life taste better', aims for an affluent market seeking quality over cost savings. While 'every little helps', targets the Tesco audience keen to save money on their weekly shop.

Some slogans are instructional. They cleverly summarize what their product enables you to do, such as Xbox 360's genius slogan: 'Life's short. Play more', or the direct slogan from YouTube: 'Broadcast Yourself'. Others clearly reveal what their purpose is and what they do: from Nokia's 'Connecting People' or Loves-truck.com's clever 'Where Busy People Click', to AudioBoo's 'Because Sound is Social'. Both Zoopla.com and Parkatmyhouse.com use the word 'smarter' before their offering: 'Smarter Property Search' (Zoopla) and 'Smarter Parking' (Parkatmyhouse.com).

Exercise

Summarize your promise

1. Clearly identify your target audience and what your product enables them to do. Refer back to your customer profile and the exercise in Step 3 p59–61 which outlines how being a customer makes your customers feel.
2. Write your slogan. Create your promise in less than five words, based on these actions and feelings, alongside your purpose, values, most compelling benefits and value proposition.

! Top Tips for Building Brands with a Buzz

1. **Have absolute clarity about what you stand for.** Become the only logical solution to a specific problem and become a 'come to' business.
2. **Design a logo that captures all that you are.** Your purpose, ethos and personality; your company's heritage or environmental stewardship; your core values and attitude.
3. **Assess your brand name.** The best names tend to share common characteristics – they infuse purpose and personality into the name, often have few syllables, are phonetic and easy to remember.
4. **Be true to yourself.** Don't try to be something you're not. There is little point in thinking, as a digital accountancy firm, that you want to be seen as funky and cool. You need to be true to yourself and your brand. Don't try to be cool and down-with-the-kids if you aren't. Focus instead on what your target audience sees you as, on

(Continued)

what you really are: such as efficient, fresh and reliable. Focus on your true strengths. Keep it real.

5. **Have a brand champion.** Give someone on your team – who understands your brand personality, vision and core purpose – the role of protecting the brand by ensuring that new ideas fit with the brand. This focus will ensure that ideas which don't fit are either discarded or become the roots of a separate brand. Strengthen your brand and protect it by having total clarity in what you are trying to do.

6. **Communicate honestly and transparently.** Share every ingredient and fact with your customers. Be proactive about sharing rather than reactive and defensive. Don't put up a smokescreen or PR wall or patronize customers.

7. **Unify your brand.** Ensure that each of your disparate online profiles and identities are consistent. Speak with the same tone of voice and create a singular experience across all properties.

By creating a brand identity that people who buy from you and work for you will respect and buy into, you'll not only benefit from a united culture, productive workforce and increased sales, but you'll make more people want to talk about your brand more often, thus creating a media buzz and viral marketing punch. Now that you have laid the foundations by building a website, a team and a brand, it's time to spread the word.

Part 3

Running And

Growing

Your

Business

Step Nine

Effective Online Marketing

'Know your user, and you'll be able to work out what's the best marketing effort fit for them.'
Sarah Beeny

Effective marketing is about getting the right message to the right person at the right time. Marketing is also about the provision of amazing products and services that make customers want to return and share their experience with others. We'll focus on the latter: exceeding expectations, building relationships and harnessing the power of social in Step Eleven. In this section, however, we shall focus on the nuts and bolts of traditional online marketing; the different methods to choose from and how to select the right marketing channels to suit both your objectives and those of your target market.

Having a fantastic value proposition and amazing website won't amount to much unless you tell people about it. If you don't allocate time and money to promoting your site, it's a bit like putting up a dazzling billboard on a disused motorway. Nobody will see it. Yes, your product might be so amazing that word of its greatness will spread virally like wildfire from a few hundred people to many millions, but you still need to inform those first few hundred people of its existence. You need to tell people then tell them again. Reminding people about what's in it for them is how marketing works.

So, by the end of this chapter you will understand:

■ **The fundamentals of online marketing: from outbound push-marketing such as PR, e-mail marketing and advertising, to inbound marketing, such as pulling traffic in via search engines.**

■ **Which marketing strategies will best suit your audience, your objectives and your stage within the marketing cycle.**

■ **How to generate interest in your product or service before you even launch.**

Spark Interest Before Launch

The good news is that there are a lot of early adopters out there who like to hear about new digital start-ups. They are keen to be the first to know about a new product or service and equally keen to share that knowledge. The bad news is that competition for early adopters is fierce.

To stand a chance of adopting their interest you should have, at the very least, a 'coming soon' landing page which enables users to enter their details and sign-up to find out more and share with their friends. To add to their intrigue, you could add a short viral video providing a teaser of what users can expect. Or turn your page into a social game and incentivize people to share it, via a site such as LaunchRock.com.

At the time of writing, I noticed a new moving billboard ad on the walls of the tube station for Freebearhug.com. The interesting domain name sparked my interest. I had no idea what this site does or will do, but I signed up to get my free bear hug out of curiosity. (Turns out its a free download called Bear Hug from a band called The 2 Bears.)

Invest in Your First Customers

Just as Hugh Chappell of TrustedReviews.com gave his first advertisers a 'preferential rate' for being first, Rowan Gormley came up with a similarly attractive tactic to convince customers to commit to pay for products they couldn't see in advance. He made sure they could taste in advance. In order to persuade wine-drinkers to take a risk, sign-up to NakedWines.com and pre-order wine six months in advance, he gave them free wine and gave the winemakers the working capital to make that free wine.

'Before we launched, we gave away a lot of wines for free to recruit tasters', explains Rowan. Naturally a few hundred people took up the offer of free wine (no doubt!) and volunteered. 'We sent people a few bottles of wine and those who came back and wrote well-considered reviews of the wine, we sent them more. Those who snaffled the free wine and didn't bother fulfilling their end of the bargain, we ignored them.'

'This gave us a hard core of people who were sufficiently interested in wine and sufficiently decent to put in their time and energy in exchange for getting the bottles they wanted. They became a group of people who we call our Archangels. [Having them on board] gave other people the confidence to see that they weren't the first; that there was already a group of people saying, "I've tried this wine; I like it,"' says Rowan.

This grew into the ratings and reviews system which is prevalent on the site today. If Nakedwines.com had just said, 'if you give us your money in advance we'll give you better wine for your money', the offer might have been hard to believe. But NakedWines.com has built up a loyal active community of 100,000 customers, by giving those very first customers the chance to try before buying. These days, customers can trust in what they buy by reading the reviews and ratings and by attending occasional wine tasting events. And, by giving customer the chance to pre-order the wines six months in advance, guaranteeing sales for its winemakers, between 40–70% of the costs of marketing, bottling, warehousing and commissions are avoided and the savings passed on to the customer: a win(e)–win(e) proposition.

Exercise

1. **Consider ways you can spark curiosity.** Consider ways you can use scarcity, intrigue or exclusivity to encourage wider adoption. For example, you might suggest that customers reserve their username, sale price or preferred customer status before someone else does, to stake their claim. How can you incite people to consider 'what if I don't sign up?' and make them realize that they don't want to risk missing out on something that just might be the next big thing?
2. **List ways you might persuade and reward potential customers to become your first.** Can you give away something for free in return for a review? Might you offer people a lifetime preferential rate for signing up first? Can you offer something exclusive that is only available for a limited time to a limited number of people?

Pick 'n' Mix

In order to get your messages in front of the right people, in the right places at the right time, you first need to understand who you are targeting, where they go online and what their needs are at any given time. You will already have a firm grasp of your audience having researched your market, written your customer profiles and got feedback from potential customers during the planning stage (see Step Three). Now it's time to put that information into use and draw up a list of places your customers frequent (from publications and blogs they subscribe to their favourite relevant sites).

Secondly, in order to decide which ingredients to put into your marketing mix, you'll need to consider your own needs and define exactly where you are within the overall marketing cycle.

The marketing cycle:

1. **First stage.** To source and attract prospects, get noticed and gather leads.
2. **Second stage.** To reach out, build credibility and convince prospective customers to take action: enter your website, book a meeting and so on.
3. **Third stage.** To close the deal, securing the sale.
4. **Fourth stage.** To deliver the product or service and follow up to request referral, testimonial, case study, repeat business . . .
   . . . and repeat.

You must therefore consider your campaign objective. Is it branding or direct response? Is it relationship-building or follow-up? Display advertising for example, is best for branding exercises where your main goal is to maximize reach and exposure to the largest number of people. Whereas pay-per-click search advertising is best suited to generating direct response, which can be measured.

So, if you wish to get noticed, build top level brand awareness, drive traffic and gather leads; you are at stage one of the marketing cycle and you might therefore opt to run a daily deal campaign on a site such as Groupon, announce a competition on your social network pages or run a display advertising campaign across targeted sites. If you are at stage two and hope to build credibility and establish your position as an expert in your field, you might instead focus on content marketing and write a blog. Whereas, if you are seeking to secure a sale, you might choose to use paid search advertising, or announce special offers to existing customers via e-mail or SMS marketing.

While this chapter focuses on the online marketing opportunities at your disposal, you should not ignore offline traditional media channels. TV and radio advertising, telemarketing, direct mail, exhibiting and public speaking are all valid marketing channels with high impact which can generate significant ROI (return on investment).

Take mass market brand Moonpig.com, it tried a variety of marketing methods, but none had the impact that mass market TV advertising had. 'Paid for search worked a little bit, affiliate marketing worked a little bit and PR worked a little bit, but none of those are as scalable as TV. In 2006 we invested all of our profits in a TV campaign. That helped transform the business', explains founder of Moonpig.com, Nick Jenkins. TV was right for the brand which has such a broad target market (anyone of any age who wants to send a greeting card). If Moonpig only sold children's birthday cards, they'd be better off targeting parenting forums, networks, publications and blogs.

Exercise

Who, where and what: Choosing the right marketing methods

1. Who is your target market (e.g. young car enthusiasts or over 50s)?
2. Where do they go online to find sites such as yours (TopGear.co.uk or Saga.co.uk)?
3. What is your current objective/position in the marketing cycle (e.g. to attract users, build leads and establish credibility, generate sales)?
4. What marketing methods are therefore best suited (viral social media campaign, content marketing, daily deal?)?

Marketing The Right Way: AnythingLeftHanded.co.uk

The team at AnythingLeftHanded.co.uk use a number of marketing strategies and have three main sources of traffic, each generating about a third: editorial, inbound links (including affiliate links) and search engines.

They pay-per-click on keywords such as 'scissors' and include 'left-handed-scissors' in their description to a) raise awareness that left-handed scissors exist to those wanting scissors and b) generate click-throughs from those who specifically want left-handed ones. They have a mail order catalogue and grow their distribution list through PR generated from quarterly press releases distributed to a wide range of media, from national newspapers to specialist magazines, such as *Embroidery Monthly* which focuses on individual products.

CEO, Keith Milsom uses different strategies depending on the objective and marketing cycle stage. For example, to build brand awareness rather than sales, Keith focused on the word, 'Eminem' to draw a crowd.

'When Eminem won a global music award for his album, he's a left-hander, so we put up a page about Eminem and made him our famous left-hander of the month', explains Keith. 'This brought in thousands of people who were looking for information about Eminem. Very few of them were interested in buying left-handed products, so lots of traffic, very low conversions. While that was running our conversion rate went right down, because of far more untargeted traffic coming in. It didn't cost us anything, was a bit of fun and made more people see the site, raising brand awareness.'

Conversely, if the objective and marketing cycle stage is to generate sales, Keith opts for PPC advertising linking to individual products. 'This attracts visitors who've already made a decision that they want a left-handed product and are coming to our site to buy it or price compare it, so that could put the conversion rate up to 30–40%.'

In practice, Keith aims to do a bit of both to drive in a good blend of untargeted traffic 'because some of it will skim off and buy things', and targeted traffic more likely to convert into customers.

Additionally, writing a blog and posting news and videos about left-handedness and distributing the videos and links widely online through video sharing sites, social bookmarking, other relevant blogs and on social networking sites generates more keyword-focused pages to be listed in search engine results, helps the overall site page rank and attracts additional traffic.

Digital Marketing Methods

People find websites through a number of channels and via a number of different types of screen: from TV and tablet to mobile and computer screens; by typing search terms into a search engine, clicking a link displayed on another site; via recommendations from friends; through printed media, e-mail or social networking; from a book, phone or on the box. Your own personal marketing mix will depend, not only on how your audience finds websites, but also on who your audience is, where they go online and what your objectives are.

Choose from:

* content marketing
* editorial via PR
* e-mail and SMS marketing
* affiliate marketing
* daily deal sites/competition sites
* paid search
* display advertising
* organic/natural search including local listings
* social media.

Let's examine each of these in detail so you can make an informed choice about which marketing ingredients to pick for your mix. All except social media that is, which has a chapter all to itself in Step Eleven.

Content marketing

You already know about the textual and visual content you can use to attract individual visitors and engage them once they arrive on your site (see Step Five), so I won't repeat myself here. However, as well as a tool of attraction and engagement, content is an important tool within your marketing armoury in terms of link-building, SEO (search engine optimization) and wider credibility-building.

To generate the most value from your content and position yourself and your business as a credible source of useful content, you can repackage content in a number of formats and distribute it wisely.

Written blog content, white papers, and articles containing top tips, checklists and interviews can all be turned into podcasts, webinars and videos and vice versa. Transcripts of videos, podcasts and webinars can be turned into written Q&A features and bulleted checklists.

Then, rather than merely post all of this content on your site and hope it will be shared and viewed, you can distribute your content to destinations with high visibility within your target market. As content is king, all webmasters need good content. As such, if you can supply people with content to publish on their own site which links back to yours, you're creating a win–win situation (content for them; targeted traffic and raised awareness/credibility for you).

> ❗ **Top Tips for Distributing your Content**
>
> ● 1. **Syndicate your content.** E-mail extracts of your articles and blog postings to online magazines, news sites, forums and other targeted websites, granting permission to republish. However, syndicate carefully as Google will always show the version they think is most appropriate for users in any given search. Google recommends that you 'ensure that each site on which your content is syndicated includes a link back to your original article. You can also ask those who use your syndicated material to use the "noindex" meta tag to prevent search engines from indexing their version of the content.'
>
> 2. **Contact bloggers from relevant blogs that your target audience reads.** Put yourself forward as a guest expert, willing to write a monthly or quarterly blog piece on whatever your target audience wishes to know (whether that's how to encourage creativity in their children, how to bake the perfect apple pie, or how to improve their negotiating skills).
>
> 3. **Hire a freelance writer.** If you don't have the time or skills to write good content yourself, get someone to ghostwrite it for you.
>
> 4. **Include a signature file/author summary at the foot of each piece of content.** This should explain who you are, why you are qualified to talk about this topic as an expert and your web link and social media addresses.
>
> 5. **Get your content listed in directories.** Promote your blog by listing it on blog directories. List your podcast on iTunes and podcast directories such as podcastdirectory.com. Find a list of such directories at podcast411.com. Host your video on your own site, your YouTube channel and on other video hosting platforms.
>
> 6. **Post videos.** Upload them to your site, your blog, and on video hosting websites from Vimeo to YouTube. Tag them by assigning specific keywords. Send video links to your brand advocates to distribute to their own networks.

Editorial via online PR

Submitting punchy press releases to targeted publications is a very cost-effective marketing tool. The only cost is the time to write, distribute and follow-up on your submissions (unless you pay a PR agency to do it for you) which can result in free publicity in online and offline publications that your target audience reads.

Tapping into a Trend

Publications constantly seek on-trend stories on hot topics which have a good angle; a hook to pull readers in.

During the recession for example, publications focused on the topic of making money or saving money. The Parkatmyhouse.com story appealed to editors on both levels. The site enabled people to earn extra income by renting out their driveway, while simultaneously helping people to save money they'd usually spend on high parking fees by parking in one of those driveways.

PR was the first marketing tool that Anthony used to kickstart interest in the site. He spent £1k on submitting a press release to every news agency and news wire he could find about a young British entrepreneur trying to solve the world's parking problems.

'The story got picked up in a way I could never have imagined, partly due to being a new and interesting concept; but also because it appealed to editors writing about ways to save money or clear your debts during the recession. Three hours after submitting the press release I was getting phone calls to do newspaper and radio station interviews during drive time. The *Guardian, Times, Metro, Evening Standard*, were all leaving me voicemails', explains Anthony.

The site went from having two parking spaces and four users (all family) to 200 users within a week. Five years on, having grown organically, the site has 125,000 drivers registered and 15,000 locations listed with 30,000 parking spaces. Parkatmyhouse.com has saved the public £3million in parking charges over the past 12 months while enabling customers renting out their driveways to earn between £400 to £3k per parking space per year (in excess of £1 million in total).

Top Tips for Generating Column Inches

1. **Promote your expertise to build citations and get quoted.** Write a brief 'expert biog'. If you spot an expert quote on your own area of expertise that you could have said, contact the editor, explain your level of expertise and outline what you might have said on that particular piece. Also register on Expertsources.co.uk. While I was editor of ilikemusic.com, I was regularly invited to comment in magazines and summarize key music events, such as The Grammys and The Brit Awards live on television for CNN and Sky News; a great way to boost credibility and brand awareness.
2. **Become a PR expert.** Assess news articles to find the hook of the story and consider what makes it newsworthy. Can you come up with a better angle?

(Continued)

3. **Be timely.** Create a PR calendar which lists specific, relevant National Days or Weeks, such as National Curry Week or Random Acts of Kindness Day. Write press releases which tie those specific dates into your own business news angles. (Don't forget that traditional offline publications work three months ahead of publication.)
4. **Use the right format.** Your introductory press release paragraph should provide the editor with the Who? What? When? Where? Why? outline required in all news stories.
5. **Provide links to images or other material that may add colour to the piece.**
6. **Submit your press releases yourself directly to named editors of targeted publications.** Look at media directories such as Mediauk. com or Gorkana.com to get contact information or visit publication websites directly. Alternatively or additionally use PR submission services such as prweb.com, sourcewire.com or pressbox.co.uk.

E-mail and SMS marketing

More people have access to text and e-mail accounts than any other medium. (Even my dad has a mobile phone and e-mail account, despite rarely using the Internet).

SMS marketing in particular has unparalleled immediacy and response rates. According to a white paper from Singlepoint, approximately 99% of all text messages are read by recipients, with 90% read within three minutes of their delivery.

And, according to the Direct Marketing Association's 2010 *Response Rate Trend Report*, the average text messaging CTR (click through rate) is 14.06% compared to e-mail's 6.64% and display advertising's meagre 0.76%. Conversion rates too are higher in text campaigns: with 8.22% for text messaging, 1.73% for e-mail and 4.43% for Internet display ads.

Texting and messaging have become the primary methods of communication in today's digital world. Conversely, e-mail inboxes are cluttered and spam-ridden. These are the main reasons for low conversion rates that e-mail marketing offers in comparison to other methodologies. Getting an e-mail opened and read, let alone acted upon, is a major challenge today.

That said, if a prospect or customer supplies you with their e-mail address and opts-in to be kept up to date, e-mail newsletters remain a great way to keep communication channels open, build relationships and prompt sales. They can be automated to follow-up and remind customers of special subscriber discounts and deals. And, if you use an e-mail provider such as iContact or Constant Contact to distribute your newsletter on your behalf, you can view metrics to see how many people received, opened and forwarded your e-mail.

These days, you can also use a QR (Quick Response) code (a square type of bar code) to promote your website, YouTube video, GoogleMap location, social media link or contact details which smartphone users can scan from a physical place (i.e. from a magazine ad, flyer, mug, promotional t-shirt or business card). On scanning the QR code they open your website or promoted link/text/VCard using their phone. Object hyperlinking using QR codes provides a great digital method of linking to the web from physical objects using a mobile phone and is an interesting twist on sending a text or e-mail message to promote your website or other links. Visit QRstuff.com or GoQR.me.

> ## ❗ Top Tips for Optimizing your Email and SMS Marketing Efforts
>
> Ensure that your e-mail and text messages are:
> 1. **Solicited.** Only send e-mail or text messages to those who have opted in to receive e-mail or SMS notifications or updates from you or have subscribed to your e-newsletter. Tell them immediately on sign-up exactly what they've subscribed to and how often you'll be e-mailing/texting them. Identify yourself clearly. Always give them the chance to opt-out and unsubscribe from your list.
> 2. **Timely, relevant, and brief.** Keep e-mails under 300 words in length and write short sentences and paragraphs. Limit texts to 160 characters and include just one singular marketing point per message. With text campaigns, brevity is vital. You need to convey immediately what you are offering and what to do next e.g. 'text xyz to 60099 to receive your exclusive member discount'.
> 3. **Useful.** Always provide value if you want subscribers to open subsequent e-mails and texts from you. Include answers to questions, industry news, special offers, incentives, tips and checklists, extracts of blog postings, invitations to comment, links to useful resources, free reports, competitions, and surveys. Provide mobile alerts about offers, sales and upcoming events.
> 4. **Personal.** Write conversationally, as if you are writing/texting to an individual recipient rather than to your entire list and use your customer's name if possible. Harness the one-to-one dialogue that messaging provides.
> 5. **Exclusive** to members of your VIP e-mail or text offers club and as interactive if possible. Invite response and prompt interaction to build your relationship, initiate a two-way communication and create a heightened exclusivity factor e.g. 'You are invited to our VIP club event at such and such on this date and time. Text back ☺ to qualify for 20% discount. Or take Facebook's lead with transactional alerts, e.g. 'You have been tagged in a post on Lara's wall'.
>
> *(Continued)*

6. **Likely to be opened and read.** SMS messages have a much higher open rate, particularly if they are from a recognizable source. Give e-mails an interesting subject line that will stand out from the rest and compelling headlines and sub-headings throughout.

7. **Not too frequent.** If you clog up a person's inbox, no matter how valuable your information is, they are more likely to unsubscribe.

8. **Actionable.** Include calls to action and, ideally, a time-sensitive discounted offer as an incentive. Don't forget to include a signature file containing links to all your web properties: your web address, contact information, social media profile links and rich media marketing materials.

9. **Integrated.** Insert your mobile short code within your e-mail messages and on your social profile pages. Specify different keywords for users to text back to the short code number, depending on the marketing channel you are using, so you can track whether the user took action from your site, from a print campaign or from a social network.

10. **Tested.** Have you included your web address? Is spelling correct? Send your intended messages to yourself before clicking 'send'.

Affiliate marketing

Having your own affiliate force promoting your products and services on the web can be a great way to multiply your efforts. You pay commission and provide the creative elements, while other targeted sites provide sales which you wouldn't have ordinarily made without them.

Sites such as AffiliateWindow.com and TradeDoubler.com enable merchants to add their affiliate programme to their portal, while they handle the tracking of impressions, results and so on.

Ideally, repeat business will then come directly via your site rather than through the affiliate.

Google Panda updates (a change to the algorithm by which Google ranks sites) famously penalized and demoted sites with thin or duplicate content which occasionally led to the affiliate sites achieving a better ranking than the original merchant site, if they had better quality content. To avoid being penalized by Google for having duplicate content (which your affiliates will also have) ensure the rest of the content on your site is high quality and unique. In short, if you follow the guidelines on the Google Webmaster's pages about content quality and duplicate content, you won't experience problems. As Google advises: 'If your site participates in an affiliate program, make sure that your site adds value. Provide unique and relevant content that gives users a reason to visit your site first.'

Daily deal sites/competition sites

Daily deal sites such as Groupon, Living Social, Google Offers, Yelp and Facebook Deals work on the premise that you offer a one-day discount or special offer which they distribute to a group of local customers who are encouraged to share the deal.

On the plus side, taking part in a daily group deal campaign can boost brand awareness exponentially, getting your brand in front of a high volume of consumers. On the downside, the level of discount you need to offer coupled with the high revenue share percentage you are required to provide to the deal site provider can mean that campaigns are essentially loss leaders which cost you money rather than boosting your profits.

Furthermore, the people taking up the deal are often only interested in the discounted deals which makes deal campaigns less effective in customer acquisition than other methods of marketing. So, while volume might be high, quality of customers redeeming deals may be low as they may be unlikely to become repeat customers or spend more than the deal offers. For that reason it may be worth trying out some lower volume niche targeted daily deal sites (such as TripAlertz for travel deals and Daily Gourmet for food-related offers) to see which works best to attract the custom you require.

To make group deal campaigns work for you, it's important to optimize each customer visit and put in place a long-term customer acquisition strategy. The only way to do this is by providing fantastic customer service; capturing deal-takers' details by encouraging people to sign up to your newsletter, follow you on Twitter and like you on Facebook; and making the most of the opportunity to up-sell other products or services to them.

For instance, you might offer smaller, time-sensitive discounts on other products or services only available on that day, before they leave your store or website. Your aim will be to encourage this plethora of consumers to return and buy stuff at the full purchase price in future.

> **! Top Tips for Making the Most of Group Deal Campaigns**
>
> 1. **Read terms and conditions carefully as these vary from site to site.** For example, while Groupon generally provides the highest volume of customers taking up a deal, they also spread payments out over a period of a few months and want more of the deal price than some other deal sites.
> 2. **Manage demand.** Make your deal time-specific where possible, so that your deal might be valid only from Monday to Thursday or during off-peak months. Groupon Now enables webmasters to put time constraints on their deals, which can also be more modest.
> 3. **Be aware of the cost implications.** You will need to offer a steep discount of say 50% and then give the service provider a high percentage (often 50%) of the revenue you make. If, for instance, you are providing a £100 product or service for £50 and are required to give £25 to the group deal service provider, you will be left with just £25 for a £100 service. If it costs you more than £25 to provide that product or service, you'll end up with a net loss to the business which is multiplied for every deal that is redeemed.
> 4. **Track how many people redeeming your deal are new customers.** Note how many come back and how much they spend above the amount of the voucher deal.

Competition sites are another way to drive traffic for those offering giveaways as incentives. When James and I first started ilikemusic.com we added a competition page to give away tickets, signed albums and free copies of new singles. Now this has progressed to some great opportunities to win unique items (such as t-shirts customized by James Morrison and Example) which makes for great viral marketing. If you give away stuff on your site, list your giveaways on competition sites such as Loquax.co.uk and Ukcompetitions.com and provide entrants with every opportunity to share the competition with their friends.

Paid search: PPC (pay-per-click) marketing

After you've submitted your web pages to the search engines, it can take a good few months to get listed naturally. Pay-per-click is a great way to get a new page or product listed in the search engines overnight. And you can start measuring response within a few days. Furthermore, you can use pay-per-click as a kind of test bed of which keywords and phrases convert best, then optimize other pages for those keywords to achieve a better natural search ranking.

Primarily, in order for your ad to show up as a sponsored ad (on the top or right hand side of search engine listings), you set a maximum daily spend. You bid on relevant keywords. You write compelling ads. Your ads are ranked based on the bid amount and a quality score. Your ads are clicked. You analyze your results, track what is working and tweak your campaigns accordingly. That, in a nutshell, is how paid search advertising works. But achieving a good ROI is a little more complex.

! Top Tips for Getting a Good PPC ROI

1. **Attract only serious clickers by using underused features.** For example, use negative keywords which enable you to select words that will not trigger your ad. So, if you sell second-hand goods, you could add the word 'new' to your list of negative keywords. Or vice versa. Geo-location is another underused feature which enables you to target audiences based on geo-specific keywords, IP addresses or both.

2. **Reveal value then compel to act.** Tell potential clickers what they'll get, such as 'free p&p' or 'up to 50% discount', then call-to-action using terms such as 'Learn More' or 'Download Now For Free'. Engage your target market by asking a question that includes the benefit, such as, 'Need a window spray that doesn't smear?'

3. **Choose 'long-tail' keywords to pull in users who are further along in their buying decision.** They will respond to a more precise phrase, such as 'red leather jacket' rather than 'jacket'. For example, Kiddicare.com which attracts 50,000 visitors per day sponsors a combination of generic words and long-tail product terms, such as 'Brittax car seat.' Visit Wordstream to get inspiration for long-tail keywords.

4. **Test several ads simultaneously and for a long enough time period.** This will allow you to amass and assess data properly. Avoid frequent changes over a short time period. You can split funds across each ad and display both ads the same number of times. Assess which ad works best – ad A or ad B? Assess during which time period ads convert the highest and lowest? Then limit ad impressions during time periods when conversions are at their lowest and vice versa.

5. **Track and get to know your conversion rates over a period of a few months.** Understand which ads and keywords convert best over that time period. Use the script which search engines provide for your 'thank you' page then measure your results.

(Continued)

6. **Optimize clicks.** Take users who have clicked on your ads to targeted relevant pages which continue where your ad left off. Don't simply send them to your homepage which is packed with other distracting content.

7. **Stay relevant to maximize your 'quality score'.** The more relevant (and higher quality) your ad is, the more times it will be clicked versus how many times it is viewed and not clicked. To maximize clickability include as many of the 10–15 keywords within your ad group as possible without diluting the compelling nature of the message.

8. **Seek out low competition alternatives to popular keywords.** Use keyword analyzer tools such as searchmetrics.com or live-keyword-analysis.com to generate alternative words. Uncover how many campaigns are already running using that phrase by using a keyword analyzer tool or by typing the word/phrase into the search engine and counting the number of ads.

9. **Spy on your competitors.** Use tools such as SypFu to emulate successful campaigns based on keywords that your competitors are targeting. You can use the information gleaned to enhance your campaign and gain the competitive edge.

10. **Read the rules and do your homework.** Visit Google Adwords or Microsoft AdCenter (Bing) to find out more about the how to get the best from your PPC campaigns and read up on the different features on offer, from Campaign Experiments and Conversion Optimizer to Ad Scheduling and Interest-Based Ads.

Display advertising

Placing graphical or text-based ads on targeted websites is known as display advertising. How much you pay is determined by CPM (cost per thousand page impressions) rather than CPC (cost per click). Until recently, you'd design a set of banner ads in standard formats (horizontal banner, vertical skyscraper and square MPU). You could then liaise directly with the webmaster of smaller targeted sites or join an ad network which displays ads across a number of relevant high traffic sites.

Nowadays however, there is a whole new landscape of display advertising available. Firstly, there is Google AdWords, which allows marketers to get their text ads onto a large number of targeted sites which have opted-in to display ads like yours. Additionally, Google Content Network now enables you to target users who have previously visited your website (known as re-targeting) and select specific sites based on keywords or location.

Social networks have also opened up their ad space to enable incredibly well targeted ad campaigns based on behaviour, interests, and even what people have mentioned in their Facebook status updates. The sheer volume of behavioural and geo-locational data means that Facebook can target extremely well. The size and simplicity of the ads is also a benefit to marketers who don't wish to spend out on dynamic design.

Certainly, it's a common misconception that, due to its size, Facebook ads will cost the earth. Quite the contrary. Facebook ads enable you to limit exactly how much you want to spend and narrow down the demographic you wish to reach. So you might set the limit at just £25. If you have a very clear niche product and target audience, campaigns can achieve fantastic conversion rates. For example, wedding photographers have used Facebook ads to target women between 24 to 30 whose social networking profiles identify them as engaged.

Search engine marketing

As well as paid search engine listings, (bidding on keywords to sponsor a search-engine listing, triggered when users search for those keywords) you can gain free organic or natural search engine listings which show up on Google, Yahoo, and Bing without paying to appear. Your aim is to get your web pages listed on the

---

! Top Tips for Making your Direct Ads Clickable

1. **Reward the user for clicking by using incentives.** This could be the chance to win something, special discounts and bonuses. Start text with a verb, e.g. 'Win a trip to Cuba', 'Save £25', 'Lose a stone'.
2. **Use benefit-rich engaging text which asks a question or promises a compelling result.** Show that you understand your potential cus-tomers' needs and, if they click your ad, you will reveal something amazing that can help them solve their problem and carry out a specific task.
3. **Make sure your graphical and text ads appear prominently above the fold.** You can exclude below the fold placements via a tick box in your AdWords settings or specify to your advertising agency or network that you only want above-the-fold placements.
4. **Browse the web.** Take note of creative display ads which catch your eye. Why do they stand out? Note down colours, messages, and typefaces used. Utilize sites such as AdRelevance which provide performance data to find out more about how different display ads have performed historically.
5. **Look into self-service ad portals which enable you to create, run and optimize campaigns yourself.** For instance, Tribal Fusion, Adify and AdBrite all enable mid-campaign customization by pausing, changing and trafficking creatives at any given time.

first page of search results which, with many thousands of search results appearing for any given search term, is a tough task. As Google receives the lion's share of all search queries, I shall focus on optimizing your site for that search engine.

SEO (search engine optimization)

Google's mission is to organize the world's information and make it universally accessible and useful. It also wants satisfied customers. To tick both boxes Google needs to ensure that the results it displays to you when you search for something are high quality and relevant. In order to fulfil this objective, Google makes roughly 500 changes to their ranking algorithms each year. So, good SEO involves optimizing your site to achieve and maintain good rankings while minimizing the impact of inevitable regular changes to Google's ranking algorithms. To do this you need to know the key durable determining factors that search engines use to rank pages, which have stood the test of time.

These cardinal cornerstones are the *relevance* (by examining text, headlines, titles, page descriptions) and *importance* of your pages (by examining authority of those pages via the number of quality links which act as votes for credibility). As such you can optimize your site's ranking by paying attention to the following four elements.

1. Keyword selection and research

Consider the words and terms that users type into search engines to find your web pages and related content. Then ensure that your site actually includes those words within its pages, in your URLs, page titles, meta tags, H1s (main headlines), blog post titles, video/image captions and breadcrumb/sectional navigation, so that keyword and page content is accurately reflected. Your <title> tag is the <title> page title of document</title> inserted in the back-end 'head' section of your site by your developers which shows up as the 70- character blue title heading in search results and as default text for bookmarks. Ensure it is descriptive, relevant and accurate. Don't stuff a title tag or tag cloud with keywords, just make them a clear reflection of the linked page that they lead to.

2. Technical accuracy

Ensure that search engines can easily crawl your pages. For instance, use Google Webmaster Tools (GWT) to identify any 404 errors (these appear if a page is no longer available or the link pointing to the page is wrong) and habitually 301redirect those URLs to a working web page that is the most relevant.

Submit your sitemap to Google, Google News Index and submit a mobile sitemap for your mobile site too. Ensure your site is browser and device compatible and fast-loading and abides by Google's technical specifications as presented on Google's webmaster pages.

3. On page optimization (content authority and quality)

Google only wants to direct users of its search engine and news site to websites which are trustworthy with a good reputation in their own field of content. So it signals the authority of your content via the PageRank it has assigned to your web pages and via social media authority (how often your content has been shared). The best ways to become seen as a trusted recognized source and authority in your content category are to:

- Create unique, authentic, fresh, quality content which is first published on your site (as opposed to duplicate content) and gains citations and inbound links from other reputable, authoritative sites. Content that is linked to is perceived by search engines as having more authority than content that is not.
- Break news stories where possible. Being first gives you a window of time to be indexed before competitors.
- Minimize the amount of duplicate or quoted material. Focus instead on providing fresh insight.
- Maximize your CTR (click through rate) by writing compelling, relevant and enticing headlines.
- Minimize bounce rates and maximize user dwell time by making sure that content is user-driven and delivers on promises it gives in its title and description. Ensure content is interesting, useful and engaging. Write content for your users not for search engines and deliver a diverse range of content across multiple formats.
- Encourage your users to comment, post reviews and share feedback on your content.

Crucially, in following these golden rules you will not only please search engines, you will also please visitors and create a positive loop. In a nutshell, the better your content, the better your click-through rates, and lower your bounce rates will be; the more links and citations you will gain and the higher dwell time and social sharing you will encourage. The consequence will be happier (returning) visitors and a higher perceived authority and thus ranking in Google.

4. Off-page optimization (in-bound links)

If you create a usable, useful site with great content as outlined here, you will naturally find other sites pointing towards yours. TrustedReviews.com would send award logos and link details to recipients of awards (product manufacturers) to encourage them to link to the award-winning reviews. 'We looked at as many ways as possible of trying to get people to point to us', says founder, Hugh Chappell. While this is still a worthy and creative way to generate links, it's easier to generate in-bound links nowadays.

To Google, a good number of inbound quality links pointing to your site signals that your site is relevant, authoritative and trustworthy. The volume and velocity of social shares are also vital so, to generate as many high quality links to your site as possible, as well as making your content of good enough quality to reference and share, you should:

- Make your social sharing buttons clearly visible on your web pages.
- Submit and syndicate content for use on other high traffic sites in exchange for a link back to yours.
- Register your site on targeted directories.
- Request reciprocal links from targeted niche sites.
- Post comments with links back to your site on relevant forums and user news sections.
- Create linked content on social sites such as Digg.com, Hubpages.com and Squidoo.com.
- Establish who is linking to your competitors. Do this by using a backlink analysis tool such as Open Site Explorer on the highest-ranked sites for your best keywords.
- Make your links a keyword-rich title to drive in more traffic.
- Use social search properties such as Google Hotpot, the recommendation element of Google Places. This enables users to rate, recommend and review your business and connect a user's search with those comments.

Localization: Local listings

Search engine results used to consist merely of a list of the top most relevant sites. This progressed to universal search which included news listings, video listings, shopping, images and book listings. Now local listings (Google Places) have also been integrated and are now prominently placed at the top of results alongside a Google map of the location. In order to rank highly in local listings, you need to add location information to your web pages and generate a good number of consistent citations of your business name and physical address elsewhere on the web. So, just as link popularity determines PageRank, address popularity determines your 'local rank'. Also aim to generate a significant volume of reviews on sites such as Google's Hotpot and specify a service area in Google Places. Try offering discounts through the offer coupons on Google Places to drive in more local traffic too, and make sure you claim your location on sites such as Foursquare, Facebook Places, Bing Local, Yahoo Local and Twitter, via its location support.

Top Tips for Optimizing your Website for Search Engines

1. **Be patient.** It can take from a few weeks to a couple of months before your page is initially indexed and, if you make SEO changes, to see ranking results. Gradually and patiently build upon a solid foundation.
2. **Be persistent.** Do something daily to optimize your site, whether that's publishing a new piece of content, registering on a directory or requesting a reciprocal link.
3. **Use third-party tools to improve your SEO activities.** Try Google's Traffic Estimator and Google Insights to compare popularity of specific search terms so you can determine which are best. Also try SEOmoz and Advanced Web Ranking to track changes in your search ranking positions, plus Website Grader and SEOAnalyzer.co.uk to review your ranking.

Exercise

Write a marketing plan

1. **Base your activities on your marketing cycle position and objectives**, e.g.
   - Phase one: Launch
   - Objective: To capture user details and attract interest and leads
   - Methods: Promote prize draw, submit press release, write blog post, create targeted display ad campaign, submit site to search engines.
2. **Task yourself with doing three things each day to market your website** based on your objectives and marketing cycle position; whether that's to e-mail or SMS your opt-in list, contact a blogger about featuring as a guest expert or getting a batch of promotional t-shirts printed featuring a scannable QRcode via QRstuff.com.

The only marketing method to be omitted from this chapter is Social Media which shall be covered in detail in Step 11.Notably, once you have tried a variety of marketing methodologies, you will be able to measure results to determine which audience segments, marketing messages and channels are the most productive.

The 80/20 rule states that you tend to get 80% of your business from 20% of your customers. As such, the rule of thumb is to try to replicate the 20% of customers that you generate 80% of your business from, as they are the ones bringing you the most profit and revenue. In order to evaluate the type of customers converting the most (where they are from, as well as demographic and psychographic information) and grasp which marketing channels and methods are converting the best, (so you can roll out and achieve the best return on your marketing spend) you need to analyze your data, measure your metrics and make necessary changes to your site and campaigns accordingly.

Step Ten

Measure and Improve your Marketing and Website Performance

'The most valuable thing you have to tell you what to do in your business is the information that you have about your customers' behaviour.'
Nick Jenkins, Moonpig.com

Regardless of how many people visit your website, they need to be the right people, i.e. people who are most likely to need and want whatever you are offering and are therefore most likely to spend their hard-earned cash on your goods or services. Think quality over quantity. With so much of a marketing campaign's success reliant on getting your messages in front of those 'right people' (and in the right places at the right time), it surely follows that you should know who is visiting your website, why they are there, and where they are coming from.

Additionally, to really maximize performance, you should know how many of those people convert into customers; how many of them revisit the site; how long they are staying around; which pages they are landing on (and converting from) the most; and which search terms are they using to reach your pages.

Once you know who your visitors are, and what their behaviour is, and your website's most viable pathways are crystallized, you can apply what you have learned to tweak your website and your marketing strategies accordingly.

By the end of this chapter you will know how best to:

- **Analyze your website traffic; understand what to assess and how to use the tracked activity to your advantage.**

- **Monitor marketing performance to determine which of your marketing efforts are working and roll-out to maximize them fully.**

- **Monitor website performance and tweak your pages based on your analysis, testing and feedback.**

- **Improve your marketing ROI and website conversion rates on a continual basis.**

The 'right people' (i.e. those most likely to convert into customers) are 'hunters' or 'trackers' who know precisely what they want; whether that is the exact solution to their problem or the exact make and model of product, as opposed to unqualified browsers or those who are searching using loosely associated generic terms.

Thanks to the evolution of marketing towards metrics, analysis and evaluation, you can now pinpoint the terms people are using to find you, and even adjust specific content and offers tailored to suit individual visitor's browsing habits, dependent on their geographical location (such as informing overseas customers that you are currently offering international shipping discount), which marketing channel they came from and their browsing history. Indeed, by paying attention to an anonymous user's browsing history – what they search for, click on and buy – you can tailor what you put in front of them. For example, if they prefer a certain brand of running shoe, that's what you can lead them to.

'Digital advertising is very powerful. When done correctly it allows you to track the sale of your product or service to the individual ad served. You can track where they saw it, when they saw it and how often they saw your ad before making a purchase. The science of successful digital advertising is all about continued optimization.'

Seb Bishop, co-founder of eSpotting.com

The Evolution of Marketing

Once upon a time the impact of marketing and advertising was not instant. You'd see an advert or marketing message on screen or in print and would have to remember next time you were going to buy that particular type of product to buy the brand you'd seen advertised. Today, you see or hear, you click (or hit the 'red button') and you buy.

In those days, to make any kind of impact you needed to focus primarily on the big creative idea. Placement was more of an afterthought. But, as metrics and the ability to track your customers' journey and behavioural habits came to the fore, big ideas and blockbuster ads were superseded by placement and metric-driven campaigns. These days though, with increasing competition, marketing has evolved further and come full circle to create an equilibrium between creativity and analytics; a balance between the idea and the output.

Consequently, companies struggling to achieve high search engine listings due to the crowded marketplace in which they operate are now running search campaigns with a big idea associated with them.

Measured Creativity: The Meerkat Way

As an insurance comparison provider facing high cost-per-click (CPC) and cost-per-acquisition (CPA) rates, CompareTheMarket.com needed a high impact idea and brand to separate it from the crowd and give it ownership of a keyword category. BISL Limited, the relatively small company behind the campaign, wanted a dual-pronged approach: a viral promotion that would create a buzz on social networks, plus clever use of keywords to gain and sustain strong search engine visibility. They hired VCCP advertising agency and created a clever TV ad which had high viral impact across social networks and gained keyword category ownership in the process.

According to recent research by Internet marketing tools and software provider, WordStream, the most expensive English-language keyword fetching the highest CPC in Google AdWords Solutions is the word 'insurance', which can cost as much as £34 per click. In fact, the word 'insurance' topped their list of the 10,000 most expensive keywords, followed by 'loans', 'mortgage' and 'credit'.

(Continued)

If it takes 10 clicks to sell an insurance product at £34 CPC the CPA would be £340. However, by creating the 'comparethemeerkat' campaign, BISL were able to bid on the inexpensive word 'meerkat' without competition from other credit card or insurance comparison companies.

The result was a dramatic reduction in both CPC and CPA and a consequential dramatic increase in profit and ROI.

Admittedly, now competitors are bidding on this search term, but BISL were able to own the category and generate additional viral impact as a result of this campaign which had a strong balance between a big idea and the use of metrics. The charming meerkat mascot of the campaign, Aleksandr Orlov has over 780,000 fans on Facebook and almost 50,000 Twitter followers. He's even launched a 'meerchat' podcast which features him being interviewed by Piers Morgan and there are now a range of Aleksandr soft toys and associated merchandise. That's a lot of exposure for a lot less than mainstream channels would have cost. By tightly integrating the marketing channels of the ad and YouTube video with the website, blog and social networking profiles and by keeping their message, theme and brand consistent and freshly updated, the insurance comparison company has harnessed the power of every marketing channel available to them. The success of the campaign has also led to some positive PR – everyone's talking about CompareTheMarket/CompareTheMeerkat . . . even me. I've just dedicated a page to them.

Whatever way you look at it, this is a campaign that worked on every level and balanced creativity with analytics.

Exercise

Get creative

Brainstorm ways in which to find ambassadors for your brand – human, animal or celebrity ;-) In 2011, the Comparethemeerkat campaign added a new viral campaign – to find a human ambassador to promote its brand via social media and at sporting and music events (basically recruiting a student and paying him £40k to promote the brand on their behalf, while making a campaign about the recruitment process itself). The winner, Josh Mitchell, beat 1500 other applicants by creating a digital campaign including a website and YouTube videos to win the role, which garnered support from Davina McCall and Sara Cox.

Research online to find ways that big brands have created a buzz for their products. Get inspired. Similar campaigns have included Green & Blacks recruitment of a Taste Assistant, and Kleenex's Facebook campaign for friends to send real and virtual packs of tissues to each other.

Brainstorm ways in which you can tie in your big idea with keywords or search terms which have a low CPC rate.

Monitoring Marketing Performance: Accountability of Expenditure and Results

With such hyper competition in the digital space, it is certainly critical to have a firm grasp of your marketing and sales results, as well as the journeys that your customers take when they buy from you. Today's marketers must know which marketing methods and customer segments generate the best response, the best return on investment (ROI) and the lowest cost per acquisition (CPA), i.e. in addition to knowing the long-term value of a customer and maximizing that value, marketers need to know what it costs to acquire a customer in the first place. Thankfully, digital companies now have the tools to gather all of that information and use it to their advantage.

Paid search, for example, lets you know that if you sell one product for every 10 clicks and you are paying £1 per click, then your CPA is £10.

The accompanying web analytics means that you can now unravel a whole host of additional data to discover where on the Internet your best quality customers are coming from and view the journey they take from arriving on your home page to converting or exiting. Through online registration, you can also collect data to build a more rounded picture about who your customers are demographically and psychographically.

But, perhaps most importantly, based on the metrics of CPA and ROI, you can determine which marketing activities and sales channels are working the best and are the most cost effective at any given time, then roll them out, thus minimizing your CPA and maximizing your ROI: a marketer's dream! You can also fine tune and tweak those activities and channels that have failed to measure up to improve their impact too.

'Every marketing activity we've ever done, we've measured in terms of the cost per customer acquisition', says Nick Jenkins, founder of Moonpig.com. 'Our business is based on two things: what it costs us to acquire a customer and what a customer is worth to us over time. We've been very good at measuring both of those metrics, so every marketing activity we've ever tried to date we've measured on a basis of whether it's an affordable cost of customer acquisition. Once we find something that gives us a decent CPA, we keep spending money on it until the cost of customer acquisition rises and is no longer viable.'

Exercise

Evaluate your marketing methods and ROI

The means to measure marketing performance are many. While measuring brand awareness can be a somewhat ambiguous metric, direct response lead generation and other objectives are easier to measure. Finding out how successful specific marketing campaigns have been via hard data means that you can now determine the link between your marketing investment and the results they achieve, i.e. your return on investment (ROI)

Web traffic

- How many people are visiting your site?
- Where are they coming from? Are they a direct source (arriving on your site by typing your web address directly into the address bar), via referral (via inbound links from other sites) or via the search engines?
- What percentage of visits come from which marketing channel/campaign?
- What percentage of visitors are new and what percentage are returning? (While a high percentage of new visitors means that some marketing activity is working, it may also mean that visitors are not loyal and, if bounce rate is also high, it could mean that your site isn't good enough to persuade visitors to return.)
- Which day of the week gets the most traffic/conversions? If this is consistently the same regardless of when you have marketed, this is the day you should spend actively marketing and distributing your campaigns.

Response and conversion rates

- What are your conversion goals? To increase net sales billed (NSB), mailing list or RSS subscriptions, user sign-ups, number of leads, or other specific user interactions, such as arriving on your site via a Facebook post to view a promotional offer?
- How many times are these conversion goal actions being completed?
- What is your current baseline, i.e. how many user sign-ups or sales are you generating now, from which sources? Your aim is to measure results against that baseline from the moment you begin your marketing activity. And, when setting specific user interactions as goals, to track how many people follow the paths you specify.

You should then track:

- What results are you gaining *above* that baseline?
- What percentage of those response/conversion goals come from which marketing channel/campaign?
- What percentage of your overall marketing efforts (in terms of time and budget) do you spend on each channel?

If you are generating 25% of your traffic from a channel that you only spend 10% of your time/budget on, bingo! But if you are generating 10% of your traffic from a campaign you've spent 50% of your time/budget on, it's time to call it a day on that particular medium or make changes to improve results.

As well as tracking conversion goals, such as how many sign-ups or blog comments you have had this month compared to three months ago, you should also measure the length of your sales cycle, value of each lead, retention period and how many new customers have been referred by another customer. All of this will help you define the quality of each lead. Cross-check how you secured those best quality leads and then focus on marketing to more of those 'right people, in the right places at the right time.'

Once data is collated and the level of success for each message, target sector, media channel and method is known, you can assess which combinations achieved the best results, tweak areas that need improving and roll out with the best marketing mix to maximize response.

Monitoring Website Performance: Using Analytics, Tests and Feedback to Improve Results

'People often think they'll get someone to develop a website and carry on using that forever, but actually it's not like a piece of equipment; you're constantly changing it, working with it; manipulating it, squeezing it, adapting it', says Nick Jenkins, founder of Moonpig.com. 'It's a work in progress.'

Certainly, to produce optimum results and response rates, you need continually to monitor and measure, test and analyze, tweak and improve your website and its performance.

As well as uncovering areas of frustration and sticking points that can be ironed out during the testing process, you might find that changing the colour of a button, the call-to-action of a message, the positioning of a privacy assurance, the layout of a form or the design of product page, may greatly impact your conversion rates. As such, testing, checking and improving various elements of your site to ensure an optimum visitor journey and experience can pay remarkable dividends.

Indeed, testing and tweaking sites based on user analysis and site testing is something that all of the digital business leaders featured in this book adhere to. Knowledge is power in every applicable way. The more you know about how your website visitors react to certain messages, pieces of content, buttons, design elements, and so on, the better placed you are to make informed decisions about improving every variable to maximize results.

Whether your goal is to improve the user experience, make the site easier to navigate, increase conversions or, as is the case with MySingleFriend.com, to make the site more scalable before launching overseas, your website should be organic and changing.

'Our websites are constantly evolving all the time', says Sarah Beeny. 'There's rarely a day that goes by when we don't find a new way of doing something or think of something new to add. I think it's important not to confuse your users, but at the same time content does need updating and things need to be kept fresh to really thrive.'

Ex-MD of Play.com, Stuart Rowe agrees. 'We were constantly testing things. We used multi-layering testing to check if we get better results out of certain areas within the page.'

Moo.com has also focused a lot of effort on understanding the site's user base and how they behave on the website with a combination of hard and soft data; a mixture of face-to-face qualitative user research and quantitative data research using Google analytics.

'We've brought customers into the office and watched how they've used the site, we've done ethnographic research in customers homes in the US and the UK, and we've done quantitative research on the actual website itself, looking at the conversion flow and the funnel analysis', explains founder of Moo.com, Richard Moross.

Testing, testing . . .

'Test everything.

It's amazing how small changes have a much bigger impact than you would think possible.'

Rowan Gormley, NakedWines.com

Exercise

Use split (A/B) testing

1. Write down elements that you intend to test and why, i.e. your testing goals. For example, if your goal is to increase conversions/sales, you may wish to change the colour of a button from orange to green or change the position of that button and test results. Alternatively, if your goal is to increase your number of subscribers, you might opt to test positioning of privacy policy, form length, field character length, number of fields to fill out, subscription offers, calls to action, headlines, text position, subscribe button position, and so on. However, you should only test one variable at a time.

2. Create two page layouts each displaying opposing versions of the bits you wish to test. One is page A, the other is page B. Randomly display the two versions to site visitors over a two week period to discover which generates the best results. (Don't rush testing as results may change over time.)
3. Evaluate the performance of each changeable variable and collect data to see which is the most popular. You can use tools such as Crazy Egg or Google Website Optimizer to test changes.
4. Alternatively watch what users do via user testing. Invite five friends or, if you can afford one, pay a user focus group of likely users to look at site (A) and site (B). Ask them to perform a series of specific tasks, such as 'buy a present for your dad', or 'find this item'. Stand and watch them. Track what they look at, what they click on, what they do and how they interact with different versions of the site.

The team at iwantoneofthose.com did this with interesting results which they simply wouldn't have discovered had they not sat and watched people use their site. They asked users to find a new section which was clearly displayed within a menu and had a text link and a large banner pointing to it. However, the users couldn't find the section. 'We learned that people have colour blind spots and geographical blind spots (in terms of the map of the site)', says Tim Booth, the site's co-founder.

'Watching what your customers do will tell you the most about what you should be doing with your site.'

Richard Moross, Moo.com

Website Analytics: Secure All Exits

In addition to testing different variables and witnessing user reactions and inter-actions with your site (by watching them in person and through your raw log file analysis), you should also add goals to your analytics package, not only to track goal completion to see how many users are signing up and using your contact form or making a payment; but also to reveal tellingly when visitors have tried to make a purchase but have failed, have dropped out of the shopping cart process altogether, or have arrived on your contact page but haven't actually contacted you.

The vital part here is not merely to tick boxes and reach conversion goals, but to fix issues that are leading to *failed* actions and drop outs. Reject rates are as important as conversion rates, especially on contact and product pages.

'Watch the flow from page to page, watch drop off points and optimize that', advises Brent.Hoberman. 'It takes a lot of refinement, a lot of following what users are actually doing and path analysis.'

Ultimately, analytics involves following the journey that your users go on from the moment they arrive on your website to the moment they leave and then implementing changes and optimizing the site to ensure they are a) guided to the right places and b) taking a desired action before they leave.

'We have a drop off chart', explains Nick Jenkins of Moonpig.com. 'So we look at all of the stages of the website, make a change, do AB testing to see which changes made the drop off better or worse in order to make the end result better or worse [so the user completes the transaction].'

Certainly one of the most significant parts of customer behaviour worth interrogating is known as the 'drop off' or 'drop out' point, i.e. the point at which a user abandons the shopping cart process without completing a sale. When you've spent so many of your resources attracting visitors and encouraging them to place something in their shopping basket, the last thing you want is for them to change their minds, abandon cart and leave with an empty basket.

As such, it is vital to interrogate your site logs to uncover the reason for this hasty exit and amend your pages urgently.

Areas of frustration might involve doing something the visitor doesn't anticipate, such as adding a VAT or delivery charge that they weren't expecting once they've placed an item in the shopping basket, or asking for too much personal information along the way.

As well as fixing areas of frustration that you find when testing your site, you can take preventative measures by adding content that should reduce the number of drop-offs. Take Moo.com, their 'Moo Promise' and FAQs are included on the right hand side of their web pages throughout the entire buying process, every step of the way, from the moment you place something in your cart. This is a nice touch to answer any questions and deal with any objections that customers might have which might ordinarily cause them to drop out, such as 'Can I get rush printing on my order? What happens if I'm not at home? Can I still make changes to my order? What happens next?'

Avoiding Empty Basket Exits: In-Depth Log File Analysis and Site Amendments

The team at Anythinglefthanded.co.uk carefully monitor the site to check if people are dropping their basket at a certain point and aren't going through the checkout.

'We'll then have a closer look at the pages they are dropping out from and the copy on those pages to ensure that the guarantee and credit card security are being boosted to give visitors that confidence to checkout.'

'We know how the site works intricately', adds Keith.

Indeed, having run the site since 1999, this in-depth knowledge and focus on monitoring the site is one of the site's secrets of success.

'Our average visitor sees seven pages on our site before leaving, and spends around 10 minutes on our site, and with our messages and the way we layout our information, we deliberately try to push people on to the next page to make them see more', says Keith.

'We look very carefully at our site logs each month, to see which pages people are visiting, dropping-out and exiting from, and then we'll look at content on exit pages to see if there's a broken link, or a graphic hasn't loaded properly, or whether something on that page is putting people off. We then fix it and push them on further.'

Exercise

Monitor your website performance

1. **Are your web pages doing their job properly?** Which web pages are visitors viewing? Are they visiting the pages that generate sales? Are they clicking onto the pages that are meant to stimulate their interest in taking action?

   If they aren't visiting those pages, your homepage is failing to lead the user along the right path and needs urgent attention. Perhaps your navigation is not intuitive enough, your content not compelling enough, your calls to action not specific enough?

   If they *are* visiting those pages, your home page may be working. But dig deeper; are they then taking the desired action and converting from browsers into buyers? If not, you may need to amend your product page copy, update a call-to-action link, remove fields from a contact form, add a better image or more competitive special offer. And how do you know which of these changes to make? Test them all to see which works the best.

2. **Assess which search terms and keywords visitors are using to drive them to your site.** Also examine the search terms they input into your own internal site search engines. Uncover what people are looking for and reveal their motivations for paying you a visit. Then give them whatever it is they are seeking.

   'If you're using a reasonably decent internal search engine and you can see what's being searched for on your site, it isn't going to be the latest product that you love the most and place with a huge image on the home page, it's going to be something obscure', smiles Tim Booth co-founder of iwantone-ofthose.com.

   'It might even be something old and you need to be able to react to that instantly. So you might suddenly see people searching for something because they've seen an article or it's been featured on a TV programme . . . you should then react and get that product on the home page even if it is old. Give people what they want.'

(Continued)

3. **What is your site bounce rate?** If it's higher than 65%, people are landing on one page and bouncing straight back to where they came from. Evaluate the search terms that visitors are using to find your site as these will reveal if they are the 'right' people looking for what you can provide.

   If they aren't the right people, then you need to tweak your marketing activity to attract the right clientele.

   If they are the right people, then you need to address why they're not delving any deeper (is it slow page load speed? Lack of relevant content perhaps?)Then fine tune the pages they are bouncing from to reduce bounce rate and test.

4. **Examine the most popular pages and least popular pages in terms of dwell time.** Where do visitors spend the most time? Which pages generate the best response and the worst response? How many page views are there per average visitor? What pathways are visitors taking? What is the general page to page flow? All of this data will reveal which pages need correction and which pages need attention in terms of optimizing their popularity to maximize conversions. For example, you might improve the sub-categories underneath your most popular pages to better define your users' search, enhance their choices, and save them time by making it even easier to find what they are looking for by putting exactly what they want in front of them.

   Evidently, it's not all about the home page anymore. As Brent Hoberman rightly says, 'For lots of sites now the home page is kind of irrelevant. People are getting their traffic by deep linking, deep searching, and via social media communication strategies so it's important to look at where the traffic on your website is going and not spend 90% of your effort on a home page that might only be receiving 5% of your traffic.'

5. **Interrogate user session files to monitor drop off points.** Track empty baskets. Where do people go once they've abandoned a basket? Do they leave the site or click to another page? 'It's important to understand why people are dropping out', advises Moonpig.com's Nick Jenkins. 'Some people are dropping out, not because of the website, but because it's simply the stage of browsing that they're at.' If, however, they are dropping out because of an unexpected request or lack of key information, make the necessary amendments and test changes to minimize basket abandonment.

6. **Examine your content ROI** in terms of how many retweets, @mentions, shares, comments, back links, likes and follows your content is achieving compared to historical content on your site and competing sites. How do the number of tweets about your brand/specific content compare in October to June? These measurements will reveal whether the resonance and relevance of your content is growing, declining or static and whether you are building trust and advocacy in your brand on which to build conversions and monetize, now and in the future.

Using Customer Feedback: Listen Up

As well as using behind-the-scenes methods of assessing customer behaviour covertly and watching their every move to improve your offering; it's important to watch and listen directly through customer interaction. This can be done by requesting customer feedback, establishing user focus groups and, simply, through engaging in conversation with your visitors. As your enterprise expands your customers' needs become increasingly complex to understand and serve, making customer feedback all the more vital. As illustrated by eBay. Many of the auction site's new services are shaped by feedback of top customers within their Voice of The Customer system.

Ask Your Customers What *They* Want

Parkatmyhouse.com is a great example of a site which really listens to its customers and subsequently continues to differentiate itself.

The site has a feedback form and widget on every page.

One of the most important features that site founder Anthony Eskinazi was able to add to the site very quickly was the ratings and referral tool. This automatically presents users with a brief and optional feedback form whenever they log out of their account. It invites users to provide a rating out of 1–5 in terms of their experience using the site, how it might be improved and whether they'd recommend the site to friends? If so, they are invited to enter their friends' email addresses, plus any other comments they may have.

'At least 20% of our customers give us feedback in that way, 90% of which is very useful', says Anthony.

In fact, one of the website's new value-added features is a direct result of feedback from a customer. Thanks to that customer's suggestion, when a booking is confirmed, the user receives an e-mail to print out and position in their windscreen to act as a parking permit.

'You get no better return on investment than constantly adding and improving things', advises Anthony.

'If you don't listen to customers as a permanent state of affairs then you're not going to be in a good place where your customers have total confidence in you.'

Martha Lane Fox

It's important to respond quickly to feedback and, where possible, add in features as soon as they are requested. (This is where having your own in-house development can be advantageous.)

'We listen to feedback and usually publish answers to FAQs on the website before trying to find a solution', says Sarah Beeny of MySingleFriend.com and Tepilo.com. It's also wise to add modifications in a piecemeal format. 'We tweak Kiddicare.com most months', says CEO, Scott Weavers-Wright, who aims to make the customer experience easier and quicker with each site release, 'but we tend not to do a major design change as that's not commercial and upsets customers who are used to it as it is.'

Tell Your Customers What *You* Want

As the whole business model of NakedWines.com is focused on the customer, it made sense to set up a Naked Innovations group to ask customers continually for ideas about what works and what doesn't, and the kind of functionality they would like to see on the site. Customers also provide feedback on the wines themselves.

However, the team decided they should try to establish some kind of quality control on that feedback. They initially thought, 'if you open up feedback to all users when you have 50,000 or more users, you need to figure out which ones to listen to, which ones speak the most sense and which ones add the most value.' This led to lengthy process based on ranking users dependent on their Facebook popularity or how many followers they had or how many posts they'd made.

Finally, the team decided to simply tell their customers what their objective was.

'Eventually we said to our customers, "look, what we're wanting is for you to help each other; if you think a wine is good tell people, if you think a wine is bad, tell people that too. If someone's got a question about how the site works, help them. One customer suggested that we just ask, next to each post, "was this useful, yes or no?"' explains Rowan.

As soon as the team implemented that customer suggestion the decent customers who liked helping others came to the top of the pile and the quality control of customer feedback filtered itself.

'It's something that I'd never have thought of in a million years but, by asking customers, we got the answer and it has worked.'

Listen, Learn, Improve, Repeat

As a digital enterprise, with the competition constantly clipping at your heels, you have to keep on improving your website and offering just to stay ahead. Over the past 15 years, the digital businesses which Martha Lane Fox and Brent Hoberman have been involved in have made continuous improvement a focal point.

On Lastminute.com changes or new functions were added as a direct result of listening to customer feedback including the addition of the Fast Buy function: 'That meant customers were able to put in their details without having to enter them all again and could see packages of flights and hotels together and ratings from other people, and so on', explains Martha.

With MyDeco.com which Brent founded and invited Martha to join, customer feedback is used to improve functionality and usability. 'For example, the 3D room planning tool, we've made that a lot better based on customer feedback about how to make it more intuitive to use', says Brent.

'You have to listen to your customers and make changes all the time', says Martha. 'It's a constant process of iteration. When you're building big sites like Lastminute.com that's the only way that you can proceed to continue to make sure that you're testing things with customers all the time; listening to your customers is so important.'

It's equally important to keep your entire team informed of customer feedback. For example, Lastminute.com kept a daily score card based on an e-mail summary of customer feedback from the website, the numerical net promoter score and feedback on all of the key web pages 'We'd send the anecdotal comments round to our management team and technical teams', explains Brent Hoberman.

Nowadays Brent provides his users with the tools to provide and respond to feedback and his teams with the ability to act fast to remedy situations where necessary. 'On MyDeco.com we have forums where customers can help each other and members of MyDeco and the tech teams will be in the forums listening and seeing the impact of what they've made. And, if they've made a mistake, they can see that very quickly and take some personal pride in fixing it.'

! Top Tips for Testing, Analyzing and Optimizing your Site To Maximize Conversion Rates

1. **Outline the components within your marketing activity that are measurable.** Decide how often you'll measure these and in which format you'll report them. Set conversion goals and measure these against your baseline.
2. **Establish a culture of testing and log-file analysis.** Use A/B testing to test colours, design, layout, offers, icons, fonts, colours and copy on two versions of your site. Use in conjunction with focus-group user testing and customer feedback to combine hard and soft data.
3. **Take a three-pronged approach to making changes to your site.** Make changes based on a) your own site tests (split testing/ user testing), b) direct customer feedback (via forums, comments, postings, e-mails and forms) and c) results (what is actually happening on your website, using analytical tools).

(Continued)

4. **Ask for feedback from your customers.** Provide visitors with ample feedback mechanisms from forums to forms, and make them easy to use.

5. **Listen to all feedback and respond quickly.** Tell users what you hope to achieve and see what they suggest. Also enable other users to rank how useful they have found viewable feedback.

6. **Check results, always.** If you change something make sure that what you've changed is better than what was there before.

7. **Don't rely on one set of statistics.** Neil Brooks, CEO of web development firm, Bluebit.co.uk, advises: 'Use two or three sources where you can. We use Google Analytics on every site we build, but also recommend comparing this against actual log statistics on your hosting plan. Google Analytics is good for trends and pure log stats are good for true numbers.'

8. **Use Google Analytics.** This is a free package which gives you a line of code to place into your web pages in order to track and measure behaviour and goals/results. You might also choose to use Google's Urchin, Webalizer.org, Logaholic.com, or Webtrends, as well as viewing your own site log files provided by your hosting company, and monitor site load speed using PageSpeed and YSlow.

Ultimately, measured marketing is about getting to know every move your customers make and how best to encourage the response you want for them. As well as analyzing data, testing different improvements and listening to your users, you need to engage constantly in conversation with them and keep the dialogue going. If you do that you'll sustain the buzz, create a good reputation and even end up with customers marketing on your behalf.

Step Eleven

Creating a Buzz Using People Power

'A mate saying "this is great, check it out," is far more powerful than any advert.'
Tim Booth, iwantoneofthose. com and The Greenhouse Project

Business today is about connection and conversation; community and collaboration. While traditional online marketing methods and social networks complement each other, it is no longer enough to be found on Google. You need to go where the action is; where the conversations are – on social networks in social media. Not only so you can take part, contribute and be an active participant in relevant dialogue to attract and engage with potential customers, but also so that you can harness the power of the people and have others generate a buzz (and subsequent traffic) on your behalf.

Yet, with more businesses competing for an increasing number of eyeballs, (100 million business contacts on LinkedIn, 500 million Facebook members posting 700 status updates per second and 200 million active global Twitter users generating 65 million daily tweets) it's crucial to get your social media and buzz marketing strategies right.

In this chapter you will therefore learn how to:

■ **use social media to gain visibility and credibility;**

■ **find a hive of high quality influencers most likely to create a positive buzz about you;**

■ **monitor that buzz and manage your reputation accordingly;**

■ **generate social transactions by adding value and strategically collaborating; and**

■ **amaze your customers and empower them to promote your offerings on your behalf.**

Social Networking

Social media and networking is about building relationships via user engagement so that, as Seth Godin famously says in *Permission Marketing*, 'you turn strangers into friends and friends into customers.' To ensure that your foray into social media has maximum impact, you need to go on a journey which will lead you to find among the masses those people with whom you can build the most profitable relationships, who will become your advocates, partners, supporters and evangelists. En route you will engage in many conversations and interact with a wide network of people. Your aim is to get as many of these individuals and communities to know you, respect you and, ultimately, recommend you. These are the fruits of your efforts: collaborations, recommendations and transactions.

As Founder of Ecademy, Penny Power, points out in her book, *Know Me, Like Me, Follow Me*, the end goal isn't merely custom.

'What is critical to remember is that profitable relationships do not have to mean a direct financial transaction', Penny explains. 'They may help you to learn, provide knowledge that you need, tell others about you, partner with you and they may buy from you. All of these results ensure your financial wealth increases. Business is not just about closing a sale with everyone you meet.'

As such, when I refer to 'profitability' below, I mean all transactions that benefit you over the long-term, not just financially.

> *'It is important to have depth in your network. A wide network only reflects your visibility, whereas the depth of your network reflects your credibility.'*
> **Penny Power, founder of Ecademy and author of**
> *Know Me, Like Me*

Your social marketing journey should therefore take you through four key stages:

1. **Visibility.** Broadcasting and sharing your content, knowledge and expertise to a wide network of people in order to gain visibility.
2. **Credibility.** Engaging in conversations and interacting with individuals directly in order to build relationships and gain credibility.
3. **Positivity.** Uncovering the best quality influencers in order to gain a positive buzz.
4. **Profitability.** Collaborating with others by adding value; then referring and receiving opportunities and recommendations in order to gain profitability.

So let's examine each of these key stages one by one.

1. Visibility

Back in the late 1990s Martha Lane Fox and Brent Hoberman became the poster people of the emergent dot com scene. This was partly due to their knack for generating column inches and creating a buzz about their brand in a time precluding blogs, profiles and hashtags; when a tweet was just something a bird did. Their secret was to make themselves as visible as possible.

'We went to every single function we could find, accepted every invitation and talked about our product all the time', recalls Martha. 'It's tiring and can be boring but you have to go through it at every opportunity. That helped get the business out there.'

Today, similarly, you need to be smart about putting yourself where people will find you, rather than expecting people to come to you. Fortunately, the vastness of today's social networks means that you don't have to attend every event, accept every invitation or even follow everyone who follows you. It's important to achieve the right balance. The key is to push yourself out to the most relevant places and get yourself heard.

'Building a destination site is quite different now', says Martha. 'It's not so effective to say "come to our site." The home page (destination) becomes much less important. Clearly, now you have to distribute your deals, your content, how you are as a business, into places where people are. It's that model that's moved from destination site building into syndicating it out.'

So, make yourself visible.

'Success in the modern world depends on the real connections you have.'
Reid Hoffman, Founder and CEO, LinkedIn

Create your footprint

To leave a trail of footprints around the Internet leading back to your business, you need to be everywhere that is relevant and maintain active accounts on all social networks used by your audience; from Facebook, Twitter, Flickr and Foursquare to LinkedIn, YouTube, Delicious and Chatroulette. Additionally seek out industry blogs, review sites and local online communities and make your presence felt.

Reveal your value

Make it clear who you are, what you do and where you are based. Don't hide your individual value behind your job title. For example, on LinkedIn a general search will only provide you with a name, professional headline, number of connections and recommendations. If you say you are CEO of XYZ, unless your brand is well-known, nobody will know what you or your business do. Since changing my own professional headline from 'Ghostwriter/Author' to 'Bestselling Ghostwriter/Author/Business Freelance Writer – helping to bring the book out of people' I have had far more enquiries.

Be yourself and be honest

Inject your brand personality into your content, comments, postings and tweets. For instance, Moo.com's Twitter stream has 30,000 followers. Its first Twitter account, 'Overheardatmoo' started off including funny things that founder, Richard Moross heard people saying around the office, and evolved into interesting links and amusing stuff relevant to their customers that the team found and wanted to share. It's real, it's human and it enables the team's personality to shine.

As well as being true to yourself and the brand personality of your company (rather than pretending to be someone or something you are not) you should also harness the power of social media to be honest and transparent; to reveal what you are about, warts and all without hiding anything. This builds trust.

'In the beginning, it was difficult to build up trust for the brand', says Rowan Gormley, founder of NakedWines.com. 'But our use of blogs and social media means customers can see what others think about the wine and the winemakers. We want to keep everything out in the open, naked.'

Be active

Get your content onto other people's platforms and vice versa. E-mail established relevant blogs with high visibility to suggest you provide a guest post. Comment regularly on other blogs. Additionally, use other people's content on your platforms. Seek out blog postings, photos and tweets that already contain messages you wish to deliver, then retweet them or link to them. In doing so, not only will you save the time having to generate all your own content, you will create external validation and a network connection with the content's author.

Seek and connect

Gather relevant people and companies to connect with. Search for magazines, journalists, bloggers and individuals relevant to your business topics and follow/connect with them. Join relevant targeted groups on LinkedIn and Facebook, then participate actively to connect with members. Invite current and former colleagues to connect and habitually add relevant people you meet professionally within days of meeting them.

Use 'advanced search' functionality to uncover the most relevant people. For example, use search.twitter.com rather than the main screen search. Search for keywords, places, attitudes, dates, people or even anyone talking about your product or your competitors' products within a specific radius of your postcode during the previous week. Also use advanced search on LinkedIn based on what people are 'interested in' to the number of 'years of experience' they have. Use the 'Promoted Tweets and Accounts' function on Twitter to seek out and reach a highly targeted audience.

Research

Do your homework on your potential connections before initiating communication. By building a detailed profile of valued connections, you will be better placed to add value, discuss topics of interest, create a more targeted message and introduce them to well-matched connections by providing the link in the chain.

Make your connections and content count

Think *quality* over *quantity* in terms of connections. While important to broadcast your message far and wide to catch the low-hanging fruit and put in the initial legwork, also be mindful about the quality and relevance of connections. The more people who see your content, the faster your messages will be spread, but only if those people are *relevant*. The long-term impact of a hundred hardcore evangelists will outweigh 50,000 less interested followers. There's little point having thousands of fans if a minor percentage of them are actually participating and interacting while the rest are disinterested and failing to engage.

Think quality over quantity in terms of content too. Every single piece of content you add should evoke some form of reaction and engagement from users; whether that's laughing out loud, provoking a thought, clicking, sharing, liking or buying. So don't merely post random articles and blogs – everyone else does that. Instead establish your expertise as a valued resource and author authority.

To create quality connections who are genuinely interested in your content, ensure that both your audience and content are relevant. Only accept invitations that you deem to be meaningful and only post content that your audience deems to be interactive and engaging.

Do this by analyzing your audience's interactions and uncovering the content that sparks the most debate and interaction. Then post high quality content in the most qualified places you can find and ask users directly, 'do you like this?' and invite them to like, share, and retweet.

Exercise

Aim for quality connections and content to enhance your visibility

1. Which sectors or niche audiences within your overall target market are engaging most within social media platforms? Describe who they are.
2. Where is your audience going? Which social networks are they using and which communities are they a part of?
3. Evaluate the influence metrics that your audience is generating. What content are they interacting with (commenting, retweeting, liking and sharing) the most? What topics and formats are making them tweet and retweet? Blogs about this or photos of that? How can you create content that is equally tweetable and likeable?

---

2. Credibility

Social media is an interactive two-way street. As such it must be viewed in terms of *conversation*. The better quality your relationships are, the more trusted, credible and well-perceived you will be; the more people will introduce you and refer business to you; and the more business you will generate. Make your conversations meaningful to build credibility; interact, don't just broadcast.

Your followers and fans have demonstrated they have a reason to connect with you by clicking the 'Like' or 'Follow' or 'Accept' button. From that moment on, your job is to mobilize them beyond the 'like' by interacting and engaging with them.

Listen and respond to your connections

Needs, trends and opportunities change. In order to stay on top of these and continually know what they are, you must listen. Listening creates insight which, if acted upon, can create outstanding value propositions and propel growth.

Through listening, you learn and can adapt and change details of your offering that need attention, and build upon the bits that you've got right. You have one mouth and two ears for a reason, so aim to listen twice as much as you talk. Practice empathy.

Demonstrate that you are listening by responding promptly to every question, comment, direct message and invitation. Remember, when your connections engage with you, your fan page or twitter handle appears in their feed, so you can multiply the impact of your individual interactions. When you are invited to connect, don't merely click 'accept' and leave it there. Collecting connections means you are saying 'hello' and then ending the conversation. Send personalized messages and reply to connection requests or 'follows'.

Participate actively in conversations

Discussions are the currency of social media. Post in forums and on profiles, comment on blog posts and tweets. Don't just tweet or post updates about your products and services or try to control the conversation, be a part of it instead: join in.

Show an interest in your fans/followers/and prospective customers. Comment on something interesting you find in someone's profile. Seek out some common ground and start a conversation. In order to build and maintain a good rapport with your connections keep your eye on what they're doing. If they achieve something, send your congratulations.

Invite your users to contribute to your content

Look at alternative ways of encouraging contribution, from having focus groups and Q&A sessions in your Google+ 'Hangout' to holding a Twitathon or Twitter Party. For example, Innocent Drinks held a Twitter Party where they invited mums and dads across the land to contribute '140 lunchbox ideas in 140 characters'. They placed the resulting tips into a ten page PDF file, complete with recipes, funny vegetable celebrities (Quince William and Peas Morgan anyone?) and jokes, with just one of those ten pages devoted to their own lunchbox-specific product range. On the back page they thanked all the tweeters. They then linked to the downloadable document from their website, their Facebook page and other social media profiles.

Measure your engagement rate

Don't just make noise; interact. Provide people with methods of engaging in conversation with you and sharing your content with others. Ensure each piece of content includes social bookmark buttons. Then monitor the number of replies, clicks and retweets that your links and content generate. Note down the number of people to whom you are making introductions and passing opportunities, and with whom you are sharing ideas and having dialogue.

3. Positivity

Once you have done the initial legwork of broadcasting to gain visibility, then engaging to gain credibility, focus on targeting specific experts and groups of online influencers (people who have a heavy influence over their peers) within certain relevant niches. Your aim should be to get your products and services into the hands of people who have the most capacity to create a buzz and spread a viral message. To do this you'll need to source the most powerful influencers and connect with them one-to-one in a way that gives them enough confidence in you and your offerings to spread word to their large and powerful networks.

Those people will be well-connected extroverted individuals who have a high social networking potential (SNP). People who have a high SNP are those with a large online social and/or business network who are well-respected by the individuals within their network (and thus have influence over that network). If other people within their network also have high SNPs, the more epidemic the spread of your message is likely to be.

Once you've established your elite hive of influencers with the highest SNP who are deemed by their peers as being 'in the know', you can reveal information for them to spread across the chat rooms they frequent, the blogs they write and the tweets they make. In doing so, they will create an anticipatory positive buzz across multiple social networks.

Choose your 'hive' carefully to build a loyal community.

Exercise

Recruit an elite fleet: A buzzing hive

1. **Identify your influencers.** Seek blog authors, industry experts who frequent traditional media, respected taste-makers, anyone who has built authority and trust within a specific niche who has a genuine interest in your industry and its issues. Look within Facebook communities for active industry experts. Seek out expert quotes in industry publications and on news sites.

2. **Qualify and quantify them.** Make a list of up to ten names and rank them according to depth of their influence, reach and SNP (e.g. how many times their name appears in Google searches; how many followers they have; how many comments their blog postings generate, and so on) plus their impact, resonance and relevance (e.g. their ability to spark conversation on topics relevant to your brand via how frequently they are retweeted, linked to, and so on). View their Klout and Quantcast scores too.

3. **Create a profile on each person.** Outline their background, areas of expertise, shared connections, any topics you share the same opinion on or interests you have in common, and so on. Track their activity and conversations. Make sure you know who they are and what they are talking about.

4. **Get their attention, build a relationship and recruit them into your elite fleet hive via a mini-campaign.** Engage in conversation with your chosen influencers by commenting on their posts, participating in topics they are active in, addressing commonalities. Introduce yourself and connect via LinkedIn, Facebook and Twitter. Listen to their story and connect their story to yours. Send them a free sample or invite them to meet you and tell them you value their opinion. Provide means for them to provide you with feedback. Thank them for their support. Feed them with information that is not available to the general public so they can spark conversation easily among their own networks; make them feel valued, trusted and part of something special.

5. **Create a secondary band of brand ambassadors.** These are people who have already expressed some form of interest in what you offer. Invite them to attend a private screening or viewing or promotional event where you make some kind of exclusive announcement and ask those attending if they'd like to become brand ambassadors in exchange for free products for a specific time period.

4. Profitability

Social networking is about give and take. It's therefore crucial to add value when building relationships online.

Add value: Become the link in the chain

Invest time thinking whether anyone in your network can help another person in your network, then introduce them accordingly. 'Introduce your connections to your connections', says James Potter, TheLinkedInMan.com. 'Invest a little and see how many referrals you get back.'

Give before your receive. What do others need? How can you help? Invest effort in introducing people and providing advice; spend time recommending people you've done business with; you'll engender goodwill and reap the rewards via reciprocal recommendations, customer referrals, business opportunities, introductions to partners and so on.

Assess each social marketing activity in terms of how you are adding value for your users, whether that's by referring business to them, introducing relevant useful connections to them, rewarding or acknowledging them or by providing them with exclusive discounts or freebies.

Collaboration: Aligned alliances

Today we can find synergies, match competencies and create opportunities. Through positive collaborative partnerships we can share insight, audiences and revenues; we can pool resources, share risks and contribute strengths to fast-track success. So seek out companies which complement yours. Focus on sourcing potential partners for you and your connections. Creating an influential coalition of strategic alliances and joining forces with like-minded small businesses is a great way for digital enterprises to gain the competitive edge over larger competitors.

By creating an eco-system based on reciprocal win–win cooperation, you can share the upside of what you can each bring to the table. Collaboration helps aligned companies to fill gaps and work smarter to do things better and faster than the competition; to increase revenue, extend reach, open up new markets, and enhance credibility.

By forging alliances you can maximize opportunities and do so while spreading both risk and costs.

Strategic alliances help businesses to grow. Whether:

1. A partnership (an agreement with an organization – often involving revenue-share or cross-promotional activity).
2. A joint venture (a business established by two or more organizations who work together, share cost and risk and pool skills and technologies in a bid to enter new markets).
3. A licensing relationship (whereby you give other organizations permission to distribute your material by granting them with a license for a fee).
4. A franchising establishment (whereby you give other individuals or organizations permission to use your successful business model by selling them a franchise of your operation for a fee).

NakedWines.com built up brand awareness by partnering with brands which had an affinity with them, such as Amazon, JamieOliver.com, BBC Good Food and First Direct, each of whom have their own wine-loving communities. Although a third of their customers come via referral from their existing customer base, where external marketing sources are concerned, 'partnerships dominate everything', says founder, Rowan Gormley.

'Jamie Oliver kept drinking nice wines in foreign countries and then couldn't buy them when he was back in the UK', explains Rowan. 'A friend who worked there considered what could be done about this, and that's how we ended up doing business. With most of our partners there's a reciprocal element so they're acquiring customers and vice versa.'

When James and I first started ilikemusic.com, we had no marketing budget, so we chose to establish some cross-promotional partnerships. We provided competition prizes to a new digital music channel back in 2003, called Channel U. We shared the same target audience so we provided prizes in exchange for a free advert created by them. The TV channel profited from the premium rate competition entries and we benefited from the free promotion on a TV station that was already getting more than one million viewers a month. Realizing that we had something valuable that other media platforms wanted – content – we also developed promotional partnerships with the likes of Ministry of Sound Radio, Habbo, YouthNet and CNN by providing free content in exchange for promotion. As editor, I would occasionally be asked to provide a round-up of the Brit Awards or Grammy's on CNN, which would deliver a spike in traffic, build credibility and create brand awareness, as did our weekly five minute slot on Ministry of Sound Radio.

Sarah Beeny's Tepilo.com has also partnered with a number of companies. 'We didn't want to expand to flatshares for example, so collaborated with the biggest flatsharing site, Spareroom.co.uk', explains Sarah Beeny. 'Cross promotion to our audiences works very well and we have a good relationship.'

❗ Top Tips for Effective Collaboration

● 1. **Seek out the rope-bridge.** Consider synergies between yourself, those you meet and those you already know. Track down companies that have large reach in the target market that you are seeking to leverage and can act as a bridge to the customers you most desire. Then identify individuals within prospective partner companies who might advocate the proposed relationship. Consider their objectives. What can you offer them in exchange for what they can offer you? How can you complement each other? Will your mutual customer bases be excited by the collaborative proposition? Look for mutual win–win and align your goals.
2. **Invite top customers to matchmake.** They should know you and your objectives well enough to be able to suggest and connect you with potential partners and articulate the mutual gain potential for each party.
3. **Think long-term.** 'Coming up with a plan that works in the long-term and be beneficial for both parties will stand the test of time', says Nick Jenkins. So it's vital to stay focused on developing relationships that create long-term value.
4. **Ensure balance and manage expectations,** particularly if entering into a joint venture to ensure that all parties fairly contribute and mutually commit in terms of resources, assets, finances and skills.

Channel Hopping

The social media channels you choose will depend on what you aim to achieve from your social marketing activity and where your audience goes. Whether you want to crystallize a community, incentivize customer loyalty, or galvanize debate, there is a social media channel out there for you.

However, these are not interchangeable and each requires a different approach.

Business networks do not want to know what you've eaten today or view nostalgic 80s videos so don't link your Twitter and LinkedIn Accounts. As James Potter, theLinkedInMan.com suggests, 'In Twitter it is fine to send a stream of messages every hour or more about all sorts of themes, but in LinkedIn it will make you unpopular quickly.'

Here is a rough guide to each:

Twitter

Twitter is an ideal channel to build direct relationships, connect with customers, answer questions and concerns, say thank you, spark debate and enter into a two-way conversation with individuals. It has a sense of immediacy and, as your 'tweets' are limited to 140 characters, you can keep messages clear and to the point.

Ideal for: conversation, gathering instant feedback, responding quickly to customers, gaining rapid response to quick-fire questions, gaining PR (if you follow relevant editors) and stay informed about journalist requests. Follow @journorequest, for example. Encourage people to follow you by configuring a 'Follow' button on your site. Twitter.com/followbutton.

Blogs

Blogs enable more detailed discussion and reaction than other channels, so you can post success stories, commentary, opinion pieces, photos and news. You can use Tumblr, WordPress or your own platform.

Ideal for: sparking debate, building credibility as an expert in your field, attracting new visitors.

Facebook

Facebook provokes instant feedback to announcements, trials and promotions on Facebook Pages and has more of a community or 'embassy' feel as users are already there, so you can converse at their own convenience rather than expect them to come to you. It also engages users in an experience, by enabling people to connect around experiences or events that they have enjoyed or attended. And, if they haven't participated, they can now be a part of those events, thanks to live photo submissions, checkins, 'likes' and QR codes. Ultimately, Facebook is a relationship management tool.

Furthermore, with Facebook Deals, you can incentivize newcomers with coupons and other promotions and multiply the impact of those promotions as users who like your page broadcast that preference to their entire network. For example, Rob Walker at XCite Digital launched a campaign for Pizza Express to drive user brand engagement, 'The more users who liked the page, the lower the price of pizza. Users were given a discount code after liking the page. This served a number of purposes; to engage with the visitors, to be able to track and market to these visitors and, most importantly, the viral effect of each visitor having liked the page and then showing all of their friends the Pizza Express brand. If you only had 10 users who liked the page, and each user had on average 50 friends, this would be marketing to a multiple of 500.'

Facebook Ads allows you to target a specific, narrow niche of users based on the preferences stated in their profiles; while Facebook Sponsored Stories informs people that their friends liked your page or shows fans that you have posted something new. You can also analyze which content is generating the best engagement by viewing which posts your fans like, how many interact with you and where they are coming from via Facebook's 'insights' section.

Ideal for: building community, testing products, gaining feedback, building brand awareness, creating customer loyalty and sourcing targeted leads.

Foursquare

Foursquare is a location-sharing mobile app which uses the GPS locator of its users' mobile phones to work out a user's location. It then enables people to check-in to venues (including yours), share that check-in with their friends and social media sites, and tells the user what Foursquare venues are in the immediate vicinity. Users can see if friends have checked in near them and get tips on things to do close by.

Foursquare and Gowalla enable you to reward your 'uber-customers' by enabling them to win virtual badges and points for their checking-in activity, making it part social network, part game. The best-known accolade is being 'Mayor' of a venue, i.e. the user who has checked in most times over a 30-day period. For example, on Wednesdays, Domino's Pizza offers the Mayor of each store a free pizza.

Explore ways that you can join the location tagging element of social media from Foursquare and Google Places to Twitter's Local Trends, Loopt and Gowalla.

Ideal for: building community, creating customer loyalty and sourcing targeted leads (if you have an offline traditional bricks-and-mortar location).

LinkedIn

Essentially a B2B social network enabling you to network with professionals within your industry, source talent, partnerships and content providers. As well as adding connections and getting introduced via your connections, there are a variety of tools you can use to leverage your expert profile.

In addition to your own personal profile page, there are Company Pages where you can upload your company profile with product photos and information, endorsements and announcements. There's an enhanced text advertising service to help you reach specific audience segments, plus LinkedIn Signal and LinkedIn Skills, which enable you to search status updates using keywords and measure the frequency of certain skill sets, as well as many other tools being added to aid small businesses.

For example, 'LinkedIn can email you potential, easy to reach clients', says TheLinkedInMan.com James Potter. 'It has an events system, a public Questions and Answers forum, free tools for Microsoft Outlook, Internet Explorer, mobile phones, and many more functions.'

You can also use the Q&A function to understand what the burning issues are within your realm of expertise and showcase your knowledge to build your profile as an expert in your field. By answering questions that other members ask you can demonstrate your acumen on specific topics and get ranked to potentially feature on a leaderboard of the best answers from 'This Week's Top Experts.'

You can also incorporate other applications via its Application Directory, from SlideShare presentations to importing your WordPress blog posts, tweets and MyTravel trip details.

Ideal for: networking and building industry contacts, connecting with industry thought leaders, sourcing collaborative partnerships and fresh talent. Note: if you are seeking advice, join peer groups on LinkedIn. If, conversely, you are seeking custom, join one of the 950,000 groups that your target audience joins instead.

Ecademy

Ecademy is a membership organisation for entrepreneurs and business owners who belong to a community that connects, supports and transacts with one another. You can sign up for free and comment on people's blogs, however if you wish to post your own blog, you'll need to pay a monthly (or annual) subscription to become a 'Power Networker'. This can be effective, particularly if your business provides a service. It certainly worked well for me when I was running my web copywriting and critiquing business, as I would post useful 'how to' blogs, participate in relevant discussions and answer questions on my area of expertise. As a result I received a regular number of enquiries which paid for my monthly subscription many times over. As well as online groups, there are optional regional face-to-face networking groups available to join and attend.

YouTube

As the leading video-sharing website, you can upload, share and view videos on the YouTube platform and effectively 'broadcast yourself'. Ideal if you have product videos, instructional how-to footage or viral marketing video campaigns that you wish to share and promote.

Ideal for: building brand awareness and sharing visual content.

Toolbox

Other social media tools worth checking out include FriendFeed (to aggregate, discover and discuss the interesting stuff your friends find on the web), Social-Median (to aggregate and share news with your social networks), TweetDeck (to enable personal browsing by connecting with your contacts across Twitter, Facebook and other social networks simultaneously), TweetAdder (to help you maintain and manage your Twitter activity), and Socialoomph.com (to provide followers with a direct-message via autoresponder).

Exercise

Create a social media campaign

1. Select the right social media channel(s) to suit your objectives and the preferred channels of your target audience.
2. Create a campaign.
   - Hold a Tweeatathon or Tweetchat by inviting followers to participate in a hot topic debate.
   - Hold a Tweetparty. Invite connections to your themed party and recruit a team of targeted bloggers to tap into their own extensive networks to promote the Tweetparty and get your hashtag to trend; simultaneously alert your Facebook community base, e-mail your opt-in list and submit media releases to traditional outlets.
   - Hold a Twontest, where you encourage your followers to tweet a specific deal-based hashtag and follow a specific promotional account to enter the content and grab the chance to win a prize.
   - Hold a FourSquare Swarm Party. Promote your event on various social networks and get 50 or more people to check in at your venue in order to unlock an elusive swarm badge. Or offer a Foursquare 'special' for people who check-in. To claim a freebie, your customers must show their mobile's Foursquare check-in screen to the cashier.
   - Create an engaging Facebook ad campaign to promote your products to a highly targeted user base. Provide discounts to users in exchange for them 'liking' or 'following' you.
3. Follow up by continuing the conversation with your fans, followers and community.

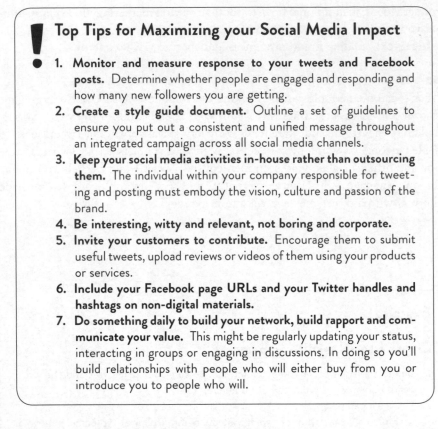

! **Top Tips for Maximizing your Social Media Impact**

● 1. **Monitor and measure response to your tweets and Facebook posts.** Determine whether people are engaged and responding and how many new followers you are getting.
2. **Create a style guide document.** Outline a set of guidelines to ensure you put out a consistent and unified message throughout an integrated campaign across all social media channels.
3. **Keep your social media activities in-house rather than outsourcing them.** The individual within your company responsible for tweeting and posting must embody the vision, culture and passion of the brand.
4. **Be interesting, witty and relevant, not boring and corporate.**
5. **Invite your customers to contribute.** Encourage them to submit useful tweets, upload reviews or videos of them using your products or services.
6. **Include your Facebook page URLs and your Twitter handles and hashtags on non-digital materials.**
7. **Do something daily to build your network, build rapport and communicate your value.** This might be regularly updating your status, interacting in groups or engaging in discussions. In doing so you'll build relationships with people who will either buy from you or introduce you to people who will.

Amaze and Empower Your Customers: Customer Retention and Referral

You can only grow your business if you continually give your customers what they want. Everything comes back to one core critical success factor – customer satisfaction. Or, should I say, 'customer delight' because satisfaction is the very least that customers expect! Delighting customers boosts your revenue, shortens sales cycles, and reduces marketing investment.

> 'It is high time the ideal of success should be replaced with the idea of service.'
>
> **Albert Einstein**

As well as deciding whether to buy what you offer and become a customer in the first place, customers now have the ability to talk about your brand to a large audience. They can paint your brand in a positive or a negative light. They can drive customers to you or away from you. Customers are now more powerful than ever before.

The good news is that great customers can fuel revenue growth. Or, to put it another way, valued customers can create value. Repeat and referred business is the best kind, because it costs you absolutely nothing.

> '*I've yet to find a business where 80% of sales don't come from 20% of customers, so stay focused on that 20%.*'
>
> **Martha Lane Fox**

> '*If you're not doing anything innovative then nobody's going to talk about you, or at least they won't more than once.*'
>
> **Brent Hoberman**

Your best customers can become an incredibly effective extension of your sales force. Testimonials, referrals, reviews and case studies involve customers sharing their *own* experiences; while social shares, likes and follows involve people giving your products or messages the big thumbs up. Those personal recommendations have far more weight and credibility than your own marketing messages or sales spiel ever could.

Ultimately, if you can maintain a cycle of delighting and listening to customers, your business is almost certain to succeed.

To do this you must:

1. Have a fantastic product and value proposition that satisfies customers' unmet needs.
2. Empower and enable your customers to promote your products and services for you.
3. Excel at customer service and satisfaction.

This all ties in with the aforementioned social media journey because, if you do all of these things, you will build Credibility and Positivity, thus enabling you to gain Visibility and Profitability.

1. Have a fantastic product and value proposition that satisfies customers' unmet needs

As I outlined in Step One, you need to have a useful product or service which solves a genuine problem for a specific market in a remarkable way in order to build up a following, generate revenue and succeed in the digital universe. Value begets value. Customers who understand and act on your value proposition will return time and time again and are likely to bring new customers with them. And it's easier for them to do that today, than ever before.

'At the core of every great business is a great product or service', says Richard Moross founder of much-loved Moo.com, which has a 75% NetPromoter rating. 'The best marketing investment we've ever made was hiring great marketing people who know that it all begins with great product, a good service and giving customers a great experience. So we're fanatical about product design, product quality, the experience that customers have on the site, the e-mails we send them, all of the content we generate around the business.'

That fanatical focus on the customer journey has paid off. 'A massive part of our business – 40–50% – is referral and that referral is free. As a result, the customers do a lot of the hard work for us.'

'It's all about the product', concurs Saul Klein, founder of Seedcamp, co-founder of Video Island (which became LoveFilm.com) and partner at Index Ventures which has invested in Moo.com, Last.fm and Tweetdeck. 'You can leverage free marketing channels like social media if your product is great. If your product's no good it's like pushing water up hill; you could be the best marketing person in the world and you'll get nowhere.'

'That's why it's important to build up fans before you spend a penny on marketing. You need a great product that customers love and can't do without that meets a need. That way, either they're going to spend a lot of time on it (a la Facebook and Twitter), or they're going to pay money for it!'

'If you have a good product, it will sell itself', adds Nick Jenkins, founder of online greeting cards retailer Moonpig.com, which brings in 100,000 new customers a month – at least 40,000 of whom come through word of mouth.

'The most important element of our growth [from £3m in 2005 to £38m in 2011] has been the product', says Nick. 'That's been 75% of our growth, because people like the product and they want to spread the word.'

Conversely, if you have an inferior product, you won't generate word-of-mouth and will have to spend vastly increased sums of money on spreading the word yourself.

However, even if your product is superb, you shouldn't rest on your laurels. It's still worth backing up self-selling products by pushing them out there and directly requesting your customers' help to generate repeat and referred business. Send out SMS or e-mail alerts with special offers or pre-order information to generate repeat business. MyDeco.com does this to notify customers when the price drops so they 'never miss another sale' and Play.com does this to enable people to order certain albums early. Establish a referral programme too. Even Facebook suggests that you invite your friends to join.

2. Empower and enable your customers to promote your products and services for you

In today's connected world, people power has never been so effectual. People now have direct access to multiple media platforms. We can all be taste-makers and we can all influence outcomes. Thanks to the Internet, the buzz effect is enabled and can take hold and be spread far more easily than ever before.

Take the phenomenon that saw rock band *Rage Against The Machine* achieve the Christmas Number One spot as a direct result of the grassroots movement on Facebook. After deciding they wanted to stop the X-Factor machine from securing yet another number one single, a couple called Jon and Tracy Morter changed the course of history and broke chart records with the viral power of their group, entitled 'Rage Against The Machine For Christmas No. 1.'

The campaign picked up pace virally and mobilized the general public to take action. A large percentage of the 750,000 people who joined the Facebook group also purchased the alternative single, resulting in a band which had done zero marketing of their own and didn't have a UK single out at that time, reaching Number One during the incredibly competitive Christmas period.

People were also encouraged to donate to the homeless charity, Shelter. The couple who started the viral buzz enjoyed notoriety and, although Sony ended up winning as the label behind both artists, the campaign had worked. The people had exerted their power to get a message across, the people had responded, the people had won.

Community counts

Many companies have wondered why businesses that have 'Freemium' or open-source business models, or no business model at all for the first few years (such as Twitter), are succeeding and being valued so highly. Apart from creating great products and services, one key reason is their ability to build loyal communities of people who spread the word exponentially about what they do without even being asked to.

Facebook founder Mark Zuckerberg understood the capacity of the web as a social rather than purely transactional channel. His aim was always to grow the Facebook community first rather than grow revenue, an objective confirmed by his decision to turn down a billion dollar offer from Yahoo two years after launch and his decision to go open source in 2007. This enabled anyone to create applications for Facebook users and provided a much-improved service for its users. These decisions certainly paid off. The company is now worth an estimated $80 billion (based on private sales of stock), has a community of over 500 million active users, while half of comScore's Global Top 100 websites have integrated with the site.

MySQL, the world's most popular open-source database software company is another people-powered business which grew exponentially due to its focus on community.

'We LOVE users who never pay us money', MySQL CEO, Mårten Mickos told Guy Kawasaki in an interview. 'No marketing could do for us what a passionate MySQL user does when he tells his friends about MySQL. Our success is based on having millions of evangelists around the world. They also help develop the product and fix bugs.'

Proof of customer satisfaction is powerful. 'It makes my day when I hear about someone getting together or married after meeting on Mysinglefriend or having a baby', says Sarah Beeny who has tried everything from press, advertising, radio and SEO to promotions, partnerships, affiliates and social media to generate new and repeat business. 'And on Tepilo.com, selling or letting your own property is pretty satisfying. There's nothing stronger for a website than good testimonials.'

As well as securing testimonials from your happy customers and creating a community of evangelical users, you can go one step further and enable your customers to represent you quite literally.

The Customer as Champion: Recruit your customers to Represent You

Kiddicare.com has taken the social recommendation element further by promoting their customers to become 'customer product champions' in return for loyalty points.

'We are allowing customers to answer other customers' pre-sales questions', explains Scott Weavers-Wright, CEO of Kiddicare.com. 'Something which frightens most retailers.'

'If you bought a car seat and rated it as quite good, we'll invite you to become a product champion/advocate. So if anyone asks questions of Kiddicare on that product in future we'll ask if you wish to provide input, which could be about whether that product can fit into a certain car or whether the cover comes off to wash the fabric.'

This method of marketing builds up additional trust for customers concerned that the retailer might answer questions based on what they think you want to hear in order to make the sale. This method puts the customer in control, to communicate with other potential customers truthfully in a transparent fashion.

'We're brave enough to let that debate go on and we're rewarding people for their involvement', says Scott. 'Rather than traditional loyalty where you checkout and get points like Nectar, we're giving you a content reward. You've helped us out, that then goes onto our forum and the product pages, so you've answered that question, other customers can see that as well, which prevents further similar questions.'

'For a retailer it's quite hard to gain trust. I like to sit in the middle and become a facilitator', says Scott. Five days after delivery, Kiddicare.com sends its customers an open email inviting them to rate the company and the product. 'If you give us a one star review on the product, we publish it, because we shouldn't be selling products that warrant a one star. A consumer who sees just five star reviews will think "that's a lie," a consumer who sees a balance of good and bad reviews will think its real.' This transparency gives Kiddicare the chance to adapt what they supply to constantly improve their offering.

'Our one star reviews also go to the buyers who agree that it's not good enough; you listen to the feedback, modify it and make it better. So, we've got customers driving our buying; driving the business', adds Scott.

Referral preferences

As well as letting your customers drive your business, it's worthwhile letting them drive how you secure referrals from them. Find out how they would prefer to refer people and whether they'd like to be incentivized to do so. That's what Rowan Gormley did at NakedWines.com.

'Every Christmas we send out a gift card for customers to give to a friend. But we don't remunerate our customers for referrals. The majority said they didn't want to be paid to refer because it looks tacky. They want their friends to know that this recommendation is a favour', explains Rowan. Conversely, Amazon dished out cash incentives to both customers and referred friends. While Moo. com has a 'refer-a-friend' programme which enables customers to 'earn MOO Money off their next order'. Each customer is given a unique 'refer a friend' link to share with friends or via social networks and, for every new-to-MOO person who buys from them using that URL, they give the referrer MOO Money off their next order. 'You scratch our back, we'll scratch yours', says the web page which appears after an order has been placed.

Conversely, Moonpig.com doesn't even ask for referrals at all. It simply includes its web address on all products and lets the product do the referring for them: 'We discovered that, if we tell our customers to tell their friends, they're less likely to tell their friends than if we don't, so the answer is, just make a good product and let them get on with it', says Nick Jenkins. 'Often people will happily spontaneously refer others, but they often don't like having it asked of them.'

Clearly it's important to find out whether your audience will happily refer without prompting/incentivizing or needs a nudge.

Exercise

Referred custom is vital for digital survival: Let your customers do the talking

1. **Create a referral plan.** Contact your delighted customers to request referrals, testimonials and case studies in addition to the regular feedback they are hopefully providing you with. Incentivize them or provide them with referral tools, if they have specified a preference for that.
2. **Interview your best customers and build up a story.** What challenges have they faced and how have you helped them to overcome those challenges and solve their problems? What specific benefits and results did they gain as a direct result of being your customer? Hire a writer if necessary.
3. **Post your case studies on your website** and submit to influencers and media. After writing the case study, ask them for referrals. Ask them how you might improve your offering or do more business with them next year. As existing believers in your products, it's worth getting as much as you can from your relationship with them.

3. Excel at customer service and satisfaction

'The principal way to get customers to return is to be absolutely wonderful. Nothing beats customer service.'
Tim Booth, iwantoneofthose.com and The Glasshouse Project

If you make your customer journey an enjoyable one they will come back, with friends. So, as well as making your product outstanding, your customer service should stand out. Go the extra mile for your customers and they'll return the favour. Consider how your customers like to buy from you – from the moment they arrive on your site to the minute their order is delivered – make each touch point a positive one and, on those occasions when you make a mistake or do something wrong, respond with speed.

'Say sorry when you make mistakes, which we've made many', advises Moo. com Founder, Richard Moross. 'We've found that people who've had a positive experience via customer services tend to spend much more money with us and be much more loyal than the people who haven't had a problem to fix.'

Be proactive and pre-emptive as well as reactive by taking a guerrilla type approach to customer service. Search Twitter and other social networks for terms that highlight issues customers might be facing but not telling you about. Look for 'xyz company sucks', and 'xyz product broken' to seek out issues and publicly post a reply using @reply. Support users who haven't even requested support and you'll turn detractors into advocates. Find ways to put your customers at the heart of your operation in as many ways as possible.

Putting the Customer at the Heart of the Business: From Purchase to Delivery

While natural and paid search marketing are significant traffic drivers to Kiddi-care.com (which attracts around 55,000 visitors per day), customer referrals generate the most traffic. Excellent customer service has helped this family business to outshine big corporations and be voted the seventh best website in the UK in *WHICH?* magazine.

'Recommendations are the main driver to the business', says CEO, Scott Weavers-Wright. 'We get 30–40% recommendations from old customers to new customers; that's huge.'

'We have made a huge effort to put the customer at the heart of our whole business, because, in the baby/mum vertical, we can't fail without being slaughtered. You can't upset a pregnant lady or a mum with a toddler on her hip, so it's very important that we get it right first time.'

To do this Kiddicare.com has:

1. Published stock figures. 'We said, "if we were a customer, how would *we* want to buy online?" We'd want to see that we had stock before ordering, so we published our stock figures online at individual skew level. Commercially we only have a 2.2% returns rate across the whole business despite having a 365 day returns policy.'

    Scott doesn't mind if this means his competitors can see his stock movements because, most importantly, his customers can: 'it's about customers not competitors', he says.

2. Minimized mistakes by tackling a main source of problems – order fulfilment. 'We made a large investment in the picking system space so we avoid those "I'm going on holiday tomorrow and you've just delivered a pink pushchair for my little boy," because that's just a whole tragic mess', says Scott.

    For a company shipping 200,000 items per month, only making on average five picking mistakes a month is a worthy achievement. Each of those is investigated by the general manager with a report then sent to the CEO.

3. Developed delivery slots to suit busy parents and put them in control. 'The problem with online is that you order and, in a few days time it'll be dispatched and you'll be asked to wait in all day for it', says Scott. 'Add school runs and all the other issues with pregnancy and babies, and that's just a mess. So we developed a next day delivery option, but that wasn't good enough. So we developed the one hour delivery slot, notifying customers which hour we'd deliver on the morning of delivery and we deliver 98% of our products within that hour. But that's still not good enough. Because what happens if the customer can't make that hour? So we developed the text and e-mail solution with our couriers which contacts the customer on their mobile asking "are you in? We're going to do the 11–12 delivery, if this is unacceptable press number 1 for Thursday, press number 2 for Friday." It's about giving the customer control. It's made a huge impact; it's doubled the business.'

! **Top Tips for Amazing your Customers and Generating Referred and Repeat Custom**

1. **Be brilliant.** Produce great products and services that people want to share.
2. **Stay focused.** Don't lose sight of what customers want, what they really think or why they care. Successful companies sometimes get so wrapped up in doing well that they take the eye off the ball and lose touch with building long-term value for customers. Empathize with the customer and be on their side. Put them at the heart of your business.

(Continued)

3. **Don't edit negative comments.** Keep reviews, star ratings and comments transparent. People see through moderation which only displays positive reviews. A mixture of good and bad reviews creates authenticity which builds trust.

4. **Create a system that amplifies the positive word-of-mouth and generates a buzz.** Don't just send trial products to traditional media, send to civilian media as well; bloggers, high SNP influencers and your community of evangelical customers. As well as providing a compelling product or service that isn't a me-too offering, identify your hive and get your messages to them

5. **Treat people as you'd wish to be treated yourself.** Treat people with respect, take an interest, be honest and keep your promises. Be like a good friend who's fun to have around and doesn't talk about themselves the whole time, so people enjoy hanging out with you and introducing others to you.

6. **Go the extra mile to delight customers by over-delivering and exceeding expectations.** For example, you might phone a customer who has had an operation to check on their recovery and nothing else (no sales pitch or follow up, just to check on how they're doing). You could deliver before deadline or hand write thank-yous on statements or send audio books to delegates travelling to your event. You could provide free goody bags to customers who wanted something that was out of stock. Brainstorm ways to excel in every customer-facing action.

7. **Create a pleasing and positive customer experience through your customer services team.** Don't use scripts; let your team speak with their own voice to ensure that your customer services touch point leaves a good impression. Act fast. Respond quickly. Tell people you are working on a solution or, at the very least, on finding an answer. Answer phones within 30 seconds, empower staff to do whatever they need to do to keep the customer very happy. Create a positive conclusion to any problem or complaint and turn dissatisfaction into loyalty.

8. **Show people that you are listening and that you care.** Join the conversation, even on negative comments and blog posts; just don't get too defensive . . .

Reputation Management and Buzz Monitoring

'We've got a million different ways that we can publicly bad mouth a company and I think it makes companies more honest; it's a good thing.'
Richard Moross, Moo.com

Word spreads very quickly online. Great if that's someone raving about you in a positive way; not so great if the word being spread is a bitter one. Previously, if you stayed in a hotel and had a bad experience you would merely complain to the manager and threaten to tell your tour operator. Not a lot would happen. These days you can tell the manager that you will be posting your comment on TripAdvisor.co.uk, other online travel review sites and on your own social networking networks complaining about your experience. That will have a far greater impact and urge him or her to make positive changes and do things better.

That's because people trust customer feedback. So, just as glowing recommendations are more effective than in-house sales patter, negative comments and ravaging reviews can drive customers away in droves.

Buzz and social has become an important part of the marketing mix because the way people make their buying decisions has changed. We are now far more likely to read restaurant reviews online before we book a table, or read product reviews before we hand over our credit card details to an online store. The power

---

❗ Top Tips for Managing your Reputation

1. **Set up a Google Alert for your company and product names.** You'll then receive an e-mail each time your company and products are mentioned on websites that are within the Google Index.

2. **Use tracking services such as Wikio and eBuzzing.** These services allow you to aggregate all comments being made about your company and its offerings in real-time across all the social networks. They then give you the opportunity to respond to comments accordingly.

3. **Pay a reputation management service.** Just as you might pay a company to get you a high listing on the search engines, you can now pay companies to get listings pushed down. Use these if the press have written an inaccurate or unfair account or have over-exaggerated the scale of a past problem which has long since been dealt with. Services such as Vizibility or Brand Yourself track your reputation and pre-select information you wish to be displayed in search results or create and raise new and existing positive content above negative content.

4. **Create a profile with plenty of content and in-bound links within a site which has negative content about your brand.** The aim is to create a page on that domain which ranks better than the offending page, and knocks the negative article off the Index. Alternatively, create relevant high quality content to push negative content down.

of community and conversation has replaced the power of search and companies. The marketing world has gone full circle as we have become more reliant on recommendations from friends and reviews, just as we were pre-Internet. Today we share what we like and dislike and post freely about our good and bad customer experiences. This gives digital businesses the opportunity to use good feedback as collateral and negative feedback as insight to improve.

So how can you manage your reputation when anyone has the ability to say anything about you (even if it's not true)? You need to take time to gain knowledge about the buzz, i.e. what your customers are saying about you; and you need to use the available tools to act fast and limit any damage caused.

The key is to be aware of how your company is positioned online, what people are saying about you, and which news stories and comments are predominant in search engine listings and blogs.

Some companies have found out the hard way the online impact of dissatisfied customers. Influential blogger Jeff Jarvis created a new verb to describe his dissatisfaction with computer company Dell. Soon 'You got Dell'd' was in use across the world as a way to explain poor customer service. While United Airlines refused to own up to breaking a musician's guitar and suffered the consequences when the musician wrote a song about his experience entitled 'United Breaks Guitars'. The video was subsequently viewed on YouTube over three million times which led to a confession and apology from the company who are now using the video as a customer service training tool.

This merely highlights the importance of giving your customers what they need so that, rather than shouting about how you failed them, they shout about how you delighted them.

To create and sustain a positive buzz and amaze customers, it's important to balance your efforts between product development, feedback monitoring and two-way communication.

To paraphrase blip.tv co-founder, Dina Kaplan, as a business owner you should split your time between getting your 'head down' to focus on creating a remarkable product and excellent customer service and keeping your 'head up' by connecting, conversing and collaborating.

Digital businesses which achieve that balance should enjoy and sustain success. In doing so, you'll hit the big time, by making yourself attractive to bigger businesses as a target ripe for acquisition.

Step Twelve

Selling Up

'All the world's a stage, And all the men and women merely players; They have their exits and their entrances; And one man in his time plays many parts, His acts being seven ages.'
William Shakespeare

A successful exit is the ultimate destination for an entrepreneur. When you implement your exit plan, you are putting in place the final piece of the puzzle, realizing that long-held vision. And therein lies the key to a successful exit strategy – the importance of having a clear vision from the very beginning. Hatching your escape route is part and parcel of setting up a business. As anyone growing a business knows, you need to know exactly where you are headed from the outset in order to arrive.

Yet, surprisingly, despite being one of the biggest financial decisions they are likely to make, not all business owners have the end in mind when they start. Many don't plan their exit until it's too late.

In this chapter, you will learn how to:

- **sell or pass on your business at the right time;**
- **prepare and plan your exit strategy;**
- **groom your business to maximize capital value;**
- **reduce owner dependency and find the right successor; and**
- **sell your business to the right buyer for the right price.**

Of course, not every business is established to be sold; it might be passed on down the family. Indeed, the majority of small businesses never get sold; they just make the owner and his or her employees a good living. However, many business owners, particularly in the digital space, have an exit within their long-term plan and see selling up as their eventual goal.

Hugh Chappell is one such entrepreneur. 'From the very start my plan was to exit', says Hugh who sold TrustedReviews.com in 2007 to Time Warner/IPC Media, and bit-tech.net in 2008 to Dennis Publishing. 'And from day one as part of my research I thought about who I would sell to. I made everyone in the industry aware of my intentions. I told them, "I'm going to build the most successful publication in the sector and one day I'm going to sell it."' And so he did.

If you plan to sell your business at some stage, you have two options. You can either consider who your potential suitors will be and groom the business for exit to suit the strategic needs of those suitors. Or, rather than build a business with exit and potential acquirers in mind, you can build a business with 'sustainability in mind'. If you create a sustainable successful business with a strong brand and a good reputation, you will attract interest anyway; buyers will find you.

Saul Klein, founder of Video Island (which became LoveFilm and was acquired by Amazon) and an investor in many other businesses, from TweetDeck (sold to Twitter) to Last.fm (sold to CBS) prefers the latter approach.

'The only way you ever make a company worthwhile to someone else to want to own is by building a good company that has lots of customers and revenues which grows. And, if you do that, you're almost inevitably going to come across bigger companies in your industry or related industries that are going to be interested in acquiring you', advises Saul.

Certainly, businesses with a high referral rate which customers like to buy from and staff like to work for create attention.

> *'If you're building value people will approach you because you're running in to them in the market, you're outselling them.'*
> **Julie Meyer, founder of FirstTuesday.com and Ariadne Capital**

Whichever approach you pursue – exiting your business can be a difficult process to endure. Legs become heavier as an athlete nears the finishing line and many take a tumble at the final hurdle. Just because you are within touching distance of the final deal – the sale of your business – does not mean that you'll actually reach your destination. It is very easy to fall like the proverbial race horse at the final furlong, especially when you have such strong emotional ties to a business that you have founded and run for many years. It's tough passing 'your baby' over to someone else.

Exit is the final chance to be rewarded for all of your efforts, to bring your vision to fruition, to potentially prosper and earn your fortune. The pressure involved in the final challenge – of maximizing value from the sale of your business, whilst managing a smooth and timely selling process – is therefore ramped up. Selling at the right time to the right buyers to achieve the right price is no easy task. Importantly then, the right external advisors should be on board for this vital final phase; for there is a lot to consider.

Timing: When is the Best Time To Sell?

Timing a sale to maximize value for shareholders and creditors is one part of the challenge. The business must be ready, the marketplace must be hungry and buyers must be buying.

Therefore business owners should:

1. Evaluate market dynamics and conditions.
2. Sell high: on the way up – *before* the peak of a cycle.
3. Consider what is driving the sale of the business.
4. Know when to let go.

1. Evaluate market dynamics and conditions

'Once your business is well established and you feel confident that you've got a good product, customers, and visibility in what your revenue may look like, you can start making sure that you understand the larger context of your industry and the other players within that', advises Saul Klein.

Getting to know what companies in your space are doing and planning to do strategically is important in any case, to enable you to compete effectively.

'For Lovefilm.com, it was important to know what Amazon or NetFlix or Apple or TimeWarner were up to, not because you want to sell the business to them, but because you want to compete with them, and the best way to understand how to compete with them is to understand their business as well as possible', adds Saul.

The knock-on effect of that knowledge is that you can guide your own strategic path to ensure that you create added value as a potential synergistic acquisition target. So, if a big company comes knocking to check you out, Saul suggests that you 'pick their brains as well'.

Exercise

Assess your market position

1. Assess where you are in the economic cycle. This will determine whether it is a buyer or seller's market.
2. Keep your eye on M&A (mergers and acquisitions) activity within your specific sector. Read trade journals and publications, speak to advisors about activity within your industry.
3. Look at what larger competing companies are doing. Get to know them and try to understand their business. Read their public profiles, press releases and annual statements. How you are positioned in the market comparatively to your competitors will determine whether you will be a likely acquisition target.

---

2. Sell high: On the way up – *before* the peak of a cycle

You should ideally aim to sell near the top of a rising market, when a valuation is at an appealing level to generate a decent return, but still leaves enough room for growth.

En Route to the Moon

In July 2011, Moonpig.com merged with PhotoBox for a total transaction value of £120m to create one of Europe's largest personal publishers. The shareholders of Moonpig.com took a combination of cash and shares in the merged company. Founder of Moonpig, Nick Jenkins retains 5% in the combined company and both strong brands will continue to operate separately, leveraging increased scale and their complementary customer bases to deliver growth. Having founded the company in 1999 and taken it from loss making to £3m turnover in 2005, and from £21m in 2009 to £38 million in 2011, Nick knew it was the right time to sell.

'You've got to be at the right point of growth. A buyer is looking for growth', says Nick. 'If you're shrinking nobody is going to buy you. If there's no growth left, nobody will buy you. But if there's too much growth a buyer will not give you the credit. So the timing is based around how much can you grow? Whoever's going to buy it will want to end up with a bigger business than the one you sold them. So you want to catch it at just the right point of the growth curve, so there's still something left for the next guy.'

That's exactly the time when Moonpig.com sold. Having had 90% market share of the online card market for a number of years, traditional card retailers were jumping on the digital bandwagon and competing sites such as Hallmark, Snapfish and FunkyPigeon.com were springing up, the latter being acquired by WHSmiths in 2010. Yet there was still ample room for growth as only 4% of the entire £1bn greeting cards market is fulfilled online.

'Over a period of two years we'd been approached by a lot of people so there was a point when we thought, it's probably the right time to sell and now is the point to call these people back', explains Nick.

PhotoBox operates in 15 European countries so will be able to expand the Moonpig brand and product set overseas to fit with their own growth strategy.

'Finding the right fit was important for me', admits Nick, 'particularly as I was rolling over into the new company. There were a number of deals on the table which I thought would be a bad fit. If you're selling the whole business then there is a point where you might think, for a little bit less money I'd rather it went to a good home. I think PhotoBox is a great home for it, and Moonpig will be the dominant part of the business.'

Selling to a company which can add value, at the right part of the growth curve, is the optimum win–win exit for all parties. It's also vital to have your finger on the pulse of the economic climate and what is going on within your industry in terms of technological advances and competitive threats.

The Bookseller

Judy Piatkus of Piatkus Books had a five year growth and exit plan and was aiming to make an exit at the end of that five years. However, as a result of hitting targets early and evaluating the economic climate and growth cycle of the company, the decision was made to exit a year earlier than planned.

'We decided that spring 2007 would be a good time to go, because we could see the company still had a lot of growth and hadn't peaked', explains Judy.

'It was doing very well, but a purchaser could also see that the next year's sales were going to be growing at the same rate and essentially they could add value.'

The process of selling a business takes a lot of time so Judy feels it's important for people to contemplate how long they want to stay with the business. 'Some entrepreneurs hang on to their businesses too long because they are worried about what they're going to do when they don't have their business', says Judy. 'They don't maximize their potential sale because of that and the business goes past its sell-by date.'

Being a lifestyle publisher, Judy and her team were used to looking at forthcoming trends, so they were expecting that the financial bubble was going to burst fairly abruptly at some point in the future and were keen to sell before it did. Had they waited to sell the business until autumn 2007 they'd not have got the valuation they had gained before the credit crunch set in and before technological advances such as digital book readers began to disrupt the traditional publishing industry.

3. Consider what is driving the sale of the business

In an ideal world you will sell your business when you have no need to; when you are being approached by others, rather than the other way round; when a window of opportunity presents itself and you and your business are performing well and are ready. Conversely, if personal circumstances dictate the sale during a less buoyant period when the business is not performing well, the timing will be wrong.

Take MySpace.com for example. The site was acquired by Rupert Murdoch's News Corp in 2006 for $580m. A year later it had 300m registered users and was being valued at $12bn. However, a new competitor entered the market (Facebook) and grabbed significant market share leaving MySpace unable to demonstrate much growth potential. It was sold in 2011 for $35m to an advertising targeting firm, Specific Media, who saw its opportunity to add value to their existing business, but at a fraction of the price it had been bought for and a fraction of the $100m price News Corp had wanted to sell for. News Corp took the offer presented to them, as waiting to sell the business would probably have resulted in an even lower valuation.

4. Know when to let go

Generally, the time to let go is when you are no longer adding value or are no longer needed. The trick is to recognize when this time has come, remove your self elegantly and sell the business. Many businesses fail as they do not have someone at the helm able to take the business to the next level or have a founder who simply can't let go. However, if you have the right team in place to continue growing the business further but have not yet been approached by a company that is the 'right fit', it may not be the right time to sell.

Follow your Intuition

iwantoneofthose.com sold in 2004 to Kleeneze for £12m.

'We had lots of approaches over the years from people who said they were interested but we weren't sure they were the right people', recalls co-Founder, Tim Booth. 'We also knew we had a lot more growth that we wanted to experience with the business before we sold it.'

Some years later, Kleeneze approached the IWOOT team, originally to buy a 20% stake in the business and invest, but the co-founders decided it would be easier if they bought the entire business to avoid any conflict of interest.

'Because it was my baby, I needed to hand the baby over entirely, rather than say "well I'm just going to keep hold of the legs, you wave the hands around." Because then you're doing too much pushing and pulling. So it came about because they were interested in investing in the company and wanted to get into online retail. And it was the right time for us to go', adds Tim.

Reducing Owner Dependency

Succession planning is a crucial consideration when selling or retiring from a business and is critical to a company's future success and long-term security. It enables companies to reduce owner dependency, identify and develop potential successors and optimize independent value.

Businesses that are wholly dependent on the activities and performance of their owners are unlikely to attract a significant capital value on a sale. At the point of sale, the business should be able to run without the involvement of the owner, except where the owner is performing a line management role that can be filled through normal recruitment. Without a succession plan, shareholder value and credibility in capital markets can be dramatically eroded.

'Succession is critical', advises Nick Jenkins. 'If you want to make a business valuable, you need to build a management team, so the business can manage without you. Otherwise you'll be tied in as a critical part of the team. And it's no fun being in your company working for somebody else in a company that you created.'

Nick wisely handed over the running of his business to someone else four years prior to selling up. This gave him the chance to focus on working 'on' the business, rather than 'in' it, as he changed his own role from CEO to chairman and handed over the reins to a new MD.

'I brought somebody in as a Commercial Director; he worked under me for a year and, when I was finally happy, I just handed over more and more of the day to day work to him', recalls Nick, although he didn't reveal to his potential MD that he was going to succeed Nick as CEO, just in case things didn't work out.

'It got to a certain point where I felt happy that he could take it on. So there wasn't a sudden leap of faith. I'd built a business up and it was my baby and nest egg; everything I'd got was in this company, so I'd be very reluctant to hire somebody and immediately say, "here are the keys . . ." because you really need to understand whether or not they can do it', explains Nick.

Conversely, if you sell your business to a venture capitalist firm or have VCs as investors, they may choose to bring in the most expensive person they can find, based on track record. Yet there are no guarantees it'll work out. 'Just because they did a good job at one company, there's no guarantee that they can do a good job at another company', says Nick. As such, for peace of mind, it may be better to hire someone to work with you and gradually hand over to them, as Nick did. At that point, you can become chairman and strategist, and even take some time away from your business to join another board and gain some valuable executive experience from another company's perspective.

When you do hand over the reins to another MD or CEO it's important not to interfere. Give your successor ownership, freedom and authority. Keep a low profile and hold meetings with them off site. While it's important to continue to define the strategic aims of the business, operational responsibility should be entirely handed over to the successor with no meddling, except to intervene in a potential crisis if needs be.

Of course, succession plans will ultimately depend on who you're selling to and why, whether you intend to stay on in another capacity or whether you are retiring or passing the business on to family members. The key is to consider where each person will end up during the next phase of the business and whether you will need to look for successors externally or internally.

Perhaps the acquiring company has its own succession plans? If you're selling your business to the most strategic trade buyer, within six to twelve months they may want their own people in to run the company. While retaining the previous owner has its initial benefits, once an earn-out period or the transitionary handover is complete, the previous CEO may be surplus to requirements.

If that is the case, it's important to be clear on where leading executives will end up following the sale of the business. As such, it's important to gain reassurance from buyers about your future role. And this goes both ways. While the buyers should take into consideration what the founder of the company wants his or her future involvement to be, the owner/manager should also have empathy for what the buyer wants and be flexible.

Various studies reveal that most companies favour internal over external candidates as a successor to their CEO. You might hand pick and groom someone internally, set up formal interviews where internal and external candidates compete for the role, or hand over the recruitment to an external advisory company.

❗ Top Tips for Successful Succession

1. **Consider your business model, strategy, culture and corporate structure and gather feedback** from all executives and board members about ramifications for leadership around these areas. Define the required competencies and outline key criteria. Prioritize must-haves.

2. **Identify the most promising internal (or external) candidates** who have the potential to take on the role, and outline how you will implement the transition to effectively hand over the reigns.

3. **Create development plans for 'candidates in waiting' to avoid a leap of faith.** Bring one or more of those candidates to work underneath you for a year so they have the opportunity to prove themselves before you hand over the reigns entirely. A grooming period is ideal. Work together with the successful candidate to agree a fixed period within which the outgoing CEO will pass over control to the new one.

4. **Mentor and coach your candidates** or have other directors take on the role of mentor. If you are running a family business, give your successor a chance to shine. Listen to their ideas and implement them. This gives you a chance to assess their leadership and management skills in practice and guide them accordingly.

5. **Expose candidates to the board** by giving them the opportunity to attend board events and present to the board on topics relating to company growth and strategy. Ask them to present on how they would make the company more efficient and effective operationally and what actions they would take to pursue strategic growth plans.

6. **Expose candidates to core business areas outside of their comfort zone** and set tasks to evaluate how they run day-to-day operations.

Due Diligence and Value: Preparing For a Successful Exit

In a recent report entitled *The Long Goodbye: Myths, realities and insights into the business exit process*, commissioned by Coutts & Co, David Molian highlights that 'only seven percent of businesses offered for sale attract a buyer – partly because they're marketed really badly and partly because there is not value in the business'.

Therefore, readiness and preparation for sale are of critical importance. As well as being profitable and deemed as valuable, there will be a variety of loose ends that will need tidying up prior to marketing the business for sale. Essentially, the more planning that has gone into an exit strategy in the run up to the sale, the less likely that a potential deal will collapse.

> *'Plan your exit so that you feel in control, rather than finding yourself in a position when you look back at the last three years' figures and you see that you peaked three years ago.'*
>
> **Judy Piatkus, founder Piatkus Books**

! **Top Tips for Planning an Exit Strategy**

- 1. **Give yourself plenty of time way ahead of selling.** Plan a couple of years in advance. Identify potential suitors; ask yourself what sort of value you'd like to gain. Are you in the right shape? And are you making the right strategic decisions to be attractive to the suitors you've identified? Assess what their reasons might be for acquiring your business – would it be to extend their geographical reach and footprint? To enter a new market? To bolster existing revenues? Where are their weaknesses? And how might your strengths make you an attractive acquisition proposition? What assets would prospective suitors place the most value on and how can you focus on strengthening and securing those assets?

  2. **Prepare properly.** Get your paperwork in order. Start gathering data. Get all your leases and contracts together, gather financial data, health and safety policies and make sure all data is instantly accessible and available to any potential acquirer as soon as they need it. Put it on 'the cloud' if necessary. The information they request at due diligence phase can be quite complex to assemble, so save time by having everything in order to keep the sale process momentum going.

  3. **Outline in your plan exactly how you will groom the business** into the best shape for exit and which vital characteristics to focus on to make the business as attractive and valuable as possible. From

optimizing efficiency and creating a strong management team to increasing the future prospects of the business. Update your business plan with detailed KPIs (key performance indicators) and assess the market growth and size against your own growth projection figures.

4. **Tidy up loose ends.** Do you have contracts in place outlining who owns or has rights to own the technology that employees and contractors have built? Are shares and IP ownership clear? Have you considered the impact of over-committing to long leases on premises or other large costs which could affect the valuation of the business? Do you have stock sitting in the warehouse? It's important to do everything you can to ensure that your business is operating at maximum strength when it goes on the market. Efficient housekeeping is essential.

5. **Outline what is important to you from the sale of the business.** Is it price and continuity of the business? Long term security of the company? A clean and fast exit?

6. **Create a 'customer satisfaction portfolio' to demonstrate your good reputation within the market.** Include case studies, testimonials and referral rate. Being able to showcase the strength and clarity of your value proposition from a customer's perspective will be attractive at exit stage.

7. **Consider how you will sustain your trading performance and continue to hit targets during the sale process.** You want sellers to be assured that the business is growing rather than declining, so put in place processes to ensure you don't take the eye off the ball while you try to sell the business. Balance costs and investment so that you continue to operate at optimum efficiency while still feeding forecasted growth during the two-year exit phase.

How To Maximize Capital Value

Ultimately, to achieve the best price you need to optimize value by creating a sustainable business and then validate that value and upside to potential acquirers.

While the balance sheet and profitability of a business can be key criteria for buyers (particularly financial buyers rather than trade buyers), historic profitability is likely to hold less importance than the company's potential for future profitability and growth. It is equally likely that the buyer will add value by investing their own money, energy, customer base, and product line into the business to further augment its scalability. As such, there are many criteria that should be considered when grooming a business for sale to maximize its value, many of which have little to do with how much money it is making or has made in the past.

If you can tick all of these boxes then you are likely to command the best capital value possible.

Does the business have:

- **A strong management team?** Remember, people buy from people, and acquirers of businesses only buy businesses with people at the helm and staff that they can confidently back.
- **A robust succession plan and independent value?** Management quality is vital in any instance but particularly so if you intend to leave the company or step back from your CEO role once the business is sold. Buyers must have confidence in any succession plan and in the management team, while the business must have value independent of its owner to avoid owner dependency or reliance on certain individuals.
- **Scalability?** Can you demonstrate that you have a good quality list of active clients generating regular income which can be built upon? Scalability can command a high valuation multiple. As well as having the capacity to grow in size and expand geographically, scalability is also about streamlining (to reduce the cost of sales as the business grows) while simultaneously generating recurring revenue from customers, services or products. Scalability is fundamentally about making more for less by either selling more: a) existing products to existing customers, b) existing products to new customers, c) new products to existing customers, or d) new products to new customers.
- **Robust yet scalable organizational and product development processes and systems** that optimize efficiency but are adaptable to market changes and scalable enough to withstand growth spurts?
- **A growing profit base?** Can you prove that your business has historically improved profits? Can you provide clear data and supporting evidence to back up your assumptions regarding future profitability?
- **Strong prospects within a sector that has growth potential?** There must be room for growth.
- **Reachable targets, particularly during the time period when you're being evaluated by a buyer?** It is vital to ensure that you deliver the target numbers you say you'll deliver during the lengthy time period that potential buyers are looking closely at your company and watching you like a hawk. If you get it wrong and fail to deliver these targets, the buyer will lose confidence.
- **A strong market position with a good reputation and clear value proposition?** Can you create a coherent mission statement that outlines

Scalability = Sellability

In February 2011 Scott Weavers-Wright sold Kiddicare.com to Morrisons for £70m after receiving 17 trade bids from all the big high street retailers (including Argos, Tesco and Mothercare). He cites scalability, efficiency and brand credibility as the most important variables to focus on to optimize value.

'If you're looking to sell your business and devise a strategy to exit, an acquirer must see an opportunity to scale it', says Scott. 'So three years ago when I looked at the business, I realized I needed to make the technology, processes and systems more scalable and dynamic.'

'We developed our stock control picking system technology so that it could be for 1000 orders a week or 30,000 orders a week. When an acquirer realizes they don't have to rip out all your systems and start again, that's a huge bonus.'

Systems that need rebuilding present a barrier to potential acquirers.

Systems + efficiency = scalability

'In our case I wanted to build systems to take the strain, and of course they had to be scalable', says Scott.

Another focus was increasing the efficiency of those systems, because efficient systems are scalable.

'When we receive things into the warehouse at Kiddicare, the truck comes in and we zap the barcode', explains Scott. This then reveals what the product is and the volume of stock, so 500 car seat boxes might then be 'zapped' and put online automatically. 'We don't pay someone to put stock online', says Scott. 'The warehouse operator driving around on a forklift is effectively content-managing the website.'

Scott also removed additional potential barriers by using industry standard applications which were 'plugged together properly'.

'So, when people like Morrisons were looking for a way into the dot com arena, they did their technology audit and due diligence and saw Kiddicare was using industry standard products (IBM and Microsoft) for its warehouse management systems. That made it more of a no-brainer.'

Additionally, Kiddicare.com had already carved out a strong brand having won countless technology and consumer awards. 'Having a good brand will bring people to the table, but without efficient and scalable systems they aren't going to buy you, certainly not for the money you want them to anyway.'

'If you go to market as an exit route with a scalable system, profitability, a great brand and independent awards . . . it becomes a huge proposition where buyers think "wow, we have to have this"; then you get into an auction which is what every exit wants to be in.'

why you exist? Can you demonstrate your worth within the market-place from an industry perspective and via good PR and net promoter score?

- **A strong culture and corporate structure with good talent attraction and retention levels?** Motivated staff working within a cogent, communicative and unified culture are not as likely to 'jump ship' when acquired.
- **Legal/accounting/tax issues in place and paperwork in order?** If not, this will slow the sale process down and could put a potential buyer off completely.

Selling to the Right Buyers

To find the right buyer for your company you need to consider carefully the strategic reasons that buyers may wish to acquire your business. Ideally, it's better to sell to strategic trade buyers who may place a higher value on what you can offer them (e.g. because you give them the opportunity to extend their geographical footprint) rather than financial buyers who are merely acquiring for a return on capital investment. It's therefore crucial to determine exactly how you can make the business strategically attractive to the right buyer for the right price.

Just as people buy the same products for different reasons, companies may have diverse intentions for wishing to acquire the same company. Each company may place a different value on the future potential of the business or other intangible assets.

'As you're building your business, keep in mind who might want to buy it', suggests Judy Piatkus. 'There could be a wide range of people who want to buy it. In the case of Piatkus Books, we had become very strong in mass market publishing so, in order to keep our authors happy, we would need to sell to a company that understood that market. Authors staying with us when we sold the company was a factor that we had to take into consideration. We felt someone with that mass market experience would be the best purchaser.'

> **❗ Top Tips for Attracting Acquirers**
>
> ● 1. **Be active yet cautious.** While you should definitely hire specialist advisors, you should still get involved in the sale process yourself, as advisors are just a conduit and a door opener; nobody knows your business like you do. At the same time, avoid publicizing the fact that you are selling the business to all and sundry. Discretion is important as public announcements simply create uncertainty. Far better to have a corporate finance advisor contact potential acquirers discreetly on your behalf.
> 2. **Be savvy.** Ask your advisors to send out a draft memorandum to the best potential buyers offering them a pre-emptive strike if they can offer a good price for the business.
> 3. **Look close to home first.** Investors or partners who have helped you to scale the business up may wish to buy you or know someone who would. Alternatively, consider whether your management team may be appropriate purchasers of the business and can attract appropriate funding for a management buy out (MBO).
> 4. **Build up stories in the press** via effective PR and directors' reports a year before you begin to implement your exit plan. That way, when you actively market the company for sale, target acquirers will remember who you are and what you do.

Selling for the Right Price

While you as the vendor will be hoping to boost the value of your company to get a high price, potential purchasers will seek to discount the value of your company to get a low price. Negotiations on both sides should therefore be anticipated.

> **! Top Tips for Achieving Sale Objectives**
>
> ● 1. **Use a third party to manage the sale process and listen to them.** Agree a strategy for sale, including who to approach, when to approach and how to approach. Use your advisors to negotiate, acting as a buffer between the parties. Be prepared to step in if there is a deadlock, but consult your advisor first.
>
> 2. **Know what you want to get for the business before you begin to negotiate.** Agree a base line price with your advisor and discuss the likelihood of achieving that target. Be prepared to walk away from the deal if your expectations aren't met. Be rational rather than emotional though.
>
> 3. **Agree a timetable for negotiations** to stop discussions stagnating. However, be flexible. Don't set a deadline before the date of a buyer's board meeting during which the potential acquisition may have been discussed.
>
> 4. **Ask the purchaser to make you an offer rather than telling them what you are selling for.** Your aim should always be to have the acquirer reveal their hand first; otherwise they will see your suggested price 'as a ceiling rather than a floor'.
>
> 5. **Be transparent with the buyer about potential risks or problems.** Honesty in the early stage of a negotiation can prevent the deal falling apart later on.
>
> 6. **Focus on a win–win price.** Negotiate that they pay you for future value as well as current value, but ensure that they feel they are getting a good deal. Aim for a good balance and mutual win–win.

Whatever you do after the sale, the mistakes and successes you have made during your journey will enrich your path and enable your future decision-making. In building and growing your own business you have contributed to the economy and to your own wealth of wisdom. Whatever challenges you pursue in the future will benefit from all you have learned throughout the process of business cultivation and evolution.

The Definitive Online Business Success Checklist

'Developing an understanding of the value of digital technology, digital networks and the tools they offer to business, will enable the UK economy to begin to thrive again. Britain's digital assets need to be nurtured and grown. Without them UK PLC will be poorer.'

Penny Power, founder of Ecademy

The speed and scale at which Internet usage has grown over just two decades (from 2.8 million users or 0.05% of the world's population in 1990 to nearly 2 billion: 1,802,330,457 or 26.6% of the world's population in 2010) clearly demonstrates that you are not alone in understanding its power. What will stand you in good stead against the rest is being as prepared as you are passionate.

From assessing viability, demand and customer needs to raising finance and building a strong team; from creating a strong and trusted brand to developing a remarkable value proposition that will stand out from the crowd; from attracting a steady stream of targeted website visitors to turning your customers into your best sales people; from fast-tracking your success through collaborative partnerships to deciding when, why and how to sell your digital enterprise . . . this journey you are embarking on will require passion, persistence and a large dose of belief. Yet, armed with the tools you need to succeed, you are more than likely to achieve your digital dreams.

I hope you put to good use the combined wisdom of the successful digital entrepreneurs featured in this book. I hope that you now feel fully equipped to launch forth having completed the practical exercises and having followed the action-focused tips, and can place what you have learned within your own frame of reference. Before you head off on your journey toward creating your very own sustainable and successful digital enterprise, here is a final definitive checklist to ensure that you head in the right direction and take all the required steps along the way.

As Penny Power and Bob Barker say in their *Digital Business Britain Manifesto 2011*, 'there is an urgent need to teach business people how to embrace the digital world'. I hope this book does so and enables you to put your ideas into action and harness the power of digital to its full potential.

- [ ] Choose a name, check it is available as a domain and register your chosen domain name. Register your company name (unless operating as a sole trader) with Companies House and inform HMRC of your intentions to trade.
- [ ] Summarize why your idea is ultimately better than the rest and define what makes your product or service truly remarkable. Define your value proposition and USPs.
- [ ] Write down your purposeful well-defined long-term vision. Create a vision board.
- [ ] Validate and test your business idea. Determine whether your business idea is clear and simple, useful, innovative, differentiated and/or disruptive. Make sure you believe in your idea!
- [ ] Assess different business models to ensure you have chosen the right one(s) for your enterprise.
- [ ] Get a solid understanding of your customers and their needs. Define your mousetrap. List every benefit that your product/service has which meets those needs.
- [ ] Prototype and test your wares in the market to validate your business opportunity. Know exactly what your potential customers actually think of your proposition. Ascertain demand.
- [ ] Determine how much of your product/service you need to sell in order to achieve the market share you are hoping for (and break even).
- [ ] Uncover who your customer base is, where they live/work, what they do, what their values are, where they go to buy stuff like yours. Discover where your target audience base goes online to source products like yours. Sketch out your customer vision.
- [ ] Assess the market overall including its size and direction and examine what competing digital businesses do and don't offer. Fully analyze the competition so you can differentiate accordingly. Figure out what your unfair advantage is.
- [ ] Set up relevant Google Alerts to monitor your competitors and your own online coverage and reputation.
- [ ] Define your destination (where you are headed) and your strategy/tactics/actions (how you intend to get there). Map out your target milestones.

☐ Write your business plan, action plan, marketing plan and exit plan, including all the relevant forecasts, figures and facts to back up your vision and mission statement. Ensure that your financial expectations are realistic yet demonstrate growth prospects for the business.

☐ Outline suitable sources of finance and write your shopping list detailing exactly what you need money for, when you need it and why. Know how you intend to raise this capital and prepare accordingly. Decide how much equity (if any) you are prepared to give away, how you'll reward investors and where their exit will come from. Note who your perfect investor might be and what they'd bring to the table in addition to hard cash.

☐ Design and develop (yourself or with the help of a contractor) a fresh, engaging, content-rich, usable, intuitive, clear, simple, fast loading, accessible, secure and search engine friendly website. (Or write a clear brief to do so.)

☐ Put a good web analytics package and monitoring solution in place, as well as methods for gathering customer feedback and data so you can understand the value of your traffic (cost per acquisition), the needs of your audience, plus which marketing methods and messages work best.

☐ Create a well-thought-through content strategy detailing your target audience's preferred methods of viewing information and listing the stock of content you will produce with a plan against each piece of content.

☐ Write clickable and readable web copy, evaluate your word choice and give your copy a final check for accuracy.

☐ Contact, compare and choose suppliers, payment providers and order-fulfillment processes.

☐ Optimize your site for mobile and web across multiple platforms, operating systems and browsers. Develop a mobile-specific site and/or application.

☐ Outline which skills, knowledge, industry contacts, experience are missing from your team for which you will need to fill the gaps. Outline roles you'll need to recruit and the types of staffing options to pursue. Create relevant job descriptions and person specifications.

☐ Establish how you will retain staff through motivation, environment, security, communication and culture.

☐ Define your purpose and values. Package up your brand identity so you can clearly articulate it. Summarize your promise and write a slogan.

☐ Consider how you will spark curiosity prior to launch and from then on. Consider how to persuade and reward your first customers.

☐ List your creative ideas about brand ambassadors.

☐ Find out what social mediums your audience is using and evaluate the content, topics and formats they are interacting with the most.

☐ Create relevant marketing messages that reveal the value of your company and your personal value.

☐ Set up social media profiles which reveal that value.

☐ Identify your influencers and recruit or put plans in place to recruit an elite fleet of influencers who can create a 'buzzing hive'.

☐ List potential partners and collaborators, and consider synergistic objectives and mutual win–win propositions.

☐ Put in place methods to enable your customers to promote your products and services for you. Create a referral plan.

☐ Create a top-notch customer service plan and process to exceed expectations and keep customers happy. Consider how you will put your customers at the heart of your business. Know how you intend to gain repeat custom.

☐ Establish ways to store, save and protect your data and your customers' data.

☐ Ensure you have in place the credentials required to build a sustainable and successful business that will attract acquirers. Put together a strong management team with scalable technology, processes and growth methodologies or have a plan of action to do so.

☐ Be open to learn from your mistakes, work hard, persist and believe.

Then, you are ready.:-) I wish you all the best of luck in your digital venture. May it flourish and become all that you have dreamed of and more.

> '*The Internet holds the promise to improve lives and empower people. I feel very lucky to be involved in this time of rapid and amazing change.*'
> **Jeff Bezos, Founder of Amazon**

About
Cheryl Rickman

Cheryl Rickman writes books on the big world of business from a small village in Hampshire.

After working in editorial for three years post graduation, Cheryl joined an online information publisher and wrote a number of booklets about Internet business and web marketing. In 1999, Cheryl decided to combine running her own Internet business with a freelance writing career, focusing on entrepreneurship, business start-up and company growth.

What sets Cheryl apart from many writers in her field is that she has experience of starting up and running her own businesses. She started her first Internet business, aged 25. WebCritique was a web usability and content consultancy which she sold in 2005 to focus on writing. Clients included Microsoft, Business Link and Motorola.

Additionally, together with her partner, Cheryl co-founded online music magazine, ilikemusic.com (I Like Music) in 2000, which her partner continues to run. During her time as editor of ilikemusic.com, Cheryl spent seven years interviewing popstars and developing the business.

Indeed, from popstar Katie Melua to rapper 50 Cent; from a death row prisoner to multi-millionaire business leaders, Cheryl has interviewed a variety of incredible people with extraordinary stories to tell.

Fifteen years after beginning her writing career, Cheryl continues to bring the stories of successful people to life. She's interviewed more than 100 entrepreneurs running businesses of all sizes, from one-man bands to large corporations; equally dedicated, passionate and insightful.

Founding and running two businesses from the age of 25 taught Cheryl about survival and enhanced what she was learning as a writer. This combination of knowledge and understanding gave her the confidence to write her first bestseller, *The Small Business Start-Up Workbook* ('probably the best book for Start-Ups ever written!'). The book went straight to number one in the Start-Ups category on Amazon when it was published back in 2005. It has remained in the top ten of the best-seller charts in its categories ever since. The late, great Dame Anita Roddick kindly wrote the Foreword to this book.

Since then Cheryl has ghostwritten a number of best-selling books, including *Sunday Times* best-seller, *Tycoon*, for Peter Jones of BBC *Dragons' Den* fame, and *Born Global* by Neal Gandhi of Quickstart Global. She also contributed to *1000 CEOs* and recently helped write *From Vision To Exit: The Entrepreneur's Guide to Building and Selling a Business* for Guy Rigby of Smith & Williamson.

Cheryl lives near Winchester, Hampshire, with her partner and their daughter.

References

1. Langer, David, 'Start-Up 100: The European ecosystem has arrived – or weren't you paying attention?' *The Daily Telegraph*, January 2009
2. Ostdick, John, 'E-vangelist', *Success Magazine*, July 2011
3. Page, Larry, 'Our Philosophy', *Google.com*
4. Page, Larry, Techcrunch.com, by Alexia Tsotsis, July 14 2011
5. Anderson, Chris, 'The Economics of Giving It Away', *Wall Street Journal*, January 31, 2009

Index